ACADEMIC INTERVENTION SUCCESS

A Whole-Child Approach to K–5 Achievement

SUE STROM AND LUCY L.

Publishing Credits
Corinne Burton, M.A.Ed., *President* and *Publisher*
Aubrie Nielsen, M.S.Ed., *EVP of Content Development*
Kyra Ostendorf, M.Ed., *Publisher, professional books*
Véronique Bos, *Vice President of Creative*
Cathy Hernandez, *Senior Content Manager*
Colleen Pidel, *Senior Graphic Designer*

Image Credits: page 117 Shutterstock; other images courtesy of Sue Strom and Lucy Payne.

Library of Congress Cataloging-in-Publication Data
Names: Strom, Sue author | Payne, Lucy L. author
Title: Academic intervention success : a whole-child approach to K-5 achievement / by Sue Strom, M.A., and Lucy L. Payne, M.A., Ph.D.
Description: Huntington Beach, CA : Shell Educational Publishing, Inc, [2026] | Includes bibliographical references and index.
Identifiers: LCCN 2025006161 (print) | LCCN 2025006162 (ebook) | ISBN 9798330903740 paperback | ISBN 9798330903757 ebook
Subjects: LCSH: Educational psychology | Special education | Academic achievement | Early childhood education | Education, Elementary | BISAC: EDUCATION / Special Education / Learning Disabilities | EDUCATION / Teaching / Methods & Strategies
Classification: LCC LB1051 .S7296 2026 (print) | LCC LB1051 (ebook) | DDC 371.9/0472--dc23/eng/20250526
LC record available at https://lccn.loc.gov/2025006161
LC ebook record available at https://lccn.loc.gov/2025006162

All rights reserved. No part of this book may be reproduced or transmitted in any form or by any means, electronic or mechanical, including photocopying, recording, or any information storage and retrieval system, without the prior written consent of the publisher, except for brief quotations in critical reviews and certain other noncommercial uses permitted by copyright law. For permission requests, contact the publisher.

Website addresses included in this book are public domain and may be subject to changes or alterations of content after publication of this product. Shell Education does not take responsibility for the future accuracy or relevance and appropriateness of website addresses included in this book. Please contact the company if you come across any inappropriate or inaccurate website addresses, and they will be corrected in product reprints.

All companies, websites, and products mentioned in this book are registered trademarks of their respective owners or developers and are used in this book strictly for editorial purposes. No commercial claim to their use is made by the author or the publisher.

5482 Argosy Avenue
Huntington Beach, CA 92649
www.tcmpub.com/shell-education
ISBN 979-8-3309-0374-0
© 2026 Shell Educational Publishing, Inc.
Printed by: **418**
Printed in: **USA**
PO#: **PO17715**

In fond and loving memory of our dear close friend, Principal Tom Koch. He was our thought partner, inspiration, and colleague. Throughout the writing of this book, we would frequently ask ourselves, "What questions would Tom be asking?" He saw life as a learning journey and had the unique capacity to calm discomfort and keep us focused on the big ideas, even when we were far beyond our comfort zones. He walked and sat with all community members to improve learning everywhere for everyone.

This book is dedicated to our own children, Jake, Alex, Anna, and Erik, and our bonus children, Lyreshia and Axel, for teaching us and supporting us in our journey. Watching them move through the education system deepened our perspective, which impacted our thinking and work. We would not be here without them.

Table of Contents

Foreword ix

INTRODUCTION — 1

- Our Purpose 1
- Who Is This Book For? 2
- Why This Book? 3
- About the Authors 3
- A Key Partnership 4
- How This Book Is Organized 5
- Overview of What's Ahead 5
- Reflection Questions 6

PART 1: HOW THE GEAR MODEL WAS DEVELOPED — 7

Chapter 1: The Gear Model — 9
- The Gear Model: Whole-Child Intervention Success 9
- Instructional Principles, Partners, and Assessments 13
- Foundational Concepts 13
- Closing Thoughts 23
- Reflection Questions 24

Chapter 2: A Foundation of Relationships — 25
- Building Relationships and a Partnership 25
- New Role of Achievement Interventionist 27
- Relationships Through a Neighborhood Program 33
- Closing Thoughts 34
- Reflection Questions 35

Chapter 3: Learning from Successful Programs — 37
- Connections for More Learning 37
- Identifying Barriers to Intervention Success 38
- Preparing to Visit Successful Programs 40
- Identifying Successful Programs 41
- Visiting Programs Across the United States 41

Questions and Observation Tool	44
Key Findings and Takeaways	45
Closing Thoughts	50
Reflection Questions	50

PART 2: HOW TO DO IT—THE GEARS 51

Chapter 4: Getting to Know The Gear Model 53

An Afternoon/Evening at The Gear Model Program	53
The Goals of The Gear Model After School Club	55
Program Logistics and Calendar	56
Physical Space for the Program	58
Selecting Participants	58
Ratio of Students to Educators and Volunteers	59
Launching the Program	59
Building Partnerships: Who Was Involved	62
Closing Thoughts	70
Reflection Questions	71

Chapter 5: Academic Intervention 73

What Is Tutoring and What Makes It Effective?	74
Math Tutoring	75
Program Design Considerations	76
The Gear in Motion	85
Closing Thoughts	85
Reflection Questions	86

Chapter 6: Enrichment—Arts/Culture/STEAM/Nature 87

What Is Enrichment?	88
Why Is Enrichment Worth Your Time?	89
Enrichment Access	89
STEAM Enrichment and Our Partnership	90
Building Relationships and Assessing Prior Knowledge	96
Celebration Showcase Highlighting Success	99
What We Learned from Our Experience	99
Closing Thoughts	100
Reflection Questions	101

Chapter 7: Communication 103
- What Is Communication? 103
- Why Is Communication Important? 104
- Efficient, Intentional Communication Strategies 104
- Academic Language 110
- Closing Thoughts 112
- Reflection Questions 112

Chapter 8: Attending to Emotions—Building Self-Awareness 113
- Belonging and Emotional Safety 114
- Identifying Emotions 115
- Emotions and Learning 116
- Tools for Attending to Emotions 116
- Communicating with Parents 123
- Closing Thoughts 123
- Reflection Question 123

Chapter 9: Collaborative Movement and Play 125
- The Sounds of Productive and Collaborative Play 126
- Why Are Movement and Play Important? 126
- Two Kinds of Play 127
- The State of Play: What We Have Observed 127
- Preparing for Collaborative Movement 129
- Getting Started with Partner Activities 132
- Collaborative Movement Activities 133
- Benefits for Participants 135
- Closing Thoughts 136
- Reflection Questions 136

PART 3: IMPACT OF THE GEAR MODEL AND INSIGHTS 137

Chapter 10: Evaluation of the Two-Year Program Implementation 139
- Evaluating The Gear Model After School Club 140
- Assessment of the Academic Intervention Gear 141
- Assessment of the Enrichment Gear 142
- Informal Evaluation of the Emotions and Communication Gears 143
- Assessment of Overall Well-Being and Resilience 144
- Parents' Feedback: Evaluations and Anecdotes 146

Evaluation from Partners and Volunteers 146
Ongoing Conversations Everywhere 147
Improving Feedback Collection and Evaluation 148
Reflection Questions 150

Chapter 11: Next Steps—You Can't Do This Alone 151

Start with the End in Mind 152
The Importance of Outreach and Relationships 153
Obtaining Funding: Do Not Let Money Stop You 154
Designing Your Own Gear Model 155
Data to Inform Improvements and Demonstrate Success 157
Collaborate on Goals and an Evaluation Plan 157
Youth Feedback and Evaluation 158
Parent Feedback and Evaluation 160
Volunteer and Partner Feedback and Evaluation 161
Developing a Team 162
Recruiting Participants 163
Handling Logistical Details 163
Closing Thoughts 165

Chapter 12: Final Thoughts 167

Key Thinking 167
New Initiatives and Change Fatigue 168
Rethinking School Structures 169
Last Words as We Send You Off 171
Long-Term Developmental Relationships = Success 172

Appendix A: Resources 175
Appendix B: Sample Program Materials 179
Appendix C: Qualities of Effective Programs 185
Acknowledgements 187
References 188
Index 192
About the Authors 196

Foreword

by Michael C. Rodriguez

As dean of the College of Education and Human Development at the University of Minnesota and a professor of educational measurement and evaluation, my work has focused on how we teach, assess, and support student learning in ways that honor the whole child. My research has focused on accessibility in testing and assessment, with more recent attention to the measurement of social and emotional well-being and the sociocultural contexts of youth development. I have seen the power of centering students' strengths—what we call *developmental assets and supports*. When we recognize that academic, emotional, and social development co-occur, we open the door to more meaningful, equitable, and lasting learning outcomes.

My work was influenced by positive psychology and the role of assets in human development. I learned about asset framing in graduate school and it became an important component of my approach to program evaluation. Although the term *social and emotional learning* was introduced in 1994 by the Collaborative for Academic, Social, and Emotional Learning (CASEL), their work was preceded by decades of scholarship, from David and Roger Johnson's groundbreaking work in cooperative learning in the 1960s (see Johnson, Johnson, and Holubec 1994) to the introduction of developmental assets by Search Institute in 1990 (see Scales and Leffert 2004).

These efforts recognized two truths. First, there are multiple ways in which each child develops, and they are fundamentally intertwined. Developmental assets and social and emotional readiness and well-being can be taught and nurtured throughout life. Second, children and youth have an inherent capacity for positive development, and although learning is social and promoted through meaningful relationships, youth are major actors in their own development (Benson et al. 2006).

Sue Strom and Lucy Payne weave these enduring concepts aptly throughout their presentation of The Gear Model in a way that churns theory and knowledge into tools and resources for educators in any setting. Their centering of developmental relationships (the current research and practice focus of Search Institute) is well founded and appropriate. Developmental relationships are the key ingredients of effective youth development and intervention programs (Li and Julian 2012). Strom and Payne are intentional in their use of *developmental* relationships, those with high and attainable expectations with the supports, encouragement, and trust needed for students to succeed.

The evidence to support the components of The Gear Model is well summarized and framed to acknowledge the interdependence of each gear: Academic Intervention, Enrichment,

Communication, Attending to Emotions, and Collaborative Movement and Play. From decades of neuroscientific evidence, we know that little cognitive learning occurs for children and youth without social and emotional readiness and well-being; emotions shape cognition (Leighton 2023). In fact, Leighton, a cognitive psychologist and measurement specialist, argues that "students are rights holders in their own learning" (2023, 4), and successful learning requires trust, where "trust comes about when teachers recognize and nurture their role as secondary attachment figures and duty bearers in the lives of children" (2023, 4). The integration of the gears in Strom and Payne's intuitive model provides clear pathways for adults and students to establish the trust needed for successful learning.

When Strom and Payne present practical ways to employ The Gear Model, they embody these notions of trust, rights holders, and duty bearers, through approaches such as collaborating and co-teaching, building community among students, communicating with parents and engaging families, and connecting with neighborhood programs and organizations. These ensure the relevance and responsiveness of interventions that support and nurture learning. They ensure consideration of sociocultural contexts of learning. And these aren't just big ideas presented in an academic voice. Strom and Payne write in an engaging narrative style; illuminate stories and examples throughout; recount conversations between educators, students, families, and community leaders; and converse with us, the readers, as though they were sitting next to us enjoying tea.

It is clear to me that both Strom and Payne are accomplished educators; they know their subject matter and how to teach it, they are committed to students and their learning, they are reflective practitioners, and they are members of learning communities. The Gear Model provides a way for all professionals working in education settings, both schools and after-school programs, to continue to hone their craft. The model supports program design, responsive implementation, and continuous improvement for paraprofessionals, coaches, youth workers, education leaders, and so many others. The authors provide sample checklists, design principles for interventions, questions to engage parents in dialogue, example student work and reflections, and many other tools and resources. Strom and Payne narrate a comprehensive story around a natural system of gears (practices and contexts) that foster children's dignity and well-being in support of learning.

In the final chapter, Strom and Payne ask: *Can we come together and create conditions where all youth have what is needed to grow into independent, contributing, healthy adults*? The answer is a resounding YES. With The Gear Model, we have a doable, responsive roadmap to get us there, and it's closer than most may realize.

References

Benson, Peter L., Peter C. Scales, Stephen F. Hamilton, and Arturo Sesma. 2006. "Positive Youth Development: Theory, Research, and Applications." In *Handbook of Child Psychology: Theoretical Models of Human Development*, vol. 1, 6th ed., edited by William Damon and Richard M. Lerner. John Wiley & Sons.

Johnson, David W., Roger T. Johnson, and Edythe Johnson Holubec. 1994. *The New Circles of Learning: Cooperation in the Classroom and School*. ASCD.

Leighton, Jacqueline P. 2023. *Leveraging Socio-Emotional Assessment to Foster Children's Human Rights*. Routledge.

Li, Junlei, and Megan M. Julian. 2012. "Developmental Relationships as the Active Ingredient: A Unifying Working Hypothesis of 'What Works' Across Intervention Settings." *American Journal of Orthopsychiatry* 82 (2): 157–166. doi.org/10.1111/j.1939-0025.2012.01151.x.

Scales, Peter C., and Nancy Leffert. 2004. *Developmental Assets: A Synthesis of the Scientific Research on Adolescent Development*, 2nd ed. Search Institute.

Introduction

> "Start from wherever you are and
> with whatever you've got."
> —Jim Rohn, entrepreneur and author

Our Purpose

This book is a work of passion—our passion for youth and a passion to do better for them. Here we offer an all-encompassing yet simple and replicable structure for an intervention program that effectively improves outcomes for youth. Our purpose in writing this book is to help you create intervention programs and learning experiences that promote youth development and empower youth to become adults who are contributing community members.

We all know that there are a large number of (often overlapping) disparities that impact students' abilities to reach their full potential, including access and opportunity. Each individual has a unique context and story about how these disparities impact them. For too many, the results are tragic, and society loses out on their potential.

If the solution to resolving these disparities were simple, our educational systems would have already done so. We believe we all need to think differently to create something different. In this book, we share our thinking and encourage you to think about what could change or needs to change for youth and about how to intervene to ensure they are gaining the academic and social skills required to become productive community members.

This book is relevant whether you work in an urban, rural, or suburban school or community. Shifting housing patterns and changing school enrollment options are now bringing economic disparities to almost all school communities. All schools have students and families who are or have experienced isolating and under-resourced conditions. Like never before, schools need to understand, support, and integrate students of all income levels and backgrounds into their communities.

Teacher educator and author Zaretta Hammond's work inspires us to believe in the potential of ALL children. To be successful in our goal to develop independent, contributing, healthy adults, we are called to aim high:

As educators, we have to recognize that we help maintain the achievement gap when we don't teach advanced cognitive skills to students we label as "disadvantaged" because of their language, gender, race, or socioeconomic status. Many children start school with small learning gaps, but as they progress through school, the gap between African American and Latino and White students grows because we don't teach them how to be independent learners. Based on these labels, we usually do the following (Mean and Knapp 1991):

- Underestimate what disadvantaged students are intellectually capable of doing.
- As a result, we postpone more challenging and interesting work until we believe they have mastered "the basics."
- By focusing only on low-level basics, we deprive students of a meaningful or motivating context for learning and practicing higher order thinking processes. (Hammond 2014, 14–15)

Influenced by Hammond's writing and that of others, we use the term *disparities* to mean the inequities and differences we see in the treatment and achievement of youth. And to expand the circle of responsibility for learning, our use of the term *educators* includes all adults involved in the places children learn: families, schools, athletics, the arts, youth groups, mentoring programs, and civic groups. Our purpose and passion is to reach all learners by asking the right questions to move us all out of our own comfortable spaces and into better-coordinated approaches to learning.

Who Is This Book For?

The intervention model we describe is applicable to people who believe all youth can succeed. We see a place for intervention in schools, in community programs, through youth agencies, in faith-based organizations, and by anyone interested in supporting youth to learn and grow. It is for people working in diverse roles, across diverse environments, with diverse groups of learners. Our intent is to provide useful information and actionable ideas to all partners and allies who work on behalf of learner growth. Each of us has our own spheres of influence, and we hope you are able to take pieces and parts from our experiences, discoveries, and strategies into your context to support learners. We wrote this book for everyone who cares about youth in this and future generations.

As you read, consider your role in the lives of learners. What do you bring to the work? What is in your sphere of influence and control? What do you hope to learn from this book? How do you hope to change and grow? What can you implement today, tomorrow, and further in the future? How can you move forward, taking the first step toward a new approach to intervention on behalf of learners? Who could be your thought partners on this journey?

Finally, as you read and reflect on what we share, please know this is not a recipe book that needs to be followed step-by-step for success. This book shares a recipe that we have repeatedly tweaked and improved for different environments. Your version of the recipe will be highly dependent on your philosophies, your learning context, and most importantly the learners you work beside. Please take our experiences, thoughts, and ideas and use them to create your own program personalized to your learners and context.

Why This Book?

There is no shortage of resources about intervention strategies. These strategies are foundational to our work; however, our goal with this book is to inspire readers to consider the larger systems in which learning interventions are implemented. Our model, known as The Gear Model, is made up of different components, typically disconnected, that we bring together for a cohesive intervention program. You can implement our model as we present it, use only some of the pieces, or make other changes to your context based on what we share. The real power of the model is the integration of the components, but you must consider your own learners and context to determine what is possible.

This is not a technology-based or scripted program. We see technology and curricula as tools to help us implement our new and innovative Gear Model and as a support for student thinking and learning. Our philosophies are based on human-centered ideas and the relationships we build across communities with others. We purposely focus on learning interactions and individualized cohort growth.

Everyone brings a variety of perspectives and experiences to this work. As we have focused on ending the isolation of parts, we have always worked from an inquiry perspective. As a result, you will see a unique blend of both research (asking questions) and easy-to-implement ideas to break down isolated efforts and effect change for learners. We encourage you to read what we have to share; think about your context, your learning, and your goals; and then begin to ask questions and start to make changes to develop your intervention program into what you want it to be.

About the Authors

We began our teaching careers in different California cities, both teaching kindergarten. Kindergarten is a magical place. We had the flexibility to be responsive to the developmental, social, and learning needs of every child. Kindergarten teachers usually teach all subjects, which gave us the freedom to be connected and integrated across curricular areas. Five- and six-year-olds' behavior provided rapid-fire feedback as we learned, forcing us to improve instructional strategies immediately or go home frustrated and crying, something we hope to help others avoid. Especially when it was hard, children have been our best teachers.

Our philosophies and approaches to teaching were built in racially and economically diverse communities. At the time, in the late 1980s and 1990s, California ranked significantly below the national average in spending per student in school funding (Teague 2000). Resources were sparse. Elementary classrooms had thirty-two or more students, and multiple languages were spoken. The classroom teacher was also the art, music, and P.E. teacher. Creativity was the key to teacher survival. We learned a lot about whole-child development and classroom management as we taught all subjects to the youngest learners in under-resourced schools.

We both moved to Minnesota, where we continued our work with students and learned from being parents to our own children. Becoming parents allowed us to witness learning from both sides of the equation, integrating the parent world and the traditional teaching world. As we each raised our own families, our views of learning ecosystems broadened. We were fortunate to always have networks to call on when our children encountered challenges in learning.

Lucy went on to work at the university level and expanded her perspective by serving on a local school board and with various education organizations. Sue continued teaching elementary grades. Her experiences were further informed by ten summers of YouthWorks community service work across the United States, seven years as the school liaison for biweekly after-school neighborhood programs run jointly with an established and well-resourced local nonprofit, and twelve years working both in and out of school with students in reading and math intervention and special education.

Minnesota has some of the worst reading and math disparities between racial subgroups on standardized tests in the nation (Federal Reserve Bank of Minneapolis 2019). Sue's school district decided to get creative with programming for students in need of additional support. In the district, test scores improved most for learners who were seen during school for small-group intervention classes *and* after school in tutoring- and enrichment-based neighborhood clubs.

Sue's extensive experience and natural curiosity led her to think about intervention systems and how to improve them on behalf of all youth. Eventually, she took time away from the daily teaching routine to research, learn, think, and explore successful programs. This time and space to pursue her thinking (instead of continuously reacting to the emerging issues of the classroom) was essential to the development of The Gear Model.

A Key Partnership

In 2005, Lucy and Tom Koch, the principal at Sue's school, formed a partnership dedicated to reaching and teaching every student. This is when we (Lucy and Sue) first met, as Sue was a teacher leader in this work. The partnership took time to develop, but ultimately, each of us contributed to the research, the design, and the application of The Gear Model intervention program.

As a university professor, Lucy brought current research, an ability to question the status quo, and curiosity to try new things. Sue brought her expertise as a veteran classroom teacher, her passion for youth success, and her drive to make a difference. Tom Koch brought a brilliant capacity to listen carefully to all education partners while growing deep relationship roots in every nook of a changing school community and setting unbelievably high academic goals.

Since beginning our work together, we have focused on learners we teach within school buildings. We have gained broader perspectives of what it takes to develop a whole, independent human while raising our own children. We have also learned so much by sharing and discussing our successes with others through site visit tours, school board presentations, and conference presentations.

As we developed and implemented The Gear Model, we realized that it is often the spaces between the programs and groups—the relationships, experiences, and challenges—that advance all youth to the ultimate goal of education: becoming independent, contributing, healthy young adults. We hope you will find this book a helpful tool in achieving that goal in your own schools, communities, and spaces.

How This Book Is Organized

This book has three parts. Part 1 (chapters 1 to 3) gives the overall purpose of our work, a short summary of our intervention model, foundational concepts to our work, experiences and relationships that influenced our thinking and development, and what we learned visiting successful intervention programs.

Part 2 (chapters 4 to 9) covers The Gear Model. These chapters take a deep dive into each component, or gear, of the model. We introduce each gear, present a rationale for the gear, share stories from our experiences and work with learners, and explore application of the ideas to intervention.

Part 3 (chapters 10 to 12) summarizes our learning from our experiences, discusses our current thinking and wondering, and explores next steps. We aim to offer you hope and excitement for what is next in your work supporting youth.

Overview of What's Ahead

In the coming chapters, you will first hear about a fledgling community-based kindergarten-through-eighth-grade Neighborhood Homework Club that grew and developed at two community locations over seven years. You will learn how it became a powerhouse program others visited to learn from as they built their own out-of-school academic and/or enrichment youth development programs. With a teacher partnering beside a nonprofit neighborhood outreach manager, the program evolved to its fullest potential. By listening responsively and continuing relationships over learners' lifespans, rich long-term relationships between teachers, youth workers, children, and their families led to amplified success. A microcommunity raised a cohort of independent, contributing, healthy young adults.

You will then hear about the two-year full implementation of our Gear Model After School Club. This newly created, multifaceted program ran for two hours twice a week and was conducted with third through fifth graders who qualified for intervention service. Both the Neighborhood Homework Club and The Gear Model After School Club supported the classroom and intervention learning occurring during the school day.

Both programs focused on uniting cohorts of students in upper elementary school, since those years are uniquely important for development. Our goal is that students at this age are empowered to become more independent as they begin to move their learning into the real world. As we consider youth and their development, we think about how to harness their energy and focus it to the desired outcomes. We work to stay focused on the question "Who do *they* see themselves becoming?"

> *As we consider youth and their development, we think about how to harness their energy and focus it to the desired outcomes. We work to stay focused on the question "Who do they see themselves becoming?"*

Both programs utilized partnerships to surround youth and their families with layers of academic and social supports steeped in multi-age, longer-term developmental relationships. Both were multi-year programs that resulted in learners showing up to school more bright-eyed, enthusiastically asking questions such as, "Will I see Mr. Ryan in school today for reading (or math)?" and "Do we have After School Club today?"

Our curiosity and the needs of our students outrank the need to stay in our comfort zone. Ideally, this book about the intervention program we created will help you examine and create your own balanced, learner-focused intervention programming for your community.

The Gear Model provides the essential parts, or gears, to create a balanced approach to learning and belonging focused on the learner. It will help you create a truly difference-making intervention program during the traditional school day and/or outside of the school day and school year with partnerships with youth development groups. This program provides learners with needed academic intervention and enrichment experiences, and develops their own beliefs that they can be who they aspire to be. The model has been shown to increase student motivation and individual academic outcomes, and it sets the conditions where growth accelerates because all gifts and talents contribute to the shared success of the microcommunity of learners where everyone is highly bonded and mutually connected.

Reflection Questions

- What experiences and hopes do you bring to your work?
- Where are all the places learning is happening for children and youth in your community?
- How will you share your learning and thinking as you continue reading?

PART 1

How the GEAR MODEL Was Developed

CHAPTER 1

The Gear Model

"Learning is rooted in relationships, and supportive relationships can unleash the potential of every student."
—Michael Fullan and Maria Langworthy,
educational researchers and authors

We developed The Gear Model based on our professional experiences working at a university and in school districts, combined with all we have learned by visiting evidenced-based, long-established, successful, and growing intervention programs across the United States. The model is informed by conversations with participants and leaders about how their programs personalized their work to individual learners' needs, what roles parents were playing, what assessment tools were most helpful, what kept youth engaged, and much more. Chapter 3 provides details on the sites we visited across the country and what we learned from them.

The following questions are answered in this chapter:

- What are the basic components of The Gear Model?
- What gear drives the entire model?
- What are the foundational concepts that support the development of The Gear Model?
- How do these concepts work together for a cohesive model?
- What can we learn from the youth we seek to further develop?

The Gear Model: Whole-Child Intervention Success

Our work strives to put a simple, replicable structure around intervention strategies by connecting effective practices to improve learners' outcomes. We know that reactive problem-solving and patchwork solutions are the reality of many intervention programs. Developing programs and improving them at the same time is less than ideal, especially when educators and youth development professionals are exhausted and overtaxed. Currently, intervention programs are typically separate from family systems and support services. The Gear Model unifies families, schools, and communities to streamline interventions for the maximum benefit of the whole child. It represents the important moving parts that are interconnected and drive the program, leading to stronger outcomes for students.

There are five main components (gears) that surround the largest gear, which is Relationships. The five gears are Academic Intervention, Enrichment, Communication, Attending to Emotions, and Collaborative Movement and Play. In this section, we provide an overview of the components. We examine them more fully throughout the book.

Relationships

The Gear Model is built around authentic, positive, growing, and loving relationships. Little to nothing occurs without reciprocal, intentional, ongoing personal relationships. We have found over our years of experience that students and families who are truly connected with their school and community networks feel as if they belong. Then, engagement in learning increases. Students become more comfortable taking risks and tackling challenges in their learning. If students or their families feel uncertain about their sense of belonging, we have seen time and again the detrimental effects on them. These negative effects show up in many forms: reduced motivation, decreased emotional well-being, hesitation to accept feedback, and a sense of isolation. Relationships matter! Some relationships are short-term sparks of inspiration, and some need to be long term. Youth benefit from both types of relationships. Both can be transformative. Long-term relationships (beyond the family) can be harder to come by for the youth we aim most to support. But we have seen how these long-term relationships have great impact on future success.

Little to nothing occurs without reciprocal, intentional, ongoing personal relationships.

Academic Intervention

This gear requires that academic interventions and small-group tutoring tied to classroom instruction and standards be personalized based on multiple assessments and input from classroom teachers. These interventions support learners by strengthening their reasoning and critical-thinking skills. Most importantly, the work is at the right level of rigor for each learner to engage in productive struggle and for all learners to be proud of their increasing confidence and accuracy. Success builds motivation and a self-concept of being a strong learner. Chapter 5 addresses this gear more in depth. In our program, we centered on mathematics for academic intervention, but any academic area could be used. The nature of integrating learning into enrichment, movement, and social-emotional skills supports improvements in whatever academic area the leaders select, whether math, reading, writing, oral expression, the arts, sciences, and so on.

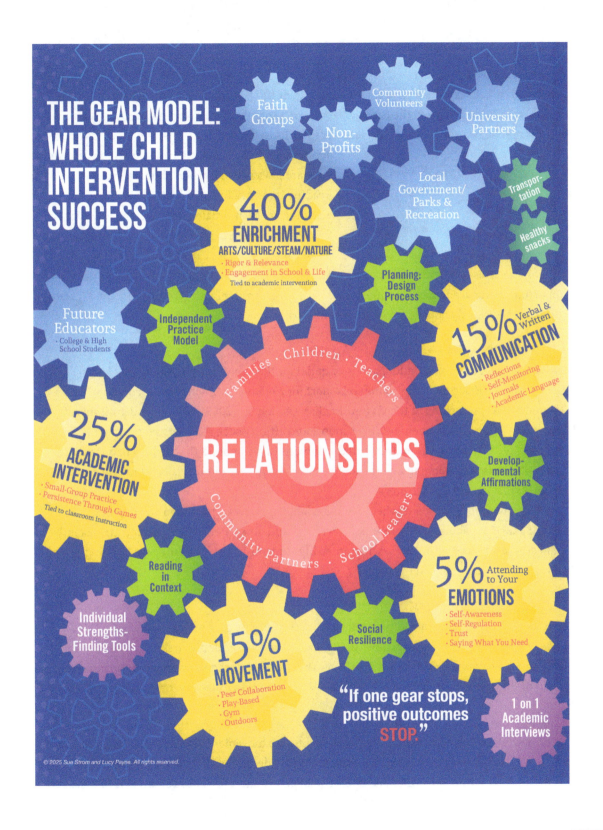

Enrichment

Enrichment through the arts, culture, STEAM, and nature are an essential part of our model (see chapter 6). When learners who are not rising to their full potential have access to enrichment in an intervention program, the experience supports them in developing positive self-image, thinking strategies, teamwork skills, leadership skills, self-advocacy skills, and more. Enrichment ignites possibilities and offers opportunities for adults to share power with learners. Integrating math and reading into enrichment activities helps learners see their relevance, ultimately motivating participants to learn even more. Enrichment activities communicate to youth that they are capable and smart. Much of our work focuses on learners from under-resourced communities; they almost always have fewer opportunities for academic enrichment than their peers from higher income brackets. The Gear Model is intentional about narrowing these disparities.

Enrichment ignites possibilities and offers opportunities for adults to share power with learners.

Communication

The ability to communicate and listen is essential for the relationship building that holds The Gear Model together. In Latin, *commun* is short for *communis*, which means "common" or "shared by all." According to the Oxford English Dictionary (2009), one of the definitions of *community* is "social cohesion; mutual support and affinity such as is derived from living in a community." Communication unites all the humans that surround the learners in our program, fostering a sense of belonging and the natural bonds required for our vision of microcommunities (more on this later in this chapter).

As former kindergarten teachers, we value language development. Our model includes oral language, vocabulary, listening skills, writing, and other literacy components consistently embedded across the entire approach, immersing students in ongoing language learning. Communication is explored in chapter 7.

Attending to Emotions

Learning to identify and attend to emotions is another mighty gear in our model. A first step in dealing with an emotion is acknowledging and putting words or pictures to it. Youth need dedicated time to practice acknowledging how they are feeling and to explore how their feelings might be impacting their learning. We include simple routines to address one's feelings in chapter 8.

Collaborative Movement and Play

We all know young bodies need to move. So, deliberate movement activities that integrate math and reading skills are part of the daily routine and are described in detail in chapter 9. We incorporate structured activities and open-ended play to meet the needs of learners and desired outcomes of the day.

Instructional Principles, Partners, and Assessments

The large gears in the model are kept turning by the small gears. These include instructional principles (green), assessments that inform and evaluate success (purple), and enrichment and community partners (blue and turquoise).

What is most important in The Gear Model is to consider the entire ecosystem and all the places and reasons that youth learn and move toward the best versions of their future selves. Ideally, intervention should be happening in school and in microcommunities around the school to enhance real learning everywhere. As you begin your thinking journey through this book, look around you to see opportunities for learning inside and outside of school and opportunities to connect parts together. The goal is for all gears to work smoothly together.

Foundational Concepts

Our work and approach are built on five foundational concepts: being learner focused, building supportive relationships, asset-based framing, influences to learning beyond the traditional three R's, and a systems orientation. These concepts are summarized below and referred to throughout the book, as they underlie and sustain The Gear Model.

Learner Focused

Being learner focused has two main components: considering the whole child and personalized learning. What do these terms mean to you? To your colleagues? To the families you serve? It is important to clarify our meanings of the terms *whole child*, *personalized*, and *learner focused* to explain how they inform program design.

Emphasis on the whole child was a focus during our teacher training and early years of teaching kindergarten and was brought into greater importance for us when we started raising our own children. We have found the Guiding Principles for Equitable Whole Child Design (figure 1.1) from the Learning Policy Institute and Turnaround for Children (2021) to be helpful in keeping our thinking learner focused. The principles are informed by decades of research that show the connection between youths' social, emotional, cognitive, and academic development, as well as their physical and mental health. According to the Learning Policy Institute, "A whole child approach understands that students' education and life outcomes are dependent upon their access to safe and welcoming learning environments and rich learning experiences in and out of school" (n.d., para. 2).

The whole-child approach changes our focus from a narrowly defined set of academic outcomes to long-term development focused on lifelong learning. ASCD, long a proponent of the whole-child approach, has five tenets to their whole-child framework: healthy, safe, engaged, supported, and challenged (ASCD, n.d.). Many people associate a whole-child approach only with young children (birth to age five). However, it applies well beyond age five and grounds us

Figure 1.1 Guiding Principles for Equitable Whole Child Design

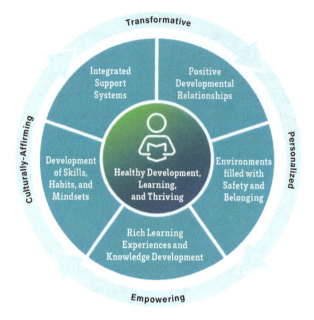

Source: "Guiding Principles for Equitable Whole Child Design." Learning Policy Institute. 2021. Used with permission.

in learner-centered thinking. A whole-child mindset causes us to start where the student is and focus on their individual social-emotional and academic growth.

When considering what it means to embrace personalized learning, we turn to Arthur L. Costa as a guide: "There is no learning that is not personalized. Anything 'learned' must first be taken in through the senses, processed and understood, interiorized in the mind and body, and emotionally charged and acted upon" (Costa 2017, ix).

Various models and graphics are used to represent what this means. Bena Kallick and Allison Zmuda's model of personalized learning (2017) resonates with us. The model has four attributes: voice, co-creation, social construction, and self-discovery.

When considering voice, we think about the student having a voice in what they are learning and how they are learning. Co-creation represents the student working with the educator on learning goals, assessments, and action plans for learning. Co-creation leads to greater student empowerment. Social construction is all about the social theory of learning. Put simply, learning is a social process that involves interaction with others. Finally, self-discovery refers to the student coming to understand themself as a learner. Personalized learning is flexible; it can be anytime, anywhere, and in partnership with communities.

Personalized, student-centered learning is one of our central beliefs and is an important aspect of The Gear Model. Assessment prior to beginning work with students helps us understand them as individuals. This initial assessment work includes learners' academic skills and their social-emotional strengths and challenges.

Developmental Relationships

Humans are wired for relationships. Relationships are complex and messy things. Most of us enter learning spaces with existing relationships with family, with friends, and with community members. However, not all families walk into schools or youth programs with relationships, and not all students have families. Acknowledging the existence or non-existence of relationships, for ourselves and our learners, informs where we invest our time and energy for the greatest impact. Though we cannot "fix" anyone's relationships, doing our part to model and build resilient, humble, vulnerable, and connected relationships supports the improvements needed to change the outcomes for youth. More and better relationships keep the systems spinning in the direction of improved learning outcomes.

To help students achieve positive learning outcomes, we strive to be warm demanders (Bondy and Ross 2008). To be warm demanders, we must establish developmental relationships, so learners know we believe in them. Being a warm demander calls us to communicate with warmth while at the same time actively "demanding" that learners perform at high levels. When strong relationships are established, youth see the positive intent within the recommendations, requests, and requirements from caring adults.

In our work, we lean into the Developmental Relationships Framework pioneered by the Search Institute (n.d.). This framework is widely considered the gold standard in youth development circles. It aligns with a whole-child approach and defines five elements of developmental relationships that inform our belief that positive relationships are central to everything we do with learners and adults. The following paragraphs provide an overview of the five elements.

Expressing Care is the first and most obvious element of developmental relationships. Educators learn about the importance of letting learners (and people in general) know they matter. Being dependable, listening, encouraging, welcoming, and so on, are part of this element. We see educators in classrooms, playgrounds, schools, and communities expressing care. Yet a strong relationship is more than a warm and fuzzy show of care.

Challenging Growth is the next element, which means to push learners to get better. Challenging growth requires timely, constructive feedback from *someone who matters*. Do youth get enough of the right kind of feedback from the trusted adults in their lives? Do they have opportunities to try, struggle, maybe fail, and try again?

The next element, Providing Support, means to help learners accomplish tasks and achieve their goals. This requires providing learners and their families with help, if needed, to navigate organizations and to advocate for their needs and desires. For example, what if parents would like access to tutoring and learning supports but do not know how to seek these resources?

Sharing Power, meaning to let youth lead, and Expanding Possibilities are the final crucial elements. To integrate these elements, we need to know the strengths and interests of learners we serve. Institutions may not know students well enough to be aware of their unique gifts, but families are often an excellent source of information about learners' strengths. To personalize whole-child intervention programs, the relationships must be deep enough to build from learners' outside experiences, strengths, and interests.

A truly developmental relationship is one in which trust and bonding are strong enough that challenging a learner's growth is understood as a belief statement. It takes spans of time and many touchpoints to grow a relationship to the point where constructive feedback can be productively considered. Connections beyond the school day provide increased opportunities to build developmental relationships.

When strong relationships are established, youth see the positive intent within the recommendations, requests, and requirements from caring adults.

Developmental relationships are at the center of The Gear Model. The model is driven by intergenerational relationships with youth, with families, with peer mentors, with classroom teachers, with community volunteers, with teen helpers, and with each other. This is a strong theme throughout this book. We often hear, "Students don't care how much you know until they know how much you care" and "It takes a village!"

Asset-Based Framing

Asset-based framing, or strengths-based teaching, in its simplest terms, focuses on learners' personal, familial, and cultural strengths. Engaging with youth within the context of their culture and in real-world settings—where rigor, enrichment, and personal interests intersect—is helpful for identifying their unique strengths and passions. Asset-based work is based on relationships. When learners are doing meaningful, relevant, self-selected activities, we see the whole child—their strengths, challenges, motivations, temperament, and so on. A key purpose of relationship building is to know learners' individual assets and tap into them to best support their learning. Asset-based work values diversity of thought, culture, and experience, and it makes room for shared experiences outside our comfort zones.

In academic settings, an asset-based approach begins with diagnostic learning activities to understand what each learner knows and can do. This allows us to focus on what each learner needs next to meet high expectations and outcomes. Knowing learners' assets helps with selecting the best instructional strategies and learning roles. This is seen in The Gear Model in how we approach each learner, select individualized work, create collaborative groups, and other ways, as discussed in Part 2.

It helps, too, to look beyond school or tutoring settings, where an even wider array of strengths can be identified and built upon. For example, consider community service work, parks and recreation programs, theatre and musical productions, sports teams, internships, mentoring programs, and more. As parents, we saw this play out with our own children. Their motivation to learn outside the school day was often higher when tied to their strengths and passions. Of course, not all students have access to out-of-school, asset-based, or passion-fueled activities.

However, our experiences have taught us that where the tiniest of connections between school staff, community partners, and learners exist, youth can gain powerful new perspectives that can change their life trajectories.

Perhaps you have memories of when you were a child out in your community and were surprised to bump into school staff. New, positive avenues for conversation could be opened. These chance real-world encounters between students and school staff have become less likely as populations have grown in many places and district employees often commute to the schools where they work. However, when chance encounters do happen, new perspectives for the learner and the educator are the result. Broader views lead to more understanding. Connections occur that can enhance the work back in the classroom.

When learners are doing meaningful, relevant, self-selected activities, we see the whole child.

We saw this when we became parents. Our own children lit up when they saw their teachers, the librarian, or cafeteria staff at the grocery store, theatre productions, or ballgames. In essence, the role of school staff being both in and of the community and in and of the school building created the conditions for the true meaning of community. We are not saying all teachers must live in the community where they teach. However, out-of-school connections can be very rewarding for students and teachers. Visiting students as they pursue their passions and watching them proudly share their skills and knowledge with others goes a long way toward building understanding and relationships.

The opposite is true also. When adults in students' lives from beyond the school building (including parents and grandparents) are seen at school, having lunch with students or attending an event, trust and bonding grows exponentially. We saw youth gain social capital and a broader sense of relationship when former After School Club volunteers attended their school choir programs. "They came to see *me*!" said a first grader, referring to a favorite volunteer who attended when the child's guardians could not get away from work.

We saw the power of relationship in our After School Club when a less-than-engaged fifth grader lifted her head and wiggled in delight as her favorite university student brought her a new book from a series they were both reading. Acquaintances from outside the school, acting with intention, became informal allies who sparked students' curiosity and ignited their thinking.

Beyond Academics

Schools have always been about academics; however, in today's world and in the future, students need to gain more than academic knowledge as it is currently assessed. Two important aspects of preparing students for productive and meaningful futures are 21st century skills and Habits of Mind.

21st Century Skills

The Framework for 21st Century Learning is focused on the knowledge, skills, and expertise needed to be successful (ASCD 2009). This framework was developed by the Partnership for 21st Century Skills, which included educators, civic and community groups, and business leaders. The framework covers the following:

1. Core subjects and 21st century themes (such as language arts, mathematics, science, global awareness, and financial literacy).
2. Learning and innovation skills (such as creativity and innovation, and critical thinking and problem solving).
3. Information, media, and technology skills.
4. Life and career skills (such as initiative and self-direction).
(ASCD 2009, para. 5–8)

When thinking of learning and innovation skills, people often include critical thinking, creativity, communication, collaboration, and character. You may have heard of these as the five C's. More recently, the idea of growth mindset, first written about by Carol Dweck (2006), has been highlighted. These are different ways of packaging the same general ideas. Twenty-first century skills are an important set of abilities needed in a highly complex and changing world.

Habits of Mind

Another important framework for our thinking is Habits of Mind, developed by Art Costa and Bena Kallick (Institute for Habits of Mind, n.d.-b). Habits of Mind are skills, behaviors, and dispositions that help learners succeed. These habits support learners in taking ownership of their learning. We lean into these habits when we run into challenging problems or situations. The sixteen habits are listed in figure 1.2. They support growing cognitively, socially, and emotionally over time.

Figure 1.2 Sixteen Habits of Mind

1. Thinking About Your Thinking (Metacognition)
2. Listening with Understanding and Empathy
3. Thinking and Communicating with Clarity and Precision
4. Taking Responsible Risks
5. Persisting
6. Thinking Flexibly
7. Applying Past Knowledge to New Situations
8. Finding Humor
9. Managing Impulsivity
10. Questioning and Posing Problems
11. Gathering Data Through All Senses
12. Responding with Wonderment and Awe
13. Striving for Accuracy
14. Thinking Interdependently
15. Creating, Imagining and Innovating
16. Remaining Open to Learning Continuously

Source: "What Are the Habits of Mind?" Institute for Habits of Mind. n.d.-a. Used with permission.

As you read the examples and stories we share in this book, watch for terms and ideas from Habits of Mind. We noticed these habits were missing or being developed as we worked with different groups of young people. We aimed to support the development of these habits for students' long-term learning success. Consider how you might use Habits of Mind in your work.

Systems Thinking

The final foundational idea is considering whether school and community structures are working in coordination on behalf of learners and families. Currently, most systems are fragmented and separated into parts, reducing their effectiveness. Families report frustration and confusion with disconnected systems and parts that do not interact or communicate with each other. Educators we have interviewed universally agree that partnerships are important, but they do not have the necessary time or resources to build partnerships. Though there are excellent intervention resources, strategies, and curricula, the implementation of well-rounded intervention programs is messy. Our work over decades has taught us that a systems approach is necessary. We need to examine the education system and surrounding community ecosystems to approach our work through broader systems thinking.

> Gil Noam, founder and director at Partnerships in Education and Resilience (PEAR), presented at a youth development conference in Minneapolis a few years ago. He spontaneously urged us to examine the multiple small streams of support available for youth and families. He challenged us to work to unite these small streams, so they become a powerful river flowing in one direction. His words and imagery helped us think about how to bring parts together.

Systems thinking puts the whole system before the individual parts (Senge 2006). In our work, this means the program structures and their places in the system come before individual intervention resources. The educational systems we aspire to create unite a wide array of people and parts that are, or should be, interconnected and interdependent. You can think of each gear in the model as a part in the system; if a single gear stops, positive outcomes stop. The parts, or the gears, must all work together for the program to successfully maximize learning for youth. Looking at the whole of the system allows us to improve the implementation of the parts to maximize impact of the interventions and support student learning and relationship building. Our vision is to bring all the parts of the student's learning environment or ecosystem together.

Within the discipline of systems thinking you can find a range of resources. We use the approach developed by the Waters Center for Systems Thinking. Their leadership team is made up of former educators who understand education systems. The approach begins with thinking about the five basic life systems: well-being, family, workplace, school, and community. Systems thinkers work to make meaningful connections within and between these five systems. The fourteen Habits of a Systems Thinker are the foundation of the Waters Center approach (Benson and Marlin 2021). We specifically lean into the following three habits:

- Seek to understand the "big picture"—we balance the big picture with attention to detail.
- Identify the circular nature of complex cause and effect relationships—we look to see how parts affect one another.
- Consider an issue fully and resist the urge to come to a quick conclusion—we take the needed time to understand the system before taking action.

Figure 1.3 gives you a summary of each habit and questions that align with it.

Figure 1.3 Three of the Habits of a Systems Thinker

Source: "Habits of a Systems Thinker." Waters Center for Systems Thinking and Thinking Tools Studio. 2020. Used with permission.

Our school and community systems are large and difficult to navigate and even more difficult to change. We do not recommend trying to take on the entire system all at once. Consider the micro-systems you work in or could create. We often think in terms of microcommunities. Microcommunities are small and include people coming together with a shared purpose.

Putting the Pieces Together

What do these influences look like when they come together? There is no single answer to this question, as the work is very contextual to the community and the learners being served. As you read, consider these influences in our work and how they could potentially influence your work. To give you a sense of what this looks like, we share the story of Jesse. For Jesse, the parts came together, and increased engagement led to increased achievement.

Jesse's Story

Jesse's mom called the school in November to enroll her first grade son. She bravely shared that she was facing her own challenges with agoraphobia (an extreme fear of entering public spaces or leaving home). Was a home visit to register possible? The next day, the principal and a social worker left school to start a relationship. In the family's living room, they warmly welcomed the family and listened as Mom shared a brief family history. When filling out forms, they noted that Mom had no one to list as an emergency contact, another indication that the family was isolated. The family was new in town.

Due to complications with Mom's anxiety and mental health, from birth to age five Jesse had only his younger brother to play with. Mom utilized assistance from county agencies. She read with the children, and played games, and the children went on some outings to the park with their maternal grandparents. Generally, Jesse had little socialization outside the family. Greeting peers, asking questions, and engaging in reciprocal conversations with other children were skills Jesse would need to develop and learn in a school community.

Sue, an intervention and outreach teacher at the time, worked with the classroom teachers to help Jesse build relationships at school. The whole school staff had a warm and encouraging relationship with Jesse, but his social development increasingly lagged behind his peers. It appeared to impact his confidence.

In the winter of second grade, Jesse refused to enter the lunchroom, hiding under a hallway table. "I'm a puppy," he whimpered. Peers were confused. His patient teacher, Mrs. H, was stumped and exhausted. Mrs. H requested help from the student support team: a special education teacher, previous teacher, current teacher, social worker, principal, and Sue, the family outreach teacher.

The meeting started by identifying Jesse's strengths. He was a bright, kind, artistic child with a limitless imagination. He had built many relationships with adults in the school and liked to stop by Sue's intervention class and the social worker's office to connect. The school nurse especially enjoyed his humorous twists of phrase.

Data showed Jesse was falling further behind academically. Although he was never overtly defiant, Jesse avoided classwork, quietly sharpening his pencil, finishing his drawings, or folding paper instead. His work completion was so minimal, and his unsuitable behavior so heightened, that the group wondered if he should be assessed for special education.

What was Jesse's new desire to be a puppy telling the adults? He was creative and persisted in independent tasks of his choice. The team wondered if the goal of developing his connections and communications with others and his genuine interest in dramatic storytelling could be integrated and tied back to the classroom. The team decided on some actions:

- In-School Idea: Jesse was already part of the mentoring program. His adult mentor had lunch with him once a week. The team hoped that if he brought a friend from class to lunch, the adult mentor could encourage peer communication between the two children.

- Out-of-School Ideas: Ask Mom for help. Sue sat with the family at community dinners to support Mom as she, with the help of her mental health counselor, worked through her own social anxiety. First, Mom registered Jesse for the After School Club in their neighborhood. Academically, that helped. Socialization was still needed at school, as evidenced by Jesse's refusal to eat lunch with peers in the cafeteria. Mom called Sue with the idea of enrolling Jesse in a community education theatre production. "You gave me a community education catalog a while back. What if we enrolled him in the play about a farm? If you could help connect me, he could be a puppy on stage instead of in class."

Sue secured a scholarship for a theatre class. Mom filled out the registration forms and told Jesse this could be his time to be creative with other kids. Sue walked Jesse down the hallway at the end of the school day for the first night of theatre class, making sure he knew the names of other learners in the class. Off to the side, Sue and the director brainstormed strategies for Jesse to verbalize with fellow actors. Jesse felt comfortable in the routine, started noticing what peers were doing, asked questions, and ultimately played *with* other youth. This was a place where he was interested in the topic and felt confident.

The afternoon of the final production, Sue met Mom, helping her avoid the crowd and enter through the back door. Mrs. H, the classroom teacher, generously made time to attend the performance and gave a thumbs-up to the proud star when he appeared.

The next morning in the cafeteria, Sue overheard Jesse talking with peers: "I think Mrs. H likes me. She told my mom I spoke clearly and made her laugh when I was on stage." It sounded as if Jesse was feeling understood. Mrs. H had always liked Jesse, but now Jesse felt seen for his talents and this helped him build connection with his teacher.

Back in class, Jesse was putting into practice critical-thinking skills. He used question-asking techniques from theatre class to solve math problems. Increasingly, he moved on from one academic task to another, proud of his completed work.

Mom gained confidence relating to teachers and other parents. Over time, she walked into the school building independently to attend parent conferences and Family Bingo Night. As Jesse's after-school and summer camp opportunities and relationships progressed, he scored well on state standardized fourth and fifth grade tests. He made and kept three close friends who remained friends all the way through twelfth grade. It likely helped that Mom became friends with the parents of Jesse's friends. This seems like a small detail, but that resulting support system may have been significant, especially during the COVID-19 pandemic. Jesse and his mom found safe places where they belonged and mattered.

Seven years later, in June 2024, when the high school seniors visited their former elementary schools in their graduation gowns, Sue felt a tap on her shoulder. It was Jesse. Sue instantly recognized him. She and other staff had informally remained in contact, bumping into Jesse at the drugstore and at his part-time job at a local ice cream shop where he earned money for post–high school tuition. What made the moment most remarkable was tucked behind Jesse: Mom, asking to take a picture of the teachers who helped her family reach their dreams. Jesse would be attending the art and design program at a local community college. His little brother was following in his successful footsteps too.

A microcommunity and long-term developmental relationships had grown up around this beautiful developing child, and he flourished. Within this microcommunity, the whole family had been transformed in significant and potentially sustainable ways.

LESSONS LEARNED

Fifteen minutes of a teacher's time improved a relationship. A boy's gift of being funny was affirmed and the skills he learned when pursuing his interests out of school enhanced his in-school learning. A mom came to trust the school and community environment, and the child continued his artistic passions. Small, intentional, coordinated intervention actions transformed life for a child and his family.

The gears surrounding Jesse worked in tandem across the days and weeks in his younger years, creating a self-perpetuating cycle of confidence that took the whole family through to high school graduation and beyond. Care and support were expressed. A keen focus on asset identification led to self-confidence. Social engagement increased, and academic gains followed.

Closing Thoughts

The Gear Model was built from an inquiry perspective. We are always asking questions and trying to make systems better. Our goal has been to purposefully unite people around the needs of the whole child to end isolation and reduce disparities. Though this is complex work, it is doable and has potential to be very rewarding.

We ask you to consider that though students report to school more than 170 days per year for over six hours a day, it can be almost impossible to see the whole child clearly enough during the school day to begin to harness their actual strengths and support their development as a whole human being. As you continue learning about our journey to improve intervention systems and their parts, think about your community's resources, strengths, and needs.

Here are a few thoughts we hope you keep in mind as you continue to read. Perhaps you will be inspired to develop your own multi-faceted intervention program.

- You must have many conversations across your education and community systems before you can begin to harness the collective buy-in needed to ensure success.
- Identifying and agreeing on shared beliefs and outcomes in advance increases the effectiveness and sustainability of a solid program.
- Educators overestimate and underestimate the amount of time and coordination needed to begin new programs or ideas. Overestimating can cause momentum to stall, while underestimating can reduce sustainability.

You are embarking on a learning journey. Think about who is on board with you. Remember the saying "If you want to go fast, go alone. If you want to go far, go together!"

This book aims to help you examine your unique learning environment and system(s) in order to better serve all youth. What you will ultimately do depends on your situation and what the voices in your community lead you to implement. You may need to construct an entirely new system, or you may need to tweak existing parts. We offer proven ideas to consider as you develop or refine your approach to ensure the strongest possible learning outcomes for students.

Reflection Questions

- What can larger systems learn from stories of microcommunities like Jesse's, stories where authentic relationships sustain small touchpoints over many years of a child's and family's development?
- What experiences influence your philosophies and beliefs about how and where youth learn?
- In what ways do your philosophies and beliefs align with the ideas in this chapter?
- What community and inter-district connections do you already have that you can leverage to unite the streams of interventions in your community?
- What new places or programs might you explore in your community's learning ecosystem?
- Think about the five elements of developmental relationships (page 15). Where does your community fall in terms of enacting each one on behalf of youth?

CHAPTER 2

A Foundation of Relationships

"Alone we can do so little; together we can do so much."
—Helen Keller, author, lecturer, and disability rights advocate

In this chapter, we discuss collaborative relationships and experiences that informed the creation of The Gear Model. The Gear Model was not developed in a vacuum; our work over many years in schools and in the community led to the foundations the model is built on.

The following questions are answered in this chapter:
- How can schools and universities work together?
- How can partnerships support your work?
- How can relationships be built between all interested parties?

Building Relationships and a Partnership

In 2005, Tom Koch, the elementary school principal mentioned in the introduction, and Lucy, working as a professor at a nearby university, created a school-university partnership. Sue was a teacher-leader at the school, and out of this partnership grew a twenty-year collaboration between Sue and Lucy focused on learner-centered instruction. The partnership's initial goals were to:
- improve K–5 students' understanding of, and achievement in, mathematics;
- improve the university's teaching methods course by use of real-world examples and experiences; and
- support the development of school site teachers' knowledge of best practices in teaching and learning mathematics.

Over time, Tom, Lucy, and Sue developed trusting relationships built on shared interests and goals.

Tom was thinking about how the interactions between K–12 schools and universities could be enhanced to better develop future teachers and serve students. He reached out to Lucy to build a relationship and find ways to learn and work together. The first step was spending time together in each other's spaces to understand what each person hoped to gain from the work and what each person brought to the work.

Tom was seeking action-oriented instructional practice for his demographically changing elementary school. The school was in a middle-class neighborhood experiencing a shift to having two distinct populations: white upper-middle class and racially diverse lower socioeconomic class. Tom embraced the change, but he knew the school could do better with more help.

Tom took the opportunity to develop his own future teachers by hosting student teachers from the university. As the partnership strengthened over time, Tom also hosted some of the most struggling candidates to help them evolve into great teachers.

Lucy also sought a tighter alignment between K–12 schools and higher education. She saw the importance of close interactions and relationships with teachers and young learners to inform her work at the university with beginning teachers. She missed being in community with students and teachers. She embraced collaboration across different parts, or levels, of the education ecosystem.

Lucy's role was to be a resource and thought partner for the teachers and staff while also being a site-based learner. Rather than acting as an expert, her role focused more on listening and asking questions than on telling or talking. She brought unique knowledge to the partnership. Everyone engaged in the partnership had their areas of expertise, and we all had a shared interest in student success. This is foundational in our work. The partnership was a way to blur roles and bridge gaps in the educational systems.

Throughout the years of the partnership, Lucy collaborated with teachers on planning and analyzing student work, attended PLC meetings, co-taught in classrooms, collaborated with teachers on implementing new teaching strategies, presented to parents at math-night events, wrote columns for the school newsletter, and supervised student teachers and their action research projects at the school.

Collaboration

Lucy, Tom, Sue, and other veteran teachers facilitated schoolwide staff development focused on state math standards. Rather than using test data merely to sort and classify students, they engaged teachers in using data to understand cohort and individual student strengths and needs. Lucy encouraged teachers to look for questions and trends in the data before jumping into potential solutions. A broader analysis was emphasized.

Lucy helped the grade-level PLCs address approaches to improve their instruction based on evidence. These conversations deepened teachers' understanding of pedagogy, instruction practices, research, and practical application of math standards. Math teaching became refined and more effective for all learners. Teachers felt confident in what they prioritized as most essential and what beginning or future standards they could integrate into large-group lessons. Teachers learned what lessons they could let go of.

From the beginning, this was a truly practical, pragmatic partnership for everyone. No leader or teacher had all the knowledge or answers. Tom and Lucy worked alongside classroom teachers to prioritize standards; build instructional focuses across grade levels; implement more responsive, personalized instructional practices; and ultimately improve learning outcomes. Teachers said they had never worked harder, but their successes gave them increased energy and motivation to continue to align and refine their approaches to learning.

During this time, Sue was a cooperating classroom teacher, hosting student teachers from the university. Further connecting elementary schools and higher education, Sue began working as a part-time adjunct faculty member, teaching preservice teachers under Lucy's guidance. This work allowed Sue to reflect deeply on her practice, as she had to explain her teaching practices to inexperienced teachers who asked a lot of questions. Together, Lucy and Sue taught graduate-level courses for teachers already working in classrooms. Instructing teachers from the urban and suburban districts around the Twin Cities deepened Sue's awareness of the complex reality that not all students have equitable access to rigorous learning opportunities.

> *From the beginning, this was a truly practical pragmatic partnership for everyone. No leader or teacher had all the knowledge or answers.*

Sue's understanding of the essential state standards and her ability to connect them across grade levels (known as vertical alignment) were refined too. This helped her coordinate intervention plans for groups of students who were not achieving at their known potential.

Results!

Results followed! The school was one of the most diverse elementaries in its suburban school district. The number of fifth graders who exceeded math targets on the state standardized test rose 12 percentage points in four years. The scores in the increasingly diverse school came to match or exceed those of more affluent schools in the same district. These gains were a result of the partnership and ultimately led to the school being recognized by the US Department of Education as National Blue Ribbon School.

New Role of Achievement Interventionist

As the formal school-university partnership ended, Sue's district reorganized with a focus on reducing disparities while maintaining excellence. They were decentralizing and bringing direct support services closer to the children who needed them. They also adopted a strategic plan to ensure a high-quality education that prepared every student to thrive today and to excel in the future. To inform their approach to intervention and address students' learning needs before they failed, the district created new positions—achievement interventionists. The job description had three parts:

1. Co-teaching
2. Daily small-group math and reading intervention
3. Family and community partnership building

The achievement interventionists were to be proactive rather than reactive. Sue jumped at the chance to continue her teaching work in a new way, more focused on the students who most needed support. The directives were to get out there, listen, and be responsive:

- Talk to the grade-level teachers during their PLC meetings. Figure out together what you could do differently.
- If the parents say it's hard for them to support reading or homework at home, find a way to fix that.
- If the student needs a friend, help them find a friend.
- If the student can't read, teach them to read. Be the tutor, set up tutoring, work with the classroom teacher.
- If the student isn't passing math unit tests, provide more individualized expert instruction.

In essence, the achievement interventionists sought to bring the voices and ideas of teachers, parents, and learners together to inform personalized, student-centered approaches to both social inclusion and academic skill building. This was a flexible way to bring the school to the community and the community back into the school. This intervention approach served as a natural bridge between parents, learners, and traditional school. Views of the whole child's life, even small glimpses of the child's life in context of their family were helpful in creating conditions for learning in the classroom.

In her new role, Sue was part of a small team of achievement interventionists at her school. She pulled small groups of students out of class daily for half-hour reading and math intervention lessons. This was basically an in-school tutoring model, a best practice identified by Robert Slavin's work at Johns Hopkins University. Parents had requested this for their children. ProvenTutoring, a think tank and consortium based on Slavin's research, "had reviewed research on all types of programs for struggling learners and knew that tutoring was by far the most effective solution for students struggling in reading and mathematics" (ProvenTutoring 2024, para. 1).

Over time, more students needed small-group intervention than the intervention specialists could service. Though standardized test scores improved for many, and parents appreciated the increased individualized (personalized) support, results over years at the broader scale were mixed.

Sue and other interventionists noticed a trend, however. Students receiving small-group intervention lessons during the day *and* participating in community-run After School Homework

Clubs showed the greatest growth on benchmark assessments and standardized tests. The double dose could be maximized with a few tweaks and data-informed intentionality. Having a teacher from the school work beside students twice a day, in multiple settings, might just be the magic recipe for developing relationships that empower students' own sense of success. Being together in multiple settings tapped into students' passions, ultimately empowering their own self-agency and academic motivation to persist in problem-solving.

> *Students receiving small-group intervention lessons during the day and participating in community-run After School Homework Clubs showed the greatest growth on benchmark assessments and standardized tests.*

Co-Teaching in Classrooms

To further build relationships with teachers and students, the achievement interventionists pushed into classrooms and co-taught for a small part of each week. This enabled the interventionists to see the students in the context of the classroom. Were they engaged and motivated? Could they advocate for themselves? Did they exhibit a sense of connection to others in the classroom? Spending time in the classroom deepened the interventionists' relationship with and understanding of each student.

As an example, assessment data revealed some fifth graders who needed additional learning in problem-solving and higher-order thinking skills. The interventionist modeled critical thinking and persistence (productive struggle) in math problem-solving alongside the classroom teacher. The rigor and difficulty of math instruction in classrooms increased as students' knowledge and work habits improved. Importantly, the interventionist served as a bridge between the skills taught in school and students' homework and learning beyond the classroom, too.

Growing Students' Community

Students in the fourth and fifth grade reading intervention groups who were also receiving special education services could read, but their slow fluency was holding them up. These students needed to be able to finish chapters or books during independent reading in school in order to tackle the rigor of nationally normed tests. To personalize the learning, Sue interviewed the students and found they disliked reading, which impacted their stamina to stay engaged. In response to the interviews, a socially oriented book club was formed.

Students were motivated by the idea of being part of "The Big Kids Book Club." The older struggling readers each selected a picture book (at, or slightly above, their level) to practice reading Monday through Thursday mornings at school breakfast. On Fridays, the students went to a kindergarten classroom where each student read to a pair of kindergartners.

The goal of the book club was to have the kindergartners laugh, lean in, or look surprised during the reading. Photos were taken while the fourth and fifth graders read to the kindergartners. Using the photos with the older students, Sue coached them to look for indicators of success:

- On a scale of 1–5, looking at the kindergartners' body language, how engaged do you think they were?
- Does their expression match what was happening in the story? (If it was a surprising part, do the kindergartners look surprised?)
- Do the kindergartners look like they are interested and following the story? If not, what could you do with your voice or your introduction to the book next week that would get them more engaged in the story?
- Are the kindergartners leaning in and looking at the book? If not, what will you do next week so the kindergartners lean in and giggle, look surprised, or respond in some way?

The fourth and fifth graders enjoyed seeing themselves in photos and eventually, without prompting, identified ways they could engage the kindergartners more next time. Analyzing the photos gave them a perspective of the experiences they were providing to the young children. The relational nature of this feedback seemed to foster openness and vulnerability that allowed students to hear suggestions for improvement from peers too. The older students recognized when they needed to use more expression or practice fluency to get the younger ones to lean in and react to the story. They began to select books to match the interests of the kindergartners. The photos were sent home to encourage family conversations about the experience also.

Most of these students also attended the Neighborhood Homework Club, where their academic motivation and engagement were growing. Their identities as readers were developing. Parents were pleased to report their children were initiating reading at home more often. Volunteers confirmed the growing confidence in reading they saw in these fourth and fifth graders at the Neighborhood Homework Club.

Teachers reported that the students now had more stamina in class during silent reading time, and students' fluency improved. And we saw another benefit: Book club participants receiving special education services (the students scoring the lowest on standard measures) more than doubled their reading rate (words per minute).

Our experience highlights the benefits of multi-age intervention strategies. We wondered what other simple, doable approaches could allow older elementary students, especially those who would most benefit from intervention, to act and lead in an academic area where they needed exponential growth. The Habits of Mind that support learning were strengthened when Sue was able to connect what the students were learning in different settings throughout the day.

Seeking Input from Families

Sue and other achievement interventionists viewed the family and partnership development aspect of their roles as an opportunity to learn from and empower families. Through conversations at school, at community-hosted family dinners, and in passing in their neighborhoods, the interventionists sought the guidance of the families. By conducting surveys and intentional conversations, they learned a lot about what parents were looking for and why.

First, families' aspirations were extremely high. Many of the families were recent immigrants who envisioned their children would become doctors and lawyers. The big dreams would require students to gain entry to college after high school. Teachers' expectations rose when they heard the parents' hopes and dreams.

Second, families were requesting tutoring. Not all their children were receiving reading or math intervention in school. Many of their children were a year or more behind, and the parents were uncertain how to help. Many parents wished teachers would be clearer and more direct about that truth at parent conferences. Once trust was established, they sometimes shared their own challenges with reading.

Third, access to childcare before and after school and during summer was an overwhelming, cost-prohibitive need. Many families were cobbling together bare-bones supervision for their children while they worked multiple jobs or nontraditional shifts. A small but very real and very concerning group of youth were home alone after school. According to data from the national organization Afterschool Alliance (2022), approximately 24.7 million children in the United States who are not enrolled in after-school programs would be enrolled if programs were available to them.

Tips for Conversations with Parents

When having conversations with parents, we recommend a safe, neutral environment and only a handful of parents at a time. Listen more than you talk. Explain your desire to hear their perspectives on what is helpful for their children's learning and what barriers get in the way of learning. Think of this not as an interview so much as a conversation to learn. For every question you ask, be ready with at least two possible follow-up questions to keep the conversation focused on the child. You can start with the list of questions below. It is also critical to check in a month later with each family; this will add to your credibility and help build a foundation of trust.

Family Interview Questions

1. What are your hopes and dreams for your child? What do you envision your child doing in fifteen years?
2. How will they get there?
3. What do they need *now* to get there? Next month? Next year?
4. What passions or interests does your child have? (That we could connect learning to?)

> "When people talk, listen completely. Don't be thinking what you're going to say. Most people never listen. Nor do they observe. You should be able to go into a room and when you come out know everything that you saw there and not only that. If that room gave you any feeling you should know exactly what it was that gave you that feeling."
>
> —Ernest Hemingway, Pulitzer and Nobel prize–winning writer

5. Are you aware that your child has been identified for extra supports (intervention) to help them catch up academically?
6. Do you know which areas your child is not yet working at grade level in?
7. What specific skills might your child need in that subject area?
8. What helps your child learn best?
9. What communications have you had with the classroom teacher?
10. Do you know how to get more information from the school/teacher?

As you listen, consider the level of detail you get from the parents. Can they provide specifics, or do they respond with broad topics? For example, for question 6, do they say "math," which is a broad topic, or do they say "fact families," which is a specific skill/concept? Are their words strong, sure, and direct? Or are they unsure?

If the discussion after the first question does not go well, you might be at the beginning stages of building a relationship. In our experience, when families have little to say to us, it could be from lack of trust. To have and build trust, you must have a relationship.

Honest Conversations Build Trust

"He is going to college or something beyond high school. We risked everything to come to this country to find success," a father and mother from Palestine announced, holding hands at a community dinner and parent-conversation night. The father pounded his hand on the table for emphasis. Their third grade son was still young, but their belief in his academic success was clear.

Sue engaged with the classroom teacher the next day. Jordan was behind in language acquisition and reading comprehension, though his fluency (words read per minute) did not stand out as slow. The classroom teacher and Sue coordinated consistent feedback between the student and his parents. Jordan's parents began consistently monitoring that he took his books out of his backpack at home and read daily. They asked him to talk about details from the text. He was encouraged to join the homework club in his neighborhood, where he read aloud with trained volunteers. Also at school, the teacher more frequently conferenced with him after independent reading time, having him briefly summarize the text and the author's main point. Jordan passed his reading state standardized test that spring. His growth in reading was exceptional. He was more engaged and appeared more confident in class.

The family felt successful. The momentum continued into fourth and fifth grade when the COVID-19 pandemic changed education. The parents had an established trusting relationship with Sue, who worked with the classroom teachers to support Jordan in school and virtually out of school. The parents knew how to advocate for assistance with technology devices and support, ensuring that Jordan and his sister showed up for every online lesson. Test scores for youth with the same level of support as Jordan (in and out of school) did not drop following the pandemic.

> **WHAT DID WE LEARN?**
>
> As we stated earlier, *community* is defined as a feeling of fellowship with others as a result of sharing common attitudes, interests, and goals. Thus, the availability of an educator from the school to work within and beyond the school schedule and walls strengthened connections between the school and the family. The family and child felt successful and connected. Informal time for meaningful conversations makes a difference when providing responsive intervention support.

Relationships Through a Neighborhood Program

Sue developed a close working relationship with Martha Grave, a new and enthusiastic neighborhood program coordinator at Interfaith Outreach, a nonprofit group focused on "building a vibrant community where everyone counts." As part of her job, Martha was responsible for two Neighborhood Homework Clubs. In addition, Martha coordinated with community sponsors for a monthly community family dinner. It was at one of these dinners where Sue forged a relationship with Jesse's family, whom you read about in chapter 1.

Martha's homework clubs were held two afternoons a week. One of the clubs met on Mondays and Wednesdays in a large community room at Interfaith Outreach Community Partnership and the other club met on Tuesdays and Thursdays in the refurbished former laundry room of an apartment building. This room was adjacent to the apartment manager's office. The clubs had an ample supply of community volunteers. Sue and another teacher from the district each assisted at each club one day a week. Their compensation was funded through state dollars.

Sue supported the Neighborhood Homework Clubs by selecting individualized math and reading worksheets, activities, and games that community volunteers used to work with youth one-on-one or in small groups after homework was completed. This advanced the club's mission to grow beyond being a safe place for youth to hang out and complete homework toward being a place of self-discovery. The tutoring support parents desired, but were not able to pay for, was beginning to be addressed.

In addition, as a teacher in the school the students attended, Sue was able to seek information releases from the parents to share students' academic data, skill needs, and behavior plans. She was also able to share classroom teachers' newsletters and curricular connections so volunteers were up to speed on classroom tasks and happenings. Sue was regularly communicating back to teachers and parents to connect their input and insights. Communication across these different systems was key to success.

When Martha and Sue were both new to their roles in September, parents were invited to a casual open house at the end of the first night of the program. Students and families enjoyed conversations and ice pops. Martha and Sue wanted to build relationships and learn parents' perspectives about what was most important to them. Parents made comments such as these:

- "We aren't home to help with homework or monitor that they read for their reading

calendars." (Most were working.)
- "We know it's important for our kids to read. We don't read in English."
- "We don't have a lot of books. We could use the school and community library. How do we do that?"
- "The way the school does math computation is new to us."
- "After third grade, the math homework is really hard. Frustrations run high at our house when it comes to math."

In response, the local librarian and district math specialist were invited to the next family dinner to enjoy a meal beside families and to each give a twenty-minute presentation with time for questions. Families left with library cards and resources to help their children in math. Everyone became friends while assembling math puzzles and learning to tackle open-ended math challenges. Families' input informed educational speakers and conversations at the dinners from then on.

The partnership between the school and the nonprofit's program was becoming a means to streamline and support learning in the classroom and at home. As word of mouth spread, more and more youth began attending. Across the two clubs, enrollment increased from eight to twenty-five students.

Over the next few years, the program was refined. More achievement interventionists and teachers from the school district started partnering with the Neighborhood Homework Clubs their students attended. They developed tubs of math games for each homework club location. They assembled a box of donated books for each child. The results were so strong that neighboring school districts started coming to observe and learn from the work being done.

Closing Thoughts

Cross-sector learning is a largely untapped way to improve student outcomes. Communities are full of people who care, who have important input and perspectives to share, and who can contribute to the success of young people. After-school programs and schools can be more effective by joining together to prioritize what would be most beneficial for youth to learn next. Parks and recreation leaders and summer school programs could also benefit from coordination efforts across systems. Politicians creating policy could benefit from shadowing classroom teachers periodically. Potential partnerships are all around you.

It cannot be emphasized enough that the work of the partnerships began and ended with the individual students and their families—their thinking, their experiences, and the development of the whole child. Effective ideas are often lost when we overlook the true epicenter of the child's life: the family. This can only be done at the levels needed when some school staff have dedicated time for outreach and partnership building. This work starts by showing up in the community.

We, Lucy and Sue, have combined our academic/teacher worlds—the experiences we have gained *meeting with* parents—and our parent worlds—*being* parents who look at the whole child, because that is what families do. We believe cross-sector partnerships focused on accurate pictures of a child's strengths and needs help develop the whole human being.

Listening and responding to partners, coalition building, development of mutually beneficial relationships, and laser-focused extension of the learning in the classroom to ensure essential skills are being mastered are the principal takeaways from our work. Moving beyond a narrow focus on academics to a broader focus on student thinking, Habits of Mind, and 21st century skills can help us improve learning for all.

Communities are full of people who care, who have important input and perspectives to share, and who can contribute to the success of young people.

Reflection Questions

- How can we build capacity and support principals and teachers so they have time to partner or coordinate with outside groups and vice versa?
- What do families in your community say would help their children develop into independent, contributing, healthy adults?
- What do learners say would help them engage and learn more? What motivates them to learn?
- How could the learning ecosystem become healthier with cross-sector approaches?
- Do schools and classrooms perceive they are separate from organizations working in youth development: nonprofits, homework clubs, sports clubs, theatre groups, and so on? If so, why do they feel this way?
- What would it take for all learners to have expanded critical-thinking, high-interest opportunities, both in and out of school?

CHAPTER 3

Learning from Successful Programs

"No one of us is as smart as all of us."
—Ken Blanchard, author, business consultant, and motivational speaker

If schools alone could have eliminated disparities during the time allotted to the school day in the traditional school year, they would have done so by now. If current systems of intervention implementation worked, this book would not be necessary. Clearly, existing systems need to evolve to meet the diverse needs of all learners.

This chapter explores critical questions:

- What barriers hinder meaningful change in intervention models?
- How does adopting a broader perspective drive improvement?
- What lessons can be learned from successful programs across the country?

Connections for More Learning

We believe that when youth have access to academic, emotional, and social growth opportunities beyond the school day, both engagement and outcomes improve. This belief led us to ask essential questions:

- How can we personalize in-school, after-school, and summer programs (such as enrichment, mentoring, and tutoring) to meet individual needs?

- How can we develop sustainable programming for all students?
- What does it take to scale a successful program from a single site to a districtwide initiative?

Our goal is to integrate school, community, and family systems while acknowledging that there are some parts of these systems we will not be able to change. Though we must work within the context of current school structures, we can certainly learn from programs that have very different structures or contexts.

Sue decided to take time away from the classroom to travel and study successful intervention and enrichment programs around the United States and investigate her theory that when learning opportunities in school and out of school are connected, youth make longer-term gains. Sue and Lucy decided to collaborate on this project, bringing their unique perspectives together—Sue as a classroom teacher and interventionist and Lucy as a university researcher and systems connector. This partnership enabled us to challenge each other to explore ideas beyond standard ways of thinking and give credibility to education intervention reform.

Identifying Barriers to Intervention Success

We began by examining all the barriers and challenges that overwhelm school systems and nonprofit entities when starting and maintaining intervention programs. We asked ourselves, "What stops progress for youth as we intervene to help them become independent, contributing, healthy young adults?" Confusion surrounds this "extra" work of intervening. One school system's barriers to after-school and summer intervention programs are seen in figure 3.1. Keep in mind that similar barriers often impact in-school intervention as well. In fact, we have found the barriers and questions are nearly the same for in-school and out-of-school intervention programs.

Below are nine common barriers we found and questions we used to examine the barriers:

1. **Funding**: Most conversations in education start with funding. Do we have any? Can we get some? Does it pay for everything we need? Is it enough? What happens when grant dollars dry up? We see others have funding, but we do not know how to get it. If we can overcome this barrier, then we go to staffing.
2. **Staffing, Partners, Volunteers**: People are a precious resource. Are teachers too tired to add this to their day? How will this impact a teacher's load? Will communicating with partners take too much time? How well do we really know the partners? Will adding more people/partners make the work more difficult for the lead educator? Where will we find volunteers? Who will be responsible for training, coordinating, and working with them?
3. **Transportation**: Yikes! Driver shortages have worsened over the past few years. Can we use district transportation? Is district transportation enough?

Figure 3.1 Unrecognized Barriers That Increase Disparities and Reduce Outcomes

We've inadvertently created a cyclical pay-to-play system
With good hearts and intentions

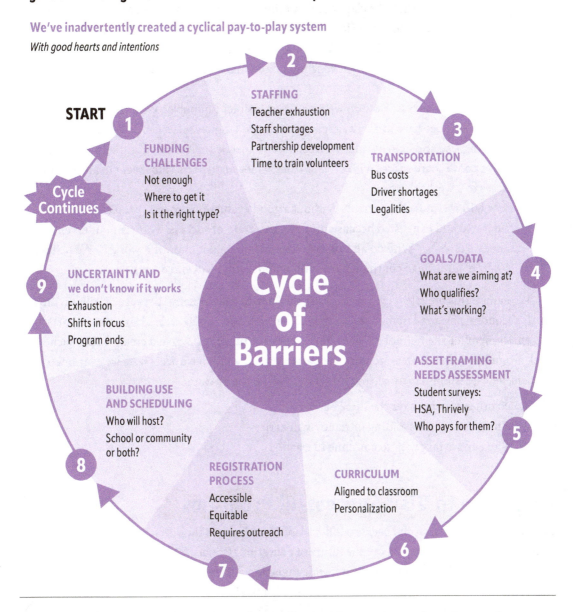

4. **Goals/Data**: Where is data housed? Is it all in one location? How do we know who qualifies to participate? How do we know if the program works?
5. **Asset Framing, Needs Assessment**: What do we have access to? Individual strengths-finding tools like Partnerships in Education and Resilience's (PEAR's) Holistic Student Assessment (HSA) (see appendix A) could help us change the conversation. Some student survey assessments charge a fee. How do we use the data from the student surveys if the data is not individualized?

Chapter 3: Learning from Successful Programs   39

6. **Curriculum**: What restrictions are tied to the funding? (In this district, instructional practices had to match the classroom, but the curriculum could not be the same as the one used during the school day.) How do we personalize the curriculum? Is the curriculum relevant and fun for the learner? Who will develop it? If program leaders are not school staff, how do they find out what vocabulary and math skills students are learning in school?
7. **Registration Process**: How do we make it accessible? Equitable? What is the process like? What if families have difficulty registering due to language barriers or lack of technology?
8. **Building Use and Scheduling**: What spaces are needed? How often and for how long? How can we share spaces with others? Chess clubs and sports clubs seem to always find access to a workable space.
9. **How will we know if it works?**: Without a good evaluation process, people tend to become frustrated and exhausted because they are uncertain of success. The entire intervention model crumbles. "Why do all this extra work if we do not know if it works?" We believe it is worth our time to continue reinventing models that will end disparities.

We named this prevalent cycle of barriers the "pay-to-play system," because families with greater economic means can more easily overcome these barriers to access learning supports and enrichment for their children. They have their own funding. We need creative approaches to work around or—even better—remove the barriers so all youth have access. As we examined the barriers, new questions emerged, and we set out to find the answers:

1. Do other systems have the same barriers?
2. What systems are avoiding or removing barriers?
3. Who can we talk with to continue to learn?

Preparing to Visit Successful Programs

Prior to Sue's site visits, we did background research to help focus the visits. Four key learning sources we used were 1) ideas about the future of education (Prince 2019), 2) a database of over two hundred schools who are doing good work aligned to student-centered learning (Canopy Project Data Portal, n.d.), 3) a webinar on the role of Multi-Tiered Systems of Support (MTSS) in personalized learning (Aurora Institute 2020), and 4) a study of out-of-school programs (McCombs, Whitaker, and Yoo 2017). A list of the specific readings we used is included in appendix A.

As we researched, we wondered what established, evidence-based, growing programs we could learn from. We were eager to share space beside them, learn together, and have in-depth discussions with their key personnel. Reading about successful programs was not enough. Sue's visits to programs to conduct informal action research, ask questions of the difference-makers and influential leaders, and see the work in action would be the next step.

Identifying Successful Programs

We talked with people in surrounding districts to identify programs in our state that were considered successful. This led to four local site visits.

Like us, a local community education leader was also running inclusive after-school and summer programs. He was animated and relieved as we discussed the pay-to-play cycle of barriers. He was from a different school district and felt isolated and disconnected from others in the state doing the same work. He too had difficulty recruiting teachers who had time and energy to individualize the academic aspect of after-school intervention. Transportation home, especially for families unable to pick up their children, was a challenge.

A district director of data and assessment pointed to the barrier at the end of the cycle, agreeing that support for extended out-of-school learning is diminished when measures for success are not clearly established at the beginning. Success comes when data is accessible, actionable, individual, and focused on a specific cohort in one place. This speaks to the power of having teachers who can see school data (following privacy laws).

Another district leader appreciated the importance of asset-based needs assessment data to personalize the approach, build engagement, and prevent the tendency to lower expectations for youth who need intervention. This reinforced the importance of implementing student surveys such as the HSA in future after-school programming. The Minnesota-based after-school and summer leaders Sue talked with struggled to find a curriculum that matched the classroom but did not repeat exactly what students did in the classroom. Doing more of the same is not best practice. Nonprofits were especially frustrated with uncertainty about how to help learners with academics. This applies to every program in Minnesota and in most, if not all, other states. Fishtank Learning's math and reading materials removed that barrier for us.

We used the barrier cycle (pay-to-play) graphic (figure 3.1) during meetings. This facilitated quick, action-oriented, and highly focused conversations largely free of blaming and finger pointing.

Visiting Programs Across the United States

Though there are many long-standing, evidence-based, growing programs across the United States, Sue was selective about the programs she would visit. She had to consider the outcomes and the learning goals of her research. With limited time to travel, it was important to get the best sites (positive reviews, good outcomes), close together (affordability), offering different perspectives (depth of learning). Sue visited, interviewed, and examined eight East Coast programs in the fall of 2021:

1. Trekkers, Midcoast of Maine

    Trekkers is a nonprofit established by Jack and Don Carpenter over 30 years ago, dedicated to building supportive, long-term relationships that help students thrive. Using a six-year group mentoring and cohort-based model, Trekkers connects young people with caring adult mentors, guiding them through experiential learning, outdoor exploration, and community engagement. The program is rooted in research-backed youth development principles and incorporates PEAR's Holistic Student Assessment to ensure that programs are responsive to students' evolving social-emotional needs. By fostering a deep sense of belonging, resilience, and self-discovery, Trekkers empowers students to envision and pursue meaningful futures.

2. Aspirations Incubator, Maine

    The Aspirations Incubator is a statewide initiative launched in 2017 by the Rural Futures Fund to address Maine's rural aspirations gap, where only 57 percent of high school seniors pursue a post-secondary plan that includes college. At the heart of the Aspirations Incubator are four key pillars: long-term mentoring, experiential learning, social-emotional development, and college, career, and life readiness. This seventh grade through high school program focuses on deep mentoring engagement through the pivotal eighth-to-ninth-grade transition, a time when many students disengage, and aspiration foreclosure—the premature narrowing of future possibilities—can set in. By providing consistent, relationship-based support, the Aspirations Incubator helps rural youth not only see more possibilities for their future but also develop the confidence, connections, and skills to pursue them.

3. Casco Bay High School, Portland, Maine

    In 2011, Casco Bay High School became an Expeditionary Learning mentor school. The school utilizes a holistic educational approach that personalizes learning and focuses on experiential opportunities, including outdoor adventure trips and comprehensive class research outside of school. This method allows students to relate their studies to real-world contexts, fostering both academic and personal development. With a maximum capacity of four hundred students, the school mirrors Portland's demographic landscape, featuring 47 percent minority representation and 34 percent economically disadvantaged students. Casco Bay High School is well-regarded for effectively preparing students for academic achievement and active participation in citizenship.

4. Yawkey Boys & Girls Club, Roxbury (southern Boston), Massachusetts

    Since 1910, this club has established a legacy of commitment to the youth of the Roxbury community. The club offers state-of-the-art facilities and provides comprehensive youth programs that focus on academic achievement, life skills, leadership, sports, and the arts. Adam Chaprnka, a licensed social worker who currently serves as director of operations, has been with the club for almost two decades.

5. City Connects, Boston, Massachusetts

    City Connects is a program founded by Mary E. Walsh at Boston College in 2001. The evidence-based program aims to improve educational success and life opportunities for children from preschool through post-secondary education. It transforms the student support function of schools to provide each and every student with an individualized plan of supports and opportunities that address their needs and strengths. It connects each student to vital resources in the school and surrounding community, such as tutoring, mentoring, and health services. As of 2024, City Connects operates in about two hundred schools across five states and has also expanded to Dublin, Ireland. Through a large body of rigorous research, the program is demonstrated to enhance educational outcomes and provide children with the support they need for lifelong success. By personalizing support and building partnerships with community agencies, City Connects helps children access the resources they need to thrive.

6. Harvard Medical School's MEDscienceLAB, Massachusetts

    Harvard Medical School's MEDscience program, founded by Julie Joyal, RN, M.Ed., and Nancy Oriol, MD, uses realistic medical simulations to engage and inspire high school students in STEM. What began in 2005 as a one-week summer immersion for twelve students has expanded into four semester-long, credit-bearing courses integrated into over one hundred high schools. Covering anatomy, physiology, immunology, genetics, and bioengineering, the program immerses four thousand students annually in real-life medical emergencies, challenging them to diagnose and treat patients as a team. Through this hands-on experience, students develop self-confidence, critical thinking, and scientific reasoning.

7. ProvenTutoring, Johns Hopkins School of Education, Baltimore, Maryland

    ProvenTutoring aims to improve educational outcomes for students in under-resourced communities through quality tutoring and academic support. They lead a coalition of organizations with the goal of enhancing student achievement, fostering academic confidence, and addressing learning gaps by leveraging evidence-based tutoring practices and building strong community partnerships.

8. Boys & Girls Clubs of Metropolitan Baltimore, Maryland

    For over 130 years, the Boys & Girls Clubs of Metropolitan Baltimore have been committed to serving youth in underprivileged communities, offering programs in education, sports, arts, and STEM. Boys & Girls Clubs of Metropolitan Baltimore focuses on academic success, character building, and leadership development, providing a safe space for children and teens to thrive. Its programs are designed to ensure all members graduate from high school ready for a post-secondary education and a 21st-century career.

In addition to her East Coast tour, Sue visited the following highly recommended whole-family and whole-child wraparound service organizations in the Midwest:

1. Operation Breakthrough—Kansas City, Missouri

   Founded in 1971 by Sister Corita Bussanmas and Sister Berta Sailer, the organization addresses both immediate needs and long-term outcomes for families by providing a wide range of services, including educational programs, healthcare, job training, and emergency assistance. This comprehensive support system aims to help families break the cycle of poverty while creating pathways for children to achieve academic and personal success. Through its multifaceted approach, the organization makes a lasting impact on the community, fostering resilience and improving overall quality of life for those it serves.

2. Banyan Community Youth Development Center—Minneapolis, Minnesota

   Founded in 1998 by Tim and Joani Essenburg, the Banyan Community Youth Development Center is a holistic program that supports youth from early childhood through high school. It offers a range of services, including academic tutoring, mentoring, and leadership programs, while actively involving families to enhance overall well-being. Located in the Phillips neighborhood of Minneapolis, Banyan places a strong emphasis on culturally relevant programming that reflects the needs and values of the community. The center leverages strategic partnerships with local organizations to provide additional resources and support, playing a vital role in helping local youth and families navigate various challenges, such as academic difficulties and economic hardships.

Questions and Observation Tool

Prior to the visits, we created a set of questions to ask and an observation tool to ensure we collected the same or similar information from each program. The questions focused on the leadership, origin of the program, mission of the program, funding and partnerships, participants, fees, attendance, registration, families, data, staff and volunteers, and programming. Some of the information was found by digging through websites, which helped focus the in-person conversations. We viewed the questions as a conversation guide. Not all the questions needed to be asked or addressed, but we felt it was important to address each broad area.

The observation tool looked at how programs use their time by noting activity segments, the cognitive demand of tasks, student engagement, and the questioning strategies used by the adults. The observation protocol also included creating a map of the space and assigning a summative observation scale. Due to the COVID-19 pandemic, use of this tool was limited. However, the tool was helpful during conversations and observations of space, even when no students were present.

Key Findings and Takeaways

Our learning through this journey was immense, and we heard stories that were very impactful. Everywhere Sue went, she was spellbound by unsung local heroes who were staffing programs. Most leaders knew of the Search Institute's Developmental Relationships Framework (n.d.) (page 15), one of our important influences. All the sites were aiming to build long-term developmental relationships. To summarize important commonalities and specialized foci that we learned from the sites visited, we have grouped the findings by the following themes: leadership, staff, students, academic support, funding, and other takeaways. A summary of these findings is in appendix C.

Leadership

Across the programs visited, leaders were able to clearly articulate the influences that shaped their approach to their work. If they weren't using the Search Institute framework, they had another research-based model. And they all had ideas regarding human relationship development. The leaders all had five or more years in their positions, which gave them institutional knowledge and community connectedness. They spoke about their own ongoing learning with people, as they were hands-on grassroots leaders even if their jobs were based in offices. Leaders were community-focused in a deep and meaningful way. They "sat beside" community members in the work. Their motivation was driven by their beliefs about the value of youth and their desire to make change. In addition, they had strong skills in motivating people around them.

When the leaders of these programs walked into neighborhoods they served, they were greeted warmly because they were known. They were respected and cared for by the community because they worked *with* the community. They were dedicated to community-based work, seeing it as more than a job. They believed in the work so strongly that they found ways for good-hearted people everywhere to contribute, to whatever degree they could or desired.

Andrea Swain was the executive director of the Yawkey Boys & Girls Club of Roxbury, one of the most robust programs Sue visited. "Robust" programming is really too weak of a description. Swain attracted innovative staff and kept them. Social worker extraordinaire Adam Chaprnka was empowered by Andrea to try new big ideas. Adam founded the Dudley Square Bike Club with a local bike enthusiast who had stepped away from his law career to pursue his passion for bikes and community engagement. He approached Adam with the idea, and together they brought it to life. They collaborated with the City of Boston, the mayor's office, the nonprofit group Bikes Not Bombs, and Boston Children's Hospital. Youth were paid minimum wage to work on bikes and lead rides for younger club members. Youth who worked in the club's repair shop received practical, marketable skills.

> *When the leaders of these programs walked into neighborhoods they served, they were greeted warmly because they were known.*

With Andrea's abilities to dream big and attract funders, Adam developed sophisticated travel experiences to Japan, India, and South Dakota Tribal Nations for selected high schoolers. These motivational experiences kept youth returning to their club through high school graduation. After high school, more than one hundred former participants have returned to visit the Yawkey Boys & Girls Club to reconnect with each other and leaders like Adam. They reveled in reflections on the multiple ways these otherwise-unattainable travel experiences broadened their perspectives and encouraged new audacious aspirations. Strong leadership is what makes life-altering experiences like this possible for high-impact clubs.

Staff

The staff at these organizations, in part, developed from within, which helped ensure the programs' sustainability over time. As staff members progressed through the programs, they carried on the techniques and values they learned along the way. This was often achieved through intergenerational staff structures, where experienced staff members were paid to work alongside newer staff, mirroring the natural relationships found in family and community. The dedicated staff saw so much value in their work that they were willing to work summers and split schedules before and after school to be available to youth when school was out. This consistent dedication—a significant portion of staff members remained with their programs for a decade or more—allowed for a sense of stability and continuity, which is critical for building strong relationships with youth as they grow and develop over time. This long-term presence was again the result of hands-on leadership, which led to staff retention. Long-term staff were able to build deep trust with the youth and their families, which is essential for fostering relationships and learning growth.

At Operation Breakthrough in Kansas City, in every neighborhood unit of the infant and preschool program, there was a staff person who had grown up there. "I love this place. I am of this place," a preschool teacher smilingly proclaimed as she shook Sue's hand.

Students

The ratio of staff to youth at the Boys & Girls Clubs of Metropolitan Baltimore was 1 to 15. To better meet individual mental health needs, they creatively used social worker interns twice a week to reduce the ratio to 1 staff to 10 youth. Staffing numbers are an important consideration.

Successful programs established cohort groups of similar-age youth who stayed together, to some degree, through high school graduation. Most cohorts focused on youth ages six to ten, ten to thirteen, or fourteen to eighteen. Cohort members had time to fully know each other. This is essential when thinking about deep, meaningful relationships and retention. When youth grow together in shared common experiences and come back together over developmental stages, their perspectives widen and their bonding deepens, cementing feelings of connectedness in profound, life-altering ways.

The adults in the programs acted as informal mentors. They truly understood the students' strengths and needs. When someone made a mistake, they knew they were, no matter what, valued for their unique gifts. This allowed them to rebound and reflect with their older mentors. Students stayed in the program and, as mentioned earlier, in some cases returned as alumni to give back to the program or to other youth. Programs were creating and building pipelines toward student success.

Don Carpenter, Trekkers' first executive director and creator of its unique six-year youth development model, said, "I never wanted to be an evangelist of an organization but an evangelist of an idea and a movement." What movement? "A movement to scale relationships between youth and caring adults throughout adolescence—not just a focus on scaling programs."

Trekkers' motto, "Six years of 360-degree support," reflects this commitment. Students join at age twelve and become part of a cohort that stays together through high school graduation. Throughout the year, they meet regularly to build an intentional learning community while collaboratively planning and implementing educational expeditions. These expeditions evolve over time, beginning with a three-day experience in Acadia National Park in seventh grade and culminating in ten- to twelve-day journeys to cities chosen by the cohort. At the heart of the model is youth voice and choice—with planning responsibilities gradually shifting to students over their six years in the program, fostering independence, leadership, and agency.

Trekkers is not just using experiential learning and travel as a carrot to incentivize youth to return each year. At its core, Trekkers is about fostering a deep sense of mattering and belonging—helping young people feel valued, seen, and connected to a supportive community. The strong, long-term relationships built between caring adults and students create a "sense of future"—a belief that their lives have purpose and potential. When youth feel that they truly belong, optimism follows. They begin to see themselves as capable, with real options and opportunities for a meaningful future. This foundation of relational trust and belonging fuels academic motivation, resilience, and the confidence to navigate life's challenges with purpose.

Academic Support

The programs selected and structured academic support in many ways. Most programs were focused on homework that participants brought with them, as few programs had proximity or connections to classrooms. In some instances, local universities were involved with programs through STEAM enrichment. Another model was working with for-profit academic (math and reading) tutoring businesses. ProvenTutoring, based at Johns Hopkins University, leads a coalition of organizations that offer evidence-based, research-supported tutoring models shown to reduce educational disparities. A database of these programs can be found at ProvenTutoring.org.

Of the ten places Sue visited, only one, the Webster Kendrick Boys and Girls Club (Metropolitan Baltimore), was located adjacent to the elementary school the participants attended. When Sue asked, "How does it make a difference being located beside a school?" the club manager replied, "We can both support gaps and needs, and provide [youth] immediate feedback." In an urban area with limited access to affordable, quality, fresh food, wraparound supports for nutritious foods could be tracked down by the Boys & Girls Clubs. The club manager went on, "It helped me realize we as an organization can't do it on our own. We need to work collectively with the local food pantry to support the school. Also, [students'] teachers say the children are doing better in class when I pick the kids up at the end of the school day to walk to our club."

Funding

Funding was a challenge for all the programs. The challenges varied depending on a program's context and structure. Funding came more easily when there were concrete results to share with the funders. Groups using the HSA attracted funders because they had students' pre- and post-self-assessments, which showed individual and cohort growth in 21st century skills. Most programs started small, with local people and funders. The first bus at Trekkers was purchased with a board member's personal credit card. Thirty years later, Sue counted two buses and a passenger van ready to haul eager youth to the outdoors.

Funders appear to shift their focus in three- to five-year cycles. Veteran leaders reported that short-term special interest trends forced their programming to focus in new directions. They had seen the funding and thus the programming pendulum swing from health, nutrition, and well-being, to inclusivity, to STEAM, and most recently to workforce preparedness and internships. Sustainability of programming and staff becomes even more challenging when the funding focuses shift. This may explain Trekkers' sustained success over the past thirty years. From the beginning they made a deliberate choice not to let funding dictate their mission, but instead to let their mission guide their funding decisions. Sadly, however, beggars cannot always be choosers when money is hard to come by.

A small but interesting fact: In places where professional sports teams are successful, a surprising amount of financial support follows. As an example, in 2006, Roxbury Boys & Girls Club was renamed after former Boston Red Sox owner Tom A. Yawkey and his wife Jean, who had been long-time philanthropic supporters of youth development in the Boston area. The year prior, this Boys & Girls Club received a $3 million capital grant from the Yawkey Foundation for the renovation and expansion of their clubhouse, bringing their swimming pool, gymnasiums, classrooms, and music and computer labs to state-of-the-art levels. When Sue visited the Yawkey Boys & Girls Club, youth had recently attended a Patriots football game, their tickets paid for by individual and corporate donors who believed in the work that was being done.

Some Kansas City Chiefs players and their families volunteer and donate financial support to Operation Breakthrough in Kansas City. Travis Kelce, Super Bowl–winning tight end with the Chiefs, provided funding to the program to expand their operations and purchase an old muffler shop next to their facility for school-age children. Their Ignition Lab is now where teens ages fourteen to eighteen learn coding, circuitry, culinary arts, construction and design, digital media, robotics, graphic design, and more. As of this writing, they are currently raffling off a cherry-red 1969 Chevelle that high school students revamped into an electric battery–operated car. According to their website, the cutting-edge opportunities they offer are a "powerful springboard for teens who live in economically depressed, often violent neighborhoods" (Operation Breakthrough 2024, para. 5). Students gain real-world work experience running a food truck, operating a container farm and selling produce, printing their graphic creations on apparel, designing and making products such as trophies and jewelry for clients, and getting certified as Chromebook repair technicians. This work could not continue without strong corporate and foundation partners and other Kansas Citians who have created a community of support.

Other Learning Nuggets

Adam Chaprnka at Yawkey Boys & Girls Club of Roxbury introduced us to Person-in-Environment (PIE) theory from the field of social work. This theory and Chaprnka's implementation of it resonate with us. PIE theory recognizes that the individual is influenced not only by their own personal characteristics but also by the environments (social, cultural, economic, and physical) in which they live. This perspective is based on the idea that individuals are part of a larger system of relationships. PIE theory also focuses on cultural competency, strengths-based approaches, mental health, and physical health.

The programs Sue visited were literally safe spaces, sometimes the only safe space participants had in their day outside school. During interviews with directors and club managers at Boys & Girls Clubs of Metropolitan Baltimore, people at every level of their organization emphasized the importance of trauma-informed staff training. It is almost impossible to center one's thinking on academics if one's body is reeling from generational stress. "We're finding kids who are numb to the trauma they have experienced, and the pandemic has made it worse," reported Amber Reed, then director of social and emotional wellness at the club. She explained, "We're learning the importance of naming our emotions and breaking the stigma of therapy. Bringing in partnerships to provide those services has been helpful but hard work."

Program leaders understood the importance of families. Y'Landa Burch, the former vice president and chief operating officer of the club, told Sue, "I know it's below my pay grade to work directly with families, but they are relying on us and they want the best for their kids, even if they come in high and expressing anger… For us in this city, emotions can run high, and sometimes we are the bridge between parents and school because we have to be."

Our question about how to include parents in the work was met with similar answers. The people Sue met valued ideas and feedback from families and had plans to seek their input and reflections, but they had not yet had time to get to that work due to their workloads.

Reflecting on Our Learning for Implementation

Several larger themes and key ideas emerged from the site visits to effective programs. (See Appendix C for a summary of the qualities of effective programs.)

1. They had the same passionate leader for five or more years.
2. They grew their own future staff.
3. They had dedicated staff sometimes working nontraditional hours: before and after school and in summers.
4. Data on individual students was driving the programs.
5. Funding emerged when data demonstrated success.
6. Intentional and close partnerships were common in these programs.
7. The focus of the programs was outreach, not in-reach.

Closing Thoughts

In writing this book, we continue to reflect on the combination of our own professional experiences, all we learned through research prior to the site visits, and what we learned during interviews and visits to proven programs. We were inspired by the passion of staff we met and the strengths of each program. All programs were beautifully supporting parts of the whole-child perspective: social-emotional learning, academic personalization, or motivation through enrichment. Few programs were addressing the whole-child needs that we identified during listening circles with local parents and interviews with youth prior to our research. We began to envision school and community partnerships, working together to do what they each do best on behalf of all learners. After making this realization, we continued to wonder how we could develop a program that capitalized on the strengths of what we had seen and addressed all areas of a whole-child perspective.

But ultimately, we saw that, yes—it can be done! The trajectory can steeply bend upward for every child. We can overcome racial, economic, and other systemic barriers. The greatest gains happen when we stop making excuses, build relationships, use data, and make families part of the equation. Cross-sector partnerships, where schools and other agencies thoughtfully share space and time, are essential for addressing the needs of youth and families.

Reflection Questions

- What is your motivation to create a program for youth?
- What are the barriers preventing change in intervention-delivery in your learning community?
- Where is there a social movement or program that you want to emulate?
- What do you hope to accomplish in your work?
- How will you gauge success after the program has run for three years? Five years? Ten years?

PART 2

HOW TO DO IT—
The Gears

CHAPTER 4

Getting to Know The Gear Model

*"Individually, we are one drop.
Together, we are an ocean."*
—Anonymous

In this chapter, we provide a high-level overview of the first two years of implementation of The Gear Model After School Club. We focus on the goals of the program we designed and the importance of establishing goals when designing your own program. We look at the process we used to select students for the program. We examine the program's twelve-week calendar and describe the daily schedule. Finally, we address how we developed partners for the work.

The following questions are answered in this chapter:
- What are the purposes of the gears in The Gear Model?
- What does the schedule for each day include?
- How are students selected? What data is used?
- How does The Gear Model approach personalize intervention for the whole child?
- How do you create developmental relationships?

An Afternoon/Evening at The Gear Model Program

It is a Tuesday in February and school has let out for the day. Sue pushes a rolling cabinet packed with program materials into the media center. University students begin arriving and start setting up a STEAM activity for later in the evening. Community volunteers sign in and help prepare and set up the snack. Greetings and hugs are happening all around. Soft music is playing. On one side of the room, the volunteers set out laundry baskets, one for each student to store their backpack and coat. They clear off six tables on the other side of the room. The students, third through fifth graders, begin entering. Sue and the volunteers greet them by name, inquiring about their school day and families. Students have assigned seats for this part of the day, so they immediately take their homework to their spots, grab their folders from the boxes in the middle of the tables, put on their name tags, and start writing in their reflection journals: "Today I am feeling _____ because I am thinking about _____."

Once everyone is engaged in their homework and the room is calm, elementary students who are serving as leaders for the afternoon deliver snacks and tutoring folder activities or games. High school volunteers arrive and go to their assigned tables, sliding in with the community volunteers to ask questions, help read directions, and drive accurate critical thinking. The room is abuzz with statements like "Oh! I get it now!" "I'm not sure how to…" and "Let's reread that part right there."

When some students realize they are reaching their learning goals—in this case, being able to flexibly tackle multi-digit multiplication and division story problems—high fives are shared. At another table, students are using geometry vocabulary cards to sort, classify, and compare two- and three-dimensional shapes. Students eventually embrace this goal, debating whether a rhombus is also a square or rectangle, and arrive at the idea that every square is a rectangle, and every rhombus is a rectangle, but not every rectangle is a square or rhombus.

Sue's co-teacher, who works at the school, arrives for the afternoon. A few of the students' classroom teachers stop by briefly, delivering homework that was left in class . . . *accidentally*. The guilty are chided in an affectionate, teasing manner: "Hmm…you must need this to advance your learning!" On occasion, teachers offer game ideas to Sue or one of the volunteers. Or they might share insights—for example, vocabulary a specific learner should be encouraged to use because it is essential for demonstrating learning on assessments. Students who are done with their homework move on to the math games that are in a tub at their table. These games were selected to reinforce needed skills.

A timer goes off, signaling a transition to community building and time for attending to emotions (although that phrase is not used with youth). The crew has been taught the routine: "Nobody is done cleaning up until the whole room is cleaned up." Everyone pitches in to clean up. Student leaders initiate the group greeting. On this afternoon, it is a group chant: "Persistence, persistence, we stick with hard problems!" Then, students' favorite activity, Affirmations Hunt, begins. One by one, tables are given the signal, and students go and find one of the colorful affirmation ovals hidden on shelves in the media center. They bring the affirmation ovals back to their seats and read them quietly to themselves, to a high school volunteer, or to each other. A tone of focused energy and positivity is setting in.

Next is collaborative movement time, but before everyone heads to the gym, volunteers distribute written directions for the activity. Small groups of four coalesce, and high school volunteers gravitate toward the youth with whom they have bonded the most. Once in the gym, the teams of four walk or run laps, hula hoop themselves across the gym, or run obstacle courses as warm-up activities. The volunteers use conversation starters to encourage communal chitchat. Earlier this afternoon, student leaders prepared a relay race and challenge course using pool noodles, balloons, and scooters. Everyone in the community tackles the course to the sound of giggling. New friendships are taking root.

Before long, the whole crew is back in the media center. The University of Minnesota's Mechanical Engineering Ambassadors introduce and discuss this week's engineering topic: "How can you build a tall tower to withstand a windstorm?" Teams of learners construct towers with straws and putty, then college students test the structures' strength by aiming hair dryers at them on full blast. The room is filled with laughter and oohs and ahs.

The evening closes with a gratitude ritual. Tables are dismissed one at a time to "pay the volunteers" with high fives, hugs, and thanks. Students line up, and Sue gives them each a cookie for the road. Sue's co-teacher walks half the students to the bus, and Sue walks the others to the parent pickup area. The high school volunteers push the rolling cart back into Sue's office and wash the tables. Sue, the co-teacher, the Engineering Ambassadors, and the community volunteers circle up for a ten-minute reflective debrief. What worked? What didn't work? What could be done to clarify directions for youth or engage them more? What student voices could be amplified and which students are showing leadership skills? Successes are celebrated with applause and high fives, and the adults head for home. The media center specialist who arrives the next morning will not know that magic happened in this borrowed space the prior evening.

Now that we have given you a glimpse of what an evening of the program looks like, let us break down the components of the model, beginning with the goals.

The Goals of The Gear Model After School Club

The Gear Model is based on our own beliefs and on the research we completed into effective programs (including Sue's travel adventure). It does not replicate an existing program; it brings together different parts of whole-child interventions. We believe the greatest gains happen when we remove barriers, take action, use data, and make families part of the work. The program goes beyond offering only tutoring, with the goal of achieving greater outcomes. Enrichment and inspirational real-world experiences are wrapped around academic interventions. We thoughtfully assembled the pieces that fit our context and strived to put together a program to meet the needs of our community of learners.

These are our goals for students:
- Increase persistence (Habits of Mind) in problem-solving (21st century skills).
- Increase independent work completion (Habits of Mind).
- Use reflection time to improve the accuracy of work.
- Increase emotional awareness and academic action orientation (strengths-finding tools like the Holistic Student Assessment).
- Identify new learning interests to increase academic motivation (personalized learning).

- Strengthen social-emotional learning (relationship orientation).
- Culminate the program with a celebratory family event to share their success.

And these are our goals for the program:
- Implement five key elements of developmental relationships (Search Institute, n.d.).
- Respond to individual learners' academic (rigor) and social-emotional needs based on multiple actionable data points.
- Implement relevant enrichment content that allows students to apply math and reading skills to real world, 21st-century career and life competencies.
- Positively impact students' math confidence and achievement.
- Increase learning, joy, and excitement for everyone involved.

The size and scope of these goals broadened as we learned more about the complexity of systems and the interconnected and disjointed parts impacting student learning. As we explain in chapter 1, our thinking is heavily informed by several conceptual frameworks—a learner-focused, whole-child approach, building supportive developmental relationships, asset-based framing, influences on learning beyond academics (including Habits of Mind and 21st century skills), and a systems orientation. So we created The Gear Model with the aim of bringing together the perspectives and uniqueness of students, families, teachers, educators, community intergenerational volunteers (teens and adults), and partners in order to have a significant positive impact on the life trajectory (outcomes) for each learner, for the cohort, and ultimately for society.

Program Logistics and Calendar

The Gear Model was designed as a flexible structure for programming. Our recent implementation was a twelve-week program. Four weeks of programming were held in the fall to jump-start students' academic year. This short time period gave us a feel for the strengths and needs of the group. Then we held eight weeks of programming from February to May, working with partners specializing in enrichment. The three-month break had two benefits. First, teachers and volunteers were more inclined to sign on when they had the choice to work a four-week fall session and/or an eight-week late winter/spring session. Second, we could use feedback and observations about the group dynamics and the results of self-surveys and the HSA to inform precise do's and don'ts that would maximize group cohesion and learning productivity during the final eight weeks. The winter break gave us time to improve our approach for the spring session.

Time Allocation for the Program

The Gear Model program was held during after-school sessions on two consecutive days each week. Based on our goals, we allocated the time as follows and developed the schedule below:
- Academic Intervention (small-group subject-specific tutoring)—25%
- Enrichment (incorporating academic skills and content vocabulary)—40%

- Communication (language development connections)—15%
- Attending to Emotions (mental wellness)—5%
- Movement (mental and physical health)—15%

In our program, this translated to the following schedule:

3:00–3:25	**Individual/Small-Group Math-Focused Time**
3:25–3:30	**Attending to Emotions**
3:30–3:50	**Collaborative Movement/Games in Gym or Outside**
3:50–4:10	**Large-Group Enrichment** - In the fall, we focused on visual arts and self-awareness surveys. - In the winter and spring, our partners, the Mechanical Engineering Ambassadors from the University of Minnesota, facilitated lessons and demonstrations.
4:10–4:40	**Enrichment Team Challenges or Projects** - Teams consisted of four students and a community volunteer (if volunteers were not available, we invited the fifth graders or oldest learners in each group to lead). - We based these on a weekly topic so they were iterative and building in complexity from Tuesday to Wednesday.
4:40–4:45	**Team Reflections/Self Evaluation**
4:45–4:55	**Reflections and a Celebration Cookie (treat for the road home)** - Tuesday: Cross-Team Verbal Reflections - Wednesday: Individual Written Reflections
4:55–5:00	**Pay the volunteers with high fives and walk to bus or parent pickup.**

Structural Considerations

As we developed The Gear Model, a number of structural considerations were important to the program design. We see these structural components as essential for success. We encourage you to think deeply about these areas as you design your program:

- Holding after-school sessions on two or three consecutive days
- Training of volunteers—high school students and community members
- Reserving physical space for the program
- Establishing partnerships—for enrichment, snacks, volunteers, etc.

Physical Space for the Program

Intervention programs can be held in many places—school media centers, multipurpose rooms, community rooms, and more. In our case, The Gear Model program was held in the school media center. As a supporter of access to creative out-of-school academic and relationship-building services, the principal granted permission for this usage. We had an interactive whiteboard, six tables and thirty chairs, and a living-room-style gathering space where we could spread out for projects. We needed thirty chairs to accommodate the twenty-four students plus six volunteers who sat beside them. Immediately after school, students walked from their classrooms to the media center. In addition to the media center, we had access to the gym or playground for twenty minutes each afternoon. Sue worked with the school-based childcare manager to coordinate schedules in order to share those spaces.

Selecting Participants

There are many factors to consider when selecting participants for intervention programs. Our goal was to identify twenty-four students in grades three through five who were not performing to their potential, with an emphasis on students not yet meeting standards on the state standardized tests. This included students who were close to meeting proficiency levels who would benefit from additional experiences.

We identified students using multiple factors, not simply their reading or math test scores (for example), as we wanted to consider the whole child's needs. Education is not a one-size-fits-all endeavor.

> *We identified students using multiple factors, not simply their reading or math test scores (for example), as we wanted to consider the whole child's needs.*

We reviewed student data using Shane Safir and Jamila Dugan's model, described in their book *Street Data: A Next-Generation Model of Equity, Pedagogy, and School Transformation* (2021). Their model focuses on recentering the learner. The first set of data is the satellite, or big-picture, view of student data. A district testing coordinator helped Sue obtain state standardized test results for youth who were not yet passing yearly academic tests. This data was placed on a spreadsheet.

The next level of data is map-level data. In our case, this was district-level assessment measures. This data was added to the same spreadsheet. More than forty students at the school were considered behind based on these measures.

Finally, we reviewed street-level data, or classroom-based measures (e.g., math unit tests). It was helpful that Sue had worked with many of these students in math and reading intervention during the traditional school day. This gave her familiarity with their street-level data. She also knew their families from outreach work she had long been doing. Relationships matter. We cannot say this enough.

As we built the cohort, we considered individual students' potential for growth in this type of setting. We held high regard for teachers' input also, as they knew which students would benefit most from the goals of the program. Finally, we studied the cohort's shared interests to identify an enrichment area students would all be interested in.

Importantly, students and families needed to be committed to coming to the sessions. This model is not a drop-in program. Group cohesion is important and is built when a stable group of individuals consistently attends the program.

We began with a cohort of third through fifth graders who were known to be a hands-on and creative group. To this cohort, we added a child who was hearing impaired and highly interested in engineering. Shy students living in sheltered family situations were also invited to join the cohort. We also included two students who were in special education with diagnosed reading impairments but were tenacious and deeply engaged critical thinkers when given real-world tasks. In addition, two recent immigrant families were seeking experiences for their girls to practice English. These very quiet English language learners were passing state math and reading standardized tests. We found a way to qualify them based on district writing assessments where they were significantly behind their peers.

All this to say, it really helps to know the cohort of participants so as to make right-fit decisions and to balance the group with a variety of personalities and strengths.

Ratio of Students to Educators and Volunteers

Our ratio was one educator—in our case, a certified teacher—to every twelve to fourteen students. We worked hard to develop a network of community volunteers and high school students and were able to reach our goal of one trained volunteer for every four to six students for most sessions. In addition, classroom teachers stopped by for brief visits and to attend special events.

Minnesota's extended learning funding provided approximately $5.50 per student per hour of the program. We combined this with other funding streams to cover the compensation for two licensed teachers and the cost of a bus to take students home.

Launching the Program

The identification of the participants led to a series of important steps to launch the program. Consider these areas and how they can be designed and implemented to extend relationships with students, families, and teachers.

Registration

We sent a cover letter and registration form home with the identified students. The classroom teacher or Sue made a follow-up phone call to each family, verifying that they had heard their child was selected and received the invitation. We personally communicated our shared belief that their child had potential. This messaging is key for families. It brings hope. Parents were especially interested in the individualized academic support and enrichment programming.

The registration form (see appendix B) made clear the program was asset and enrichment based.

> Your student is invited to the
> **After School Club** where we will:
> Celebrate individual strengths
> Laugh and play during team-building activities in the gym
> Challenge our MATH SKILLS
> And most importantly, play with building materials to take engineering to new heights

Using Student Data for Planning

Data, data, and more data. We strive to collect data that are actionable. We need data that can be used to inform and adjust our program design to ensure the development of a program that is truly student-centered. We must also be cautious with our collection and use of student data.

Our goal was to use data to develop an intervention program that addressed the needs of individual groups of learners. However, school and district student and curricular data often are not actionable. And we knew we needed the right data, data that provide a view of the whole child. Academics, peer and adult relationships, and resiliency factors such as self-awareness, empathy, and trust are building blocks to advance reading, writing, and math skills. We had to search for the data in different systems and places to gain a complete perspective of each learner.

Academics

Sue scheduled ten-minute one-on-one student interviews during the school day to identify precisely the foundational math skills students needed to advance in mathematics. In addition, she used this time to build excitement for the After School Club. To determine individual student needs, we turned to baseline assessments from the district intervention curriculum. These assessments covered number sense, place value, and computational algebraic fluency. The scoring rubric helped us identify games and practice sheets from the curriculum to use for individualized skill packets and games. This was an easy way to develop these packets.

Results of the interviews led us to four focus skill areas:

1. Number sense, specifically place value
2. Basic computation and problem-solving with addition and subtraction of one- to three-digit numbers
3. Basic computation and problem-solving with multiplication and division with one- to three-digit numbers
4. Geometry and data analysis

Anecdotal observations are helpful for assessing students' persistence in their work. This was important for the students whose test data was most discrepant from that of their grade-level peers. These are the things we considered at this point:

- What skills or concepts will advance this student the most?
- What is the outer edge of the student's current understanding?
- Would games or practice sheets best advance this individual learner?

Student Strengths and Resiliencies

Knowing what makes each student tick should inform you as you create individual work plans and group activities. We had heard from many professionals that student strengths, interests, and passions should form the foundation of program development. Programming is more intentional and impactful when student strengths drive the time together.

Thrively and Partnerships in Education and Resilience (PEAR) are two companies that provide important data that is often missing in our existing student data profiles. These companies use students' responses to online questionnaires to build both individual profiles and an analysis of the makeup of a cohort. The Thrively profiles focus on students' strengths, interests, Habits of Mind, and future aspirations, while PEAR's HSA profile focuses on resiliencies, learning and school engagement, and relationships. Though the reports are different, both hone in on what motivates a student. We have used both companies and found them worthwhile.

The key point is that you need more than academic data to meet students' needs. You can get these additional data through either of these resources, or you can create your own questionnaires and do your own cohort analysis. Whether on paper or online, questionnaires can be as simple as asking students what motivates them, what they are interested in, and how they see themselves contributing their own assistance and ideas to the program.

Figure 4.1 Sample Thrively Reports for Two Students

Student	Strengths	Interests	Aspirations	Profile Description
[name redacted]	- Coordination - Athleticism - Drive - Flexibility - Analytical	- Creative Arts - Cartooning - Ceramics - Crafts - Drawing	- Coach - Lyricist - Professional Athlete	You are extremely well-coordinated with impressive athleticism and a distinct drive to succeed.
[name redacted]	- Appreciation - Social Justice - Compassion - Analytical - Independence	- Creative Arts - Crafts - Jewelry Making - Music - Flute	- Artist - Doctor - Scientist	You have a high ceiling with particular growth potential around your analytical skills and flexibility.

Building Partnerships: Who Was Involved

We sought partners and allies who would help us move beyond barriers such as time constraints, staffing shortages, and limited access to planning time and space in order to optimize learning. We knew we would not be able to sustain the creation of materials for and management of all five main gears in The Gear Model on our own without burning out. Our goal was to locate and collaborate with partners and allies who could prepare and coordinate the parts of the program we could not do well—in this case, the Enrichment Gear.

The Importance of Volunteers

Volunteers can come from many places. We were able to tap into community volunteers (retired teachers, classroom teachers, community members, etc.) and high school students. When working with people, one of the most important things to do is establish shared understandings through clear communication. For instance, even though someone is a teacher or a retired teacher, they may not automatically align with your thinking or approach. Providing training prior to the start of the program and planning for reflective feedback conversations at the end of each afternoon helps make things run smoothly. The time it takes to clearly communicate with volunteers pays off.

Volunteers make the most pivotal impact by serving as a calming force during transitions from high-energy times to quieter, more focused moments. Transitions between activities often make or break program success. In our program, the high school students struggled to get to the building by the time we started due to their school's release time and congestion in the parking lot, so we relied on the community volunteers who could arrive earlier. They were key to making sure the space was ready so students could calmly transition from chaotic hallways into the program room. We often had relaxing music playing in the room when participants arrived.

Training Volunteers

We were fortunate to have student volunteers who were part of the local high school's Academic Mentors (Tutors) program and the Future Educators course. These students came into the sessions ready and eager to build relationships and assist. Sue and the high school teacher who supported civic engagement created a short training session for the student volunteers. This training covered behavior management, questioning techniques, and cognitive coaching. At a different time (due to schedules), the same training was given to the community volunteers.

The short training focused on moving instruction from the "sage on the stage" who knows and imparts all knowledge to a "guide on the side" who gradually inspires the learners to engage. We compared the teacher played by Ben Stein in *Ferris Bueller's Day Off*, who talks at students and repeats the same question over and over in a dry, flat voice, with Gandalf from *The Hobbit*, who joins in the group's experiences to stir their thinking. Additional role models for the high school students were Yoda from *Star Wars* and Ms. Frizzle from *The Magic School Bus*. These examples helped show volunteers how their role was different from what they might have envisioned or experienced themselves. The high school students were given our mentor motto: "Whether you know or do not know, ask a few questions to gauge where the learner is at and get the learner talking."

We gave tips on how to help students get started on their work and provided questioning prompts to use. We also provided a short in-service on conceptual math and the multiple methods students might use to solve math problems. The focus was on problem-solving and number sense. We cannot emphasize enough how important it is to teach volunteers to listen and ask questions before jumping in to solve problems for and at learners. We wrapped up the training by discussing the importance of helping clean up and reset the room for the next day. Ending the program calmly and not upsetting custodians or owners of the space keeps peace.

We also created documents to support clear communication with the volunteers. We used volunteer checklists to walk the volunteers through each session by time and task. These checklists helped the volunteers feel successful and supportive. Having the written directions in hand gave the volunteers autonomy and a timeline, and it minimized interruptions to instruction caused by questions such as, "What's next?"

Effective teachers know how to "forecast" student behaviors. They have deep relationships with students and are always watching for behaviors or body language that indicate the need to intervene. For example, if a student starts to leave their seat, avoiding the work, how the teacher responds can determine the student's next action. A teacher who has a relationship with the student can forecast that if the student is not redirected in the right way, their behavior may disrupt the entire group. Forecasting, the keen ability to observe behavior before it distracts, is a difficult thing to teach. However, we worked on this with our volunteers by providing question frames, modeling with our behaviors, and debriefing after we had used our forecasting skills. In debriefing sessions, we asked questions such as these:

- Was it during a sitting-still time or a transition time that you noticed this behavior? This information helped us monitor more closely during that time going forward.
- What happened right before the learner _____ (shut down, got frustrated, cried)? This helped us be aware of triggers in the future.
- What helped the student? What help do you need to support the student next time?

Training volunteers in advance is worth the investment of time. And setting aside ten minutes to debrief after each session helped everyone focus on building a happy community. Volunteers are an important part of the work, and their feedback is key. The debrief time allowed volunteers to express interest in working with specific students and give feedback on how the activities went. The process of reflecting collectively each evening improved the purposeful interactions the next day.

During these daily ten-minute debriefs, we asked questions such as these:
- On a scale of 1 to 5, where 1 is the least productive and 5 is most productive, how productive was the group this afternoon?

- What students were you able to help get engaged with the homework/tutoring work?
- Which students do we need to continue to help get more engaged during tutoring time?
- Did your group make a plan before tackling today's STEAM challenge?
- What good questions did you ask, or did you hear, today?
- What students are you connecting with most?
- What else is helpful for us as the leaders to know?

We also created a custom QR code that linked to an online input form and placed it near the exit for volunteers to scan so they could provide ideas for continuous improvement even if they needed to leave early and miss the debrief.

We found that high school volunteers benefit from reviewing their training every few weeks. On afternoons when the teens were less engaged, adding to the noise, or had experienced disrespect, Sue or her co-teacher brought out the written training guide to refresh their memories and refine guidance about the way volunteers could be most helpful.

Figure 4.2 Training Guidelines

Thank You for Assisting at After School Club!
Here are some questions to ask learners and tips for our time together.

Conversation starters/transitions to start building relationships:
(Alternatives to the unproductive "How was your day?")

- "What made you smile today?"
- "Who did you play with at recess? What did you play?"
- "What chapter book are you finishing these days?" (second grade +)
- "What did your teacher read to you today?"
- "Where at home do you like to do your reading?"
- "You know what I am reading at home? I am reading _____."
- "Who knows a joke?"
- "What is your favorite food?"
- "Do you prefer dogs or cats?"
- "What is your favorite video game/app?"
- "Tell me about your interest in _____."

To get learners motivated in the work:
- "You will feel proud when you're done. Let's get started." (You lean in. If they aren't leaning in, start reading the directions aloud and act like you're interested. Pat the chair next to you and motion for them to move up.)
- "Where are the directions? Read them aloud twice."
- "What are the really important words that help?"
- "What do you notice? What are you wondering?"
- "What else could we try?"

If learners are confused:
- "What is happening in this example here?"
- "What else did [the teacher] say about this?" (And point to directions.)
- "If this strategy is not working for you, are there any other tools we could use?" (100s chart, bead rack, a ruler to use as a number line, money)

If learners are confused (cont.):
- "Look around and decide who else we could politely ask." (If you are having trouble, don't hesitate to seek help from the teacher.)
- Please don't spread math phobia. (AVOID using the words *easy* or *hard*. Just start.)
- Model curiosity and growth mindset. We are all learning together.
- "We do not understand this YET, but we will figure it out!"

When learners are done with their work:
- "Go back and look it over." (And you look it over with them.)
- "Finished means you added to it or found your own mistakes!"
- "How could we make this even better?"
- "You must be proud of yourself." (Give the learner a fist bump or elbow!)
- "You look [happy]!"

During clean-up/reflection time:
- "How do you feel now that you are done with that?"
- "Look around. What else can we do to help clean up?"
- Show how you clean up after yourself!
- AVOID doing anything for learners that they can do for themselves.

How will we know if we've made a difference?
- Students will be starting their own work and initiating movement on their own.
- Students will look proud at the end and appear happy.
- Students will be finishing more work.
- Students will stick with tough problems.
- Students will talk more about their thinking.
- Students will ask another question.
- Students will laugh with you. They might even laugh about a rough spot they hit with their work and how they turned it around.

When in the gym:
- Spread out and quickly find a pair of students who need direction. Point to their paper.
- Keep them reading on their own and doing what is next.

During any large-group verbal direction:
- Stop talking and look at us.
- Stand to the side of those who are not paying attention.
- Silently point to the person talking or to the task in front of them.
- If students near you are talking, put your hand on their shoulder and point to us.
- DO NOT ADD TO THE NOISE IF WE ARE DIRECTING A CHAOTIC ROOM.

Please let us know if you have ideas for how we can provide independence for learners AND keep learners flowing from one activity to another. We love your suggestions!

We are always available at the end of the session to hear your ideas and hear observations about individual students that you are working beside.

Figure 4.3 Sample Checklist

After School Club Community Volunteer Checklist

(This could be adapted for all volunteers. In our program, the high school volunteers arrived later, so community volunteers got things started.)

2:50	Sign in at the office. Get your name tag. (You might need to remind them you have already completed a background check through the district office.)
2:55	Put any library books on the tables onto the cart. Put a pencil at each seat. ▪ Sharpen pencils at the library desk if needed. ▪ Half-fill a pitcher of water from the fountain to the left of the media center.
3:00	Check out the snacks on the front corner table to see what we are serving today.
3:05	Stand at the door and greet students. Remind them to read the screen and schedule on the board for directions: ▪ *Are you wearing tennis shoes?* ▪ *Use the bathroom now and please wash your hands.* ▪ *If you have homework, get it out and bring it to the tables.* ▪ *Please put your name tags up by your heart.*
3:10	**Homework Help and Passing Out Snacks** **MOST IMPORTANT IS PAPER HOMEWORK:** First, sit beside students who have work from their classroom teacher. This could be math workbook pages, or a worksheet labeled as homework, or something else. ▪ *Read me the directions, please.* ▪ *Would you like me to read you the directions?* ▪ *What part is confusing you?* ▪ *Can you sketch a picture quickly to get started?* ▪ *Go onto the next problem if you are stuck, and we will come back to it.* Then, look for students who are playing games and work with them. **SNACK:** When 80 percent of the students are seated, start serving. Serve students who are engaged in their work first. Use a tray to deliver small cups of water if there are no juice boxes today. ▪ *I will come back when you have gotten started with your work/game.*

3:24 **CLEAN-UP and High School Students Arrive**
- *Have you put your homework back into your backpack?*

Roll the garbage can around to the tables to encourage quick snack clean-up.

3:28 Help students find their teams and move TOGETHER to the gym or outdoors.

3:30 Students leave for physical activity while you stay behind:
- Turn each chair to face the screen.
- Triple-check the floor, so all wrappers and food are cleaned up. Check the pencils to be sure they are sharp.

3:40 **Ask the U of M Engineering Ambassadors if they need any help** setting up for their activity.

Head for home knowing we appreciate your support tremendously.

Engaging Partners with Common Goals

When thinking about programming partners, consider the goals of your program, the interests of the youth (identified by interviews and surveys), and the resources in your community.

You may need to approach a few groups to find the right fit for your students and program. Think about your existing relationships and build from them. We were looking for community partners who were free or extremely low cost and held a shared goal to support youth in finding their passions at home, at school, and with their friends by engaging in fun, purposeful activities. We were looking for fellow thinkers who believed all youth could reach their academic potential.

Sometimes, the best and most passionate partners walk in off the street to find you. There are people with a passion who want to work on behalf of youth because it is just their way of being human. Other times, organizers must seek partners matching the interests of the learners.

Remember the story from the Yawkey Boys & Girls Club (see page 45 in chapter 2)? A bike enthusiast approached the club with the idea of training some youth to work in bike shops. He was looking to help youth gain practical skills for future employment. The Dudley Square Bike Club was established, evolving into a cross partnership with the City of Boston, the nonprofit group Bikes Not Bombs, and Boston's Children's Hospital. The club included youth from Roxbury as well as from surrounding neighborhoods. Members learned to strip and rebuild bikes. They started biking in the city more. They started advocating at city meetings, eventually helping the mayor reach his goal of expanding bike lanes to make Boston a more bikeable city. Authentic relationships and passion put into practice improved the City of Boston and developed youth into future leaders.

A few words of caution about selecting and working with partners: You need to research your partners to understand their intentions and past work. You should consider any political affiliations for each group and implications of that in your community. Background checks and clear expectations when working with students cannot be overemphasized. If your partners (or you) want to be able to use data or photos from the partnership experience, you will need to obtain approvals and photo releases.

Before finalizing a partnership, both parties must arrive at agreements and boundaries. Ideally, both parties share similar values and know how to be culturally responsive to unique groups of youth. Establish and define shared goals for success. Each party needs to know their role and the requirements to set the stage for reciprocity. Both parties should be influenced by and learn from each other. Partners will need to periodically and routinely evaluate progress toward the mutually agreed-upon goals. In our work, some data were collected daily, some weekly, and some at the end of the program. You should be considering both student data and program-effectiveness data. Educators will need to provide and support the community partner with the structures and knowledge about learning to make the partnership instrumental for students' development. Identify possible barriers or knowledge gaps to set the stage for success.

You may need to approach a few groups to find the right fit for your students and program. Think about your existing relationships and build from them.

Our Partnership with University Students

We found an excellent partner in the University of Minnesota Mechanical Engineering Ambassadors program. This newly launched program was a perfect complement, providing experts in hands-on, creative, critical-thinking enrichment activities.

The Engineering Ambassadors program's mission is to improve diversity, equity, and inclusion in undergraduate and graduate programs in mechanical engineering by increasing the diversity of the pipeline. The college students (Engineering Ambassadors) and one of their professors attended the Engineering Ambassadors Network's Annual Training Workshop to learn to present information, create curriculum, and manage projects for youth. Their plan to be well prepared and think ahead matched our philosophy that training is essential for sustainability. It also fit our philosophy of partnerships being mutually beneficial and all partners being engaged in learning processes. (You can learn more about the Engineering Ambassadors Network online.)

The ambassadors developed engineering modules for the learners in the After School Club. The modules were developed in partnership with us to ensure they would match the developmental vocabulary of the students, be of high interest, and match state academic standards in science and engineering. Remember, the ambassadors were content experts, but they were not trained as teachers or to work with youth. They were learning about youth while we were learning about engineering.

They selected engineering principles important for beginning engineers. Then they identified big concepts to be gained from enrichment (objectives). Based on the big concepts, they developed two-day modules for different topics. Next, a one-hour lesson was developed for each day. The modules were based on the design process and heavy iterative inquiry. Each day, ambassadors provided a fifteen-minute presentation and demonstration, placing the engineering principle in the context of real-world engineering. Next, students engaged in a team challenge, a hands-on activity where they advanced through increasingly complex challenges.

The Engineering Ambassadors met together weekly at the university for the months leading up to the school visits. There they planned and gave practice presentations and provided one another with feedback. Once the module content was developed, Sue was invited to the university to provide feedback. She pointed out where concepts would be over learners' heads and where language supports (or scaffolds) would be needed, and she gave helpful instructional and behavior management hints for smoother presentations and transitions between the whole-group presentation and the small-group hands-on activities.

Before starting their work at the After School Club, the ambassadors delivered a final test presentation at a formal launch event. They received written feedback from funders, emeriti/retired professors, professors, peers, and local youth.

Many ambassadors volunteered to attend the Welcome Night of the After School Club and the Family Science Carnival on the final night, though these evenings were above and beyond their commitment. This attendance was important because setting aside time to build relationships and get to know one another fostered the sense of safety and connection students needed to feel motivated to engage with challenging engineering tasks.

Whether you are working with a partner or creating your own enrichment activities, we recommend you develop your own version of this planning and development process. We also encourage you to consider the learning that occurs for each partner and the impact in the larger education ecosystem.

Using Cohort Reports for Planning with Partners

As mentioned previously, we used the Thrively and PEAR HSA student assessments. We used these tools in the first few weeks of the After School Club to help learners build self-awareness and identify future ambitions. We found the cohort analysis reports based on these assessments very helpful for personalizing and planning at an individual level. The reports helped us curate the activities toward the interests of individuals in the group and to make sure that all passions and strengths were incorporated in the programming at some point (not necessarily all at once). This data was especially helpful to the Engineering Ambassadors, who had little experience with youth generally and no experience with our participants. The ambassadors were able to walk in with a sense of the personalities and interests of the students in front of them, which eased their anxiety about working with youth. Each ambassador saw a profile of a student they could relate to, and of their own volition started writing notes of encouragement back and forth or suggesting new books to read or websites for the younger students to explore.

Other Partners

We recommend developing partnerships with multiple groups. This provides flexibility when needed and supports adding variety to the program. For example, when the Engineering Ambassadors were unavailable during their university spring break, we were able to continue programming and meet our goals by leveraging other established partners. Staff from our local parks district visited to talk about the enrichment opportunities they offer when school is not in session. They shared maps of the parks, and students explored their website for free outdoor programs being held in the community. Later, some families reported they were crossing off the parks on their map as they visited them. Everyone's mental well-being benefits when families get outside together.

The local YMCA staff visited to introduce summer camp and scholarship forms, which helped fill in childcare needs and gaps for some of the families in this cohort.

Local public safety officers (police) were running a free family fishing day to celebrate the end of the school year and stopped by to invite school staff and youth. Sue spotted youth fishing with the new poles they received for many summers to follow. The public safety officers also returned the last night of the After School Club for the Family Science Carnival to listen to the students present what they had learned from the program. They served as surrogate supporters for youth whose caregivers were unable to attend the final celebration.

Any organization with a shared value of expanding access to learning opportunities and increasing critical thinking should be welcomed. Libraries, museums, nature facilities, and more often have free or very low-cost options for supporting learning and growth. Partnerships are relationships. Relationships drive our work. It was worth our time to build and leverage partnerships in order to expand opportunities and build a microcommunity of multigenerational developmental relationships. Everyone was energized when partners visited the After School Club.

Closing Thoughts

Now that we have considered the people, the place, and the schedule, we will look in more detail at how to develop a program that is high in responsiveness! The gears keep us on track to deliver an effective and engaging whole-child intervention program. As you continue to read and reflect, think about building a program based on your students and your context. We encourage you to take what fits and leave behind parts that either do not fit or are not possible in your current system. And remember, always focus on the relationships.

Reflection Questions

- What are your program goals?
- What student data is available to you when selecting participants?
- How will you coordinate with teachers to learn about the needs of the students?
- How will you incorporate academics and enrichment, the two big pieces?
- Which parts of the schedule are most important to you? To the students? To the families?
- Who do you have in your community to partner with?
- Where might you find volunteers to help with setup, cleanup, and mentoring?
- What will you provide in the way of volunteer training and written checklists?

CHAPTER 5

Academic Intervention

"What if we started with what they can do?"
—Gholdy Muhammad, author of *Unearthing Joy*

For us, after the Relationships Gear, the Academic Intervention Gear is most important. Reading, writing, and math provide the foundation for participation in society. Youth of all backgrounds benefit from one-on-one and small-group intervention. We are supporters of more academic learning for everyone everywhere. We believe all children can learn and deserve to get what they need to develop into independent, contributing, healthy adults.

That said, students from lower-income families, brimming with aspirations and talent, have the least access to academic support and often benefit from it the most. Filled with unique gifts, they too often enter school with fewer foundational skills due to limited access to early childhood education and enrichment learning opportunities outside the home. Tutoring can highlight their talents and help close these disparities by providing targeted, personalized support to fill in skills not yet mastered.

A caring, trained community volunteer can provide consistent academic and emotional support, building trust and confidence. Unfortunately, the pay-to-play system prevents too many capable youth with great potential from accessing additional learning time such as summer programs or after-school activities where nurturing, trained tutors provide structured, dedicated time to focus on academic growth outside regular classroom hours. The Academic Intervention Gear, 25 percent of our model, closes achievement disparities, which is what we are all about and why we wrote this book.

25%
ACADEMIC INTERVENTION
- Small-Group Practice
- Persistence Through Games

Tied to classroom instruction

The following questions are answered in this chapter:
- What does effective tutoring include?
- How can I personalize tutoring for students?
- How do I manage this work for multiple students?
- What resources do we already have available for tutoring?

What Is Tutoring and What Makes It Effective?

Tutoring is a form of personalized instruction to meet the learning needs of individual students. Students receive additional academic support in small groups or individually for concepts they struggle with or learning they have fallen behind in. Tutoring allows for a focus on a small set of skills and concepts through instruction designed around the students' individual strengths and learning needs.

The Academic Intervention Gear is based on research about effective tutoring. A very helpful resource that informed the structure of the program is *Design Principles for Accelerating Student Learning with High-Dosage Tutoring*, an EdResearch for Recovery brief published in 2021 (Robinson et al.). This report looks at ten areas that need to be considered when designing programs. Figure 5.1 shows a summary of the findings.

Figure 5.1 Tutoring Design Principles at a Glance

Frequency
Tutoring is most likely to be effective when delivered in high doses through tutoring programs with three or more sessions per week or intensive, week-long "vacation academy" small-group programs taught by talented teachers.

Group size
Tutors can effectively instruct up to three or four students at a time. However, moving beyond this number can quickly become small-group instruction, which is less personalized and requires a higher degree of skill to do well. One-on-one tutoring is ideal if possible.

Personnel
Because the skills required for tutoring are different from the skills required for effective classroom teaching, a wide variety of tutors (including volunteers and college students) can successfully improve student outcomes, if they receive adequate training and ongoing support.

Focus
Research has found tutoring to be effective at all grade levels—even for high school students who have fallen quite far behind. The evidence is strongest, with the most research available, for reading-focused tutoring for students in early grades (particularly grades K–2) and for math-focused tutoring for older students.

Measurement
Tutoring programs that support data use and on-going informal assessments allow tutors to more effectively tailor their instruction for individual students.

Relationships
Ensuring students have a consistent tutor over time may facilitate positive tutor-student relationships and a stronger understanding of students' learning needs.

Curriculum
Using high-quality instructional materials that are aligned with classroom content allows tutors to reinforce and support teachers' classroom instruction.

Scheduling
Tutoring interventions that are conducted during the school day tend to result in greater learning gains than those that are after school or during the summer.

Delivery mode
Most research has focused on in-person tutoring, but there is emerging evidence that tutoring can be effective when delivered at a distance.

Prioritization
Programs that target lower-performing students can support those students who most need personalized instruction but can also create a moral dilemma where tutoring is perceived as a program of last resort and not for all students. Programs that target all students in a lower-performing grade level may address the perception that tutoring is for everyone but still meet the needs of those most in need.

Source: *Design Principles for Accelerating Student Learning with High-Dosage Tutoring.* EdResearch for Recovery Brief #16. 2021.

Robert Slavin's research was important in our design of the tutoring time at The Gear Model After School Club. In his blog, Slavin wrote that well-structured programs could make an impact on students' learning (Slavin 2018). His work looked at the effect sizes of different models and structures. We incorporated the following ideas from the EdResearch brief and from Slavin's work:

- Tutoring can be done in small groups or one-on-one.
- Tutoring can be done by trained volunteers under the supervision of licensed teachers.
- Where possible, it is ideal if teachers and students work together across time and spaces, during both school-day and out-of-school programs.
- Tutoring can be especially helpful for low-income students.
- Tutoring works because of more than just individualization; nurturing and supportive attention are also important factors.

Math Tutoring

In The Gear Model After School Club, mathematics was the initial academic intervention focus for the third through fifth graders. This was about more than getting faster at multiplication and division facts, although we value computational fluency. We were striving to improve students' math achievement by strengthening their number sense. We wanted to see students increase their persistence when problem-solving and use critical-thinking skills as a social means of thinking together. Academic gains in literacy were made as well, but math was our focus. In addition to tutoring in mathematics, selecting the University of Minnesota Mechanical Engineering Ambassadors as our partner allowed for the application of mathematical content knowledge. They provided the real-world connection and purpose of learning mathematics, which supported students' motivation to learn the math concepts.

Since we were focused on mathematics and both had taught university courses for teachers using *Principles to Actions: Ensuring Mathematical Success for All* (2014) from the National Council of Teachers of Mathematics (NCTM), we leaned into the Mathematics Teaching Practices from that book. The following eight practices provide a framework for strengthening math teaching:

1. Establish mathematics goals to focus learning.
2. Implement tasks that promote reasoning and problem-solving.
3. Use and connect mathematical representations.
4. Facilitate meaningful mathematical discourse.
5. Pose purposeful questions.
6. Build procedural fluency from conceptual understanding.
7. Support productive struggle in learning mathematics.
8. Elicit and use evidence of student thinking.

(NCTM 2014)

We have used these ideas in our teaching and practice, so they are integrated deeply into our thinking. If you select mathematics as your academic focus area, these ideas and others from *Principles to Actions* are worth incorporating. If you use that resource or similar resources written for adults, we recommend that you find ways to reword the ideas using youth-friendly language to set learning goals with students. This rewording will also help volunteers understand the concepts. Although the practices are specific to math, many are relevant for other content areas.

Program Design Considerations

We allocated twenty-five minutes for tutoring. This was long enough to make a difference, but not so long that students became bored or frustrated. To support building relationships, we mixed up the seating arrangements and small groups frequently each afternoon. However, tutoring must be personalized and match a learner's capabilities, so during tutoring time, students were grouped according to their skills. When forming these groups, we referred to assessments and data indicating students' proficiency. Pairing or grouping students based on academic data gave them opportunities to collaborate with peers working on similar skills.

Grouping students for tutoring also allows the intervention staff to create materials for each group, instead of for each individual student. To us, this is the right amount of personalization.

Given the number of students who need tutoring and staffing limitations, personalization at the individual level is not sustainable over time in this type of program.

As we developed the Academic Intervention Gear, we knew we wanted to include opportunities for productive struggle that challenged students' growth. We have seen and heard of too many programs that relied on skill worksheets but failed to make a meaningful impact. Acceleration was needed. However, we were working with students who had experienced ongoing failure or who needed to develop persistence. They needed to be slowly eased into *productive* struggle, and our aim was to grow their capacity for this struggle over time. In our program, students' strong emotions about math (often negative) and failure reinforced the related importance of the Emotions Gear (see chapter 6). And by gradually increasing their productive struggle, we knew we were supporting students' ongoing classroom learning.

> *Grouping students for tutoring allows the intervention staff to create materials for each group, instead of for each individual student. To us, this is the right amount of personalization.*

Where to Start Planning

As you consider the content focus for tutoring, prioritize the skills most needed by the groups of learners you will serve. We reviewed our state's math standards, focusing on the big ideas taught at each grade level. If math tutoring is new to you, it may be helpful to meet with the participants' classroom teachers, a district math specialist, or the director of curriculum. If one of those options is not possible, ask a student if you can see their math homework or other materials they are bringing home. We were very familiar with our state's math standards. And since Sue worked at the school and knew the classroom teachers, we were aware of what was being taught in the classrooms.

Having access to student data and frequent opportunities to talk with the teachers informed us in three ways:

1. It gave us useful information about individual students and the grade-level cohort. We learned what standards and skills our learners were already working on or needed to work on.
2. We learned the computational methods and strategies students were being taught in school. We wanted to use the same language so we did not confuse them.
3. We learned the reasoning for the teaching methods being used at the school. We aligned ourselves with those instructional approaches.

As mentioned in chapter 4, we conducted one-on-one math interviews and used an assessment available with the district's intervention curriculum. This assessment had already been conducted with the students who were receiving intervention during the school day. Sue arranged with the classroom teacher to meet with the other students one-on-one prior to the first day of the After School Club. These students were sometimes fragile or not confident in math, but they could not be accommodated by the math interventionist. A handful of students chosen for the program were actually quite proficient in math but were not keeping up with schoolwork, so they were underperforming on assessments.

As you consider the content focus for tutoring, we recommend examining your state academic standards and talking with the participants' classroom teachers to determine which skills should be prioritized and taught with intensity. The level of rigor should be student specific, determined through interviews and data.

Homework Support

One of our goals was to consistently use key parts of students' homework assignments to keep students on track with their peers. We also aimed to shore up missing foundational skills for individual learners. Our focus throughout was to rapidly build their confidence, so they could return to the classroom the next day feeling competent about mathematics. We also wanted students to gain a sense of how practice leads to progress. After essential parts of homework were completed, learners moved on to practice work and math games. These were selected by Sue to help learners work on personalized skills and thinking strategies for long-term success.

Curriculum

We used math curriculum from Fishtank Learning, which we learned about from other programs that use it. This is one example of a supplemental, high-quality conceptual math resource. Fishtank Learning offers both a free and an (even better) low-cost curriculum for English language arts (ELA) in grades K–12 and mathematics in grades 2–11. The curriculum from this nonprofit is designed to meet the needs of diverse classrooms and to help students develop critical-thinking skills. Standards are linked to grade-level units but can be taught in nonsequential order if needed to personalize tutoring.

ProvenTutoring.org provides information about research-proven programs for both math and reading. This site shares each program's description, a summary of the research studies it is based on, its cost, any important additional information, and a link to its website. Sue used this resource to explore different curriculum resources and materials for potential use in the Academic Intervention Gear.

Many other resources are available, including Focused Instruction: Reading Intervention and Focused Instruction: Mathematics Intervention (Teacher Created Materials 2026). If you have funding and will be purchasing materials, a conversation with school and district leaders will help you select materials that align with students' classroom instruction.

Planning Based on Individual Student Data

In chapter 4, you read about the student selection process and how we collected data on each student. It is important to use appropriate data and assessment information when making program decisions involving the participants. The data help us identify aspects such as reading level, mathematical competency, motivations, and so on. These data points support selection of materials that will truly elevate or enhance learning with a just-right amount of productive struggle that does not frustrate and discourage students. In our program (based on our goals and our funding), we did not select only those youth who were failing tests. We also invited students with a range of skill levels who would benefit from more time on individualized math work and enrichment. These learners were underperforming, as evidenced by teacher referrals and Sue's knowledge from working with them previously.

Once we had selected participants and gathered data, we needed to prepare the materials we wanted each individual or small group of learners to work on after they tackled their homework. Homework, especially for the students far behind their grade-level peers, was sometimes minimal because the classroom content was far too difficult or the student was out of the room receiving in-school support during the lesson. In these cases, we worked closely with the classroom teacher to determine personalized work students could complete and take back to class in place of the regular classroom homework. This helped increase their confidence in their math abilities. We identified essential skills and knowledge in mathematics that lead to success. We thought about real-world application of skills and knowledge, beyond what was needed to solve the next textbook problem or be fastest at computation. We engaged in conversations based on our years of experience with struggling students and what they were missing and the research on student thinking and math success. Talking with small groups of learners through tough, relevant, interesting problems and thinking aloud together builds relationships and also strengthens everyone's persistence in problem-solving.

Talking with small groups of learners through tough, relevant, interesting problems and thinking aloud together builds relationships and also strengthens everyone's persistence in problem-solving.

Some students have experienced repeated failures, which impacts their self-esteem and confidence in mathematics. Addressing these beliefs and the resulting mindset is crucial, as our experience shows that students genuinely want to succeed. This is why we always include math games in the academic time. Games are an excellent and proven way to develop fact fluency, which often serves as a foundation for complex problem-solving tasks.

Number sense is another important area of mathematics. Our experience told us that students are often weak in two specific areas of number sense—reasonableness of answers and place value. We also wanted to incorporate the math process standards of problem-solving, communicating, reasoning, representation, and connections (NCTM 2008). We have found them to be key to students' math learning.

We prefer visual learning, so we utilized what we call sticky note planning. We wrote key ideas from our conversations on sticky notes and used them to organize our academic intervention goals. Using digital sticky notes allowed us to easily change their colors and groups. Figure 5.2 represents where our planning conversation landed. You will need to have similar conversations to develop your plans for tutoring.

Figure 5.2 Sticky Note Planning

KEY

| HSA | Dispositions | Process Standards | Content Area | objective | Curriculum | Curricular Strategy |

Critical Thinking | **Action Orientation / Engagement** | **Learning Interest** | **Assertiveness** | **Reflection**

Math Games | **Flexibility in thinking about numbers** | **Number Talks** | **Reasonableness of response (answer)** | **CGI Problems and rubric** → **Bridges** | **Problem solving**

→ **Math for Love** | **Discourse & Communication**

fact families | **estimation**

→ **Fishtank Math** | **Connections in and outside mathematics**

Base 10 - expanded notation | **ball park answers**

Composition and Decomposition of Number | **What is the question?** | **resilience - what do they do when stuck?** | **persistence - time on task**

Patterns | **Attitude** | **Love and fun in Math**

The light-pink sticky notes refer to the student data we had from the HSA (see chapter 4). The lime-green sticky notes focus on the attitudes we wanted to support, sustain, and grow. The dark-pink sticky notes reminded us of the NCTM process standards to focus on. The purple notes are the big math skills/concepts, with specific objectives on the teal notes below them. The brighter blue notes are curriculums that we decided to use for materials. The lighter blue notes list the strategies we planned to use.

Here are the beliefs and concepts informing the academic tutoring portion of The Gear Model program.

1. Use what we know about students and their interests.
   - Provide choice when possible.
   - Understand students' relationships with other students and adults in the school.
   - Be aware of their family structures and supports.

2. Tie the selection of tutoring activities to state or national academic standards.
   - Identify what we are "teaching hard" for, or our academic-focused outcome.
   - Identify the skills most needed for success.
   - Go beyond worksheets, or "drill and kill."

3. Utilize games, play, and fun (attitudes and beliefs impact learning).

4. Use resources currently accessible online or in curriculum manuals.
   - Curriculum—at grade level or dip back to earlier grade level
   - Intervention books and supplemental web-based resources

We aimed to find student work and games reinforcing concepts that would accelerate student success and build a stronger math foundation. In some cases, this involved not only considering grade-level standards but also tracing a standard back through previous grades to scaffold the learning or shore up still-developing key concepts.

Based on our goals and values, we used these materials in our work:
- The district's adopted curriculum (Bridges in Mathematics)
- Fishtank Learning math curriculum
- Games—Everyday Mathematics online games from the University of Chicago, Fishtank Learning math games, Tang Math games, card games, dice games, other games from the district's math curriculum that teachers did not have time to use during class

Planning the Small-Group Academic Activities

The interviews Sue conducted were the most beneficial way of learning where each student was in number sense, place value, and computation.

After the interviews, we determined the makeup of small groups. We used a chart to plan the tutoring activities (see figure 5.3). This chart was a quick reference to the resources we were using, the number of copies we would need, and the assessment tools we would use to check for growth.

Figure 5.3 Tutoring Outline for Program—Grades 3, 4, 5

Individualized Time (25 Minutes) to Start Each Session
Content: Flexibility in thinking about numbers and reasonableness of response
Dispositions: Time on task, resilience, reflection, learning interest

	Skill/Focus	Students in Group (names have been changed)	Extra Practice/Games	Post-Assessment
1	10 more, 10 less, 20 more, 20 less, and counting fluency to 2,000	Henry Evie Mandy* Quinn*	• Number Grid from Fishtank Learning • Tic-Tac-Toe from Fishtank Learning	• Number grid with random numbers and spaces behind to count tens forward or backward
2	Moving beyond visuals for multiplication fluency (using facts you know to help you with what you do not know)	Sterling* Sadie* Hana—6s, 7s, 8s, 9s Quincy—8s, 9s	• Ratio Table Multiplication booklet reinforcing relationship between division and multiplication • Tang Math Kakooma card games	• Ratio table assessment • Missing number equations • Observe how many cards they can play in five minutes of Kakooma card game
3	x10, x100	Harriet Judith G. Lindsey* Tracy Anna	• PIG (game from fifth grade teacher) • Fishtank Learning's third grade Unit 2: "Multiplication and Division, Part 1"	• The Powers of Ten Game in the district intervention curriculum module • Quick exit-slip quiz using Fishtank Learning's post-test
4	Rounding and estimation to check reasonableness of answer with multiplication and division	Mindy Otto Kathy	• Fishtank Learning's fourth grade Unit 1: "Rounding and Estimating with Two/Three-Digit Multiplication"	• Estimate 23 × 52
5	Multi-digit multiplication: • area model • partial products	Max—has steps but off (close)	• Fishtank Learning's fourth grade Unit 2, 3, and 4 • Emphasize games in Unit 3	• Estimate 23 × 52 • Pose 23 × 52 = • Show two ways. • What is your preferred way?

	Skill/Focus	Students in Group (*names have been changed*)	Extra Practice/Games	Post-Assessment
6	Teacher requested geometry follow-up	Isaak—second 10 sessions Louisa—no pattern in approach	• Fishtank Learning's Geometry unit on congruence and polygons, since he was absent for the vocabulary in his fifth grade class	• End-of-unit quick written assessment matching shapes to terms and comparing and contrasting two polygons using a Venn diagram
7	Comparing fractions and finding equivalent fractions	Eddy—4 sessions toward end Laquan—4 sessions toward end	• Fishtank Learning's fifth grade Fractions Units 4, 5, 6, with focus on the pre-assess and games	• Monitor their fifth grade classroom end-of-unit assessments and talk to teachers

* Read directions two times.

Assessing the Disposition for Rigor in Mathematics

Given the focus and goals of our program, we wanted to assess students' disposition for rigor in mathematics. We were continuously stepping back and observing the learners during independent and small-group academic work, asking ourselves if they were growing in persistence based on time on task.

On the first two afternoons of the After School Club, we selected specific activities to assess all learners' abilities to independently complete work. The first day, we used basic Spot the Difference or Hidden Picture activity sheets. This was not directly math, but it was a measure of a student's temperament to dig in and notice and wonder. The second day, students completed a survey (see figure 5.4) about their math goals for themselves. After they completed these tasks, students were given directions to choose a math game that matched their math goal and that would advance their math learning. We were fascinated to observe what students chose for themselves and thought would help. Many selected games that were very easy for them. Others picked games that were in keeping with the skills they said they wanted to work on. These observations gave us important insights into the learners. We learned who we would need to monitor and who we would need to encourage to push themselves.

Sue checked in with individual students to discuss their personal goals for the next few weeks and find out if their goals and the way they saw themselves matched the placement we identified for them. Notes about students' dispositions and engagement were sorted into piles based on common behaviors so we could learn how best to coach each budding mathematician in the coming weeks.

Here is what we learned about some of the students as mathematicians and thinkers at the start:

- Denny recognized he could grow more if he chose more challenging math activities/games.

(He qualified for reading intervention and was proficient in math. In our observations, he was playing very basic addition games.)
- Anna was able to get started with work when she was placed at a table with trusted friends. (If she did not feel safe and connected, she shut down.)
- Sadie and Lindsey, when given extra coaching to read and understand directions, could indeed do the work. Both were reassured they could ask for more time and seemed proud to finish. They mainly just needed help reading and understanding the directions.
- Max, Isaak, and Tracy arrived with very high energy. They needed mentors to step in at the beginning of tasks to ensure they were not rushing through the work on automatic pilot marking any answer or tearing the paper to shreds.
- Harriet was off to the races, independently pumping through work efficiently and accurately. She could be a role model and leader but did not yet appear to feel confident speaking up to the whole class. She was the only one at the table who independently found all ten differences in the two pictures and moved on to the online math games on her own. (On this particular afternoon, the cohort had access to computers.)

Figure 5.4 Survey: "What math skill would you like to improve this year?"

YOU are a growing mathematician.

Engineers need math to know how things in the world work.

What one or two things would you like to get even better at in math? Check them.

_____ I want to get better at adding and subtracting by friendly tens to 2,000. (I want to visualize a number line in my head better.)

_____ I want more strategies to multiply and divide confidently.

_____ I want to get better at estimating answers so I know if I am right.

_____ I want to get better at multiplying big numbers.

_____ I want to be able to put fractions on a number line and get better at comparing fractions.

On a scale of 1 to 5, how much do you like to challenge yourself?
(1 = not at all and 5 = I love a good stumper.)

1   2   3   4   5

The last example shows the power of access for students who do not have opportunities to be with peers after school. Harriet was frequently absent from school, and her teacher (who was at the session) was pleased, even surprised, to see her get so much work done. Harriet did not have access to a computer or the internet at home. Being in attendance helped her make up missed learning. Even more importantly, Harriet chatted and giggled with her school friends as they worked, something she rarely got to do in her neighborhood. The family lived in an isolated location, and her dad had the family's car after school. The program became a place where Harriet could gain skills she needed for school success, and this was made possible because of the opportunity to take the bus to get home.

The Gear in Motion

Once the planning, assessing, and observations were done, it was time to put the work into action. We set up a work folder for each child. The folders were color coded by groups so work could easily be monitored and replaced when completed. We placed the folders and students' writing journals in bins (one for each table group) and placed the bins on a rolling library cart along with writing utensils, paper, and games and puzzles needed for the day. This was a portable program that got moved into the media center at the end of the day and wheeled back to Sue's office at the end of the night.

Learners were assigned to the tables in mixed groups. However, we ensured that at each table, at least two students were working on the same concepts and games. We intentionally did not seat them by ability groups in order to prevent self-shaming. Third through fifth graders, like all humans, compare themselves to one another. We did not want to feed that tendency, but rather wanted to set the stage where everyone was working on improving themselves in their own way.

Figure 5.5 Portable Materials for Students

We had trained the volunteers to avoid sharing any of their own negative feelings about math. Our adage was "Don't spread math phobia!" If a student was stuck, volunteers were trained to ask if the learner would like to reread the directions or if they would like to have the directions read to them again. It is amazing how many times this simple strategy got the wheels of math productivity turning again. If a volunteer did not know how to solve a problem, other students at the table were solicited or the classroom teacher's weekly newsletters to parents were consulted. We had one iPad; sometimes it was used to look up unknown vocabulary words or to check answers.

While students were working, we were fostering strong communication skills and persistence. How did they approach their work? Were they avoiding work? Were they completing work? We affirmed desired behaviors, quietly or loudly recognizing anytime a learner reread directions, drew a picture to make sense of a story, checked the reasonableness of an answer (especially with multi-digit computation), or went back to self-correct their work.

Closing Thoughts

Initially, learners loved the math games, not realizing they were learning and reinforcing skills. Games served as a social conduit to critical thinking. Over time, as the routine set in, the learners advanced to extremely productive work on increasingly challenging math problems, often almost forgetting to move on to the games that also supported their goals. Hearing students debate and explain their thinking showed not only motivation but also growing oral language skills.

As the program progressed, almost all learners began returning to class with their homework done. Many teachers informally reported that the students in the After School Club were looking up and participating more in class. A growing sense of momentum may be what led to more classroom teachers stopping by for five to ten minutes during tutoring time to lend a hand to individual students, especially if they were close to mastering a core math standard and simply needed a refresher before an upcoming assessment. The momentum of the developing microcommunity was creating a buzz in the room. Success was breeding success.

By the end of the program, evidence on exit slips showed that students all met their personal math goals. Students and caregivers reported increased confidence in math. Parents reported great pride and were thankful that when it was needed, math support was provided. Almost all the volunteers came back the following year.

The streams of progress were coming together to make a mighty river of learning that flowed right back to the school-day classroom experiences too. A microcommunity of relationships and learning was being created, as we'd hoped.

Reflection Questions

- Will your academic focus be math, reading, or writing?
- How can you find out what knowledge and skills your students would benefit most from?
- What curriculum resources do you already have access to?
- Are your resources conceptual, requiring critical thinking?
- How will you decide what materials will move each learner forward on unit assessments and standardized assessments?
- Are the skills you are aiming at essential in your state standards?
- What simple post-assessments can you use to aid in making adjustments?
- How will you celebrate success and persistence?

CHAPTER 6

Enrichment— Arts/Culture/ STEAM/Nature

"The mind is not a vessel to be filled, but a fire to be kindled."
—Plutarch, Greek philosopher and historian

Powerful advancement takes place when youth are connected with people and places that broaden their view of the world. They find new learning interests, their confidence grows, and they are inspired to take charge of their own futures. And many times, they build long-term relationships with trusted adults, expanding networks that support their future pursuits. In this chapter, we discuss the Enrichment Gear, which is intended to help students engage in deep, messy learning and to help them find and develop passions for real-world topics.

The following questions are answered in this chapter:
- What role does enrichment have in building academic motivation and background knowledge?
- How do you find and train partners for your group of students and their learning goals?
- What do partners bring to the work, and what do you need to do to support them in working with students?
- What did we learn from our partnership experience?

40% ENRICHMENT
ARTS/CULTURE/STEAM/NATURE
· Rigor & Relevance
· Engagement in School & Life
Tied to academic intervention

What Is Enrichment?

The answer to this important and complex question has a big impact on our work. There are different definitions and understandings of *enrichment*. Its meaning can be ambiguous and unwieldy, but we have not yet come up with a better word. For now, we use the term *enrichment*, and ask that as you read and work, you determine what it means to you and your community. Having a common understanding is necessary to support impactful change.

The Cambridge Dictionary (n.d.) defines *enrichment* as "the act or process of improving the quality or power of something by adding something else." This definition led us to wonder, "What is the *something* being added?" We have heard others define it in more basic terms, such as "things beyond the standard curriculum," or in more refined ways, such as "enhancing the academic experience to challenge thinking." There are many ways enrichment activities can be presented in the classroom or in the community. We encourage you not to limit yourself to lessons from published curricula.

Our thinking around enrichment is also informed by the Habits of Mind (chapter 1). We see them embedded in enrichment work, with a focus on the following habits: creating, imagining, and innovating; thinking and communicating with clarity and precision; and remaining open to continuous learning. As you select topics for enrichment work, the idea or goal should include connecting these habits to whatever is relevant to the youth you are serving.

Wendy Taylor, host of *The Special Ed Strategist* podcast, explains that enrichment opportunities encourage learners to take an in-depth look at a topic. This could be done with further research, or by approaching a topic with a new or different perspective, or by connecting the topic to real-world work in the arts, culture, STEM, or nature (Taylor 2019). We note these two points Taylor makes:

- "Enrichment activities account for student choice. This means that, while each option for enrichment should revolve around a similar learning goal, the method by which students arrive at that objective can be vastly different depending on their interests or selections" (2019, para. 5).
- "Enrichment should connect to prior knowledge and/or account for cross-curricular and/or cross-cultural connections" (2019, para. 6).

The idea of enrichment being cross-curricular caught our attention. This led us to envision enrichment in its most ideal form, when it ties to current learning in the classroom and to students' life experiences at home. It adds to the regular curriculum with greater breadth, depth, or complexity. Combining enrichment, academics, and social-emotional learning supports whole-child development. In The Gear Model, arts, culture, STEAM, and nature are the vehicles that drive opportunities for enrichment.

The enrichment activities we are advocating for are the feeding grounds of deep, meaningful learning—learning that involves frustration, struggle, messiness, and challenge. This type of learning experience allows youth and adults to be vulnerable, which helps build and enhance relationships, bonding, and empowerment. Real-world context and application of curiosity allows students to think critically and problem-solve, and it empowers them to be leaders. Where students have opportunities for craftsmanship, exploration, adventure, and creation, their vulnerability and rapidly firing minds can lead to natural friendships and life-sustaining relationships. For us, enrichment is using student voice to achieve deeper learning or application of learning. We also think of enrichment as being the doors that, once passed through, change you forever, sometimes in small, less-obvious ways, but sometimes in profound, life-changing ways.

> *The enrichment activities we are advocating for are the feeding grounds of deep meaningful learning—learning that involves frustration, struggle, messiness, and challenge.*

Why Is Enrichment Worth Your Time?

Many schools have moved away from offering enrichment opportunities, often not by choice. This shift has occurred due to changes in priorities, budget limitations, and staffing challenges. Ongoing efforts to ensure that all students pass academic tests have reduced teachers' time for what is often viewed as "extra" learning during regular school hours. The science fairs, career days, weekly art lessons, visits to the nature center, and other field trips have been disappearing. In some places, recess itself has been greatly reduced, forcing states to enact laws requiring recess. These shifts often happen with little attention to the impact on youth mental health and learning. No wonder youth are more anxious and increasingly acting out.

In her article "Liberatory Education," Zaretta Hammond substantiates this abject truth:

> For the students most in need of enriching learning experiences, we all too often impose a pedagogy of compliance that prizes orderliness and completing work over getting to understanding. This point was highlighted in a recent report, *The Opportunity Myth*, that summarized a study in which almost 1,000 lessons in five school districts were observed. It found that although 71 percent of students were doing what was asked in their assignments (with more than half receiving As and Bs), they were meeting grade-level standards only 17 percent of the time—mainly because the assignments did not ask for grade-level work. (Hammond 2021, para. 13)

Enrichment Access

The United States has an *access-to-enrichment* gap. We believe that students are disengaging from learning in school largely because they have little access to enrichment to stimulate their minds or make the reason for learning meaningful. Enrichment has the potential to give daily lessons a purpose and engage students in learning beyond the walls of school.

For example, in Minnesota (our home state), the statewide student survey (Minnesota Department of Education 2022) disaggregated by race and ethnicity clearly shows that the majority of non-white students have very little access to school-sponsored enrichment experiences outside the school day. When school-sponsored activities are categorized into sports and non-sports, the data shows even less access to non-sports experiences for all students in fifth grade.

The United States has an access-to-enrichment gap.

Minnesota is not alone in its current lack of access to enrichment experiences. There is a similar lack throughout the United States. Tuchman and Pillow (2018) found that opportunities were not available in a way that gives all students equal access. When the researchers examined the differences in access to enrichment opportunities, they found that white families were more often located in neighborhoods that allowed them access to many out-of-school programs, while the neighborhoods Hispanic families resided in had much lower access to enrichment opportunities. When they examined the data for individual racial groups, they found that the neighborhoods Black families resided in had the lowest access to any out-of-school opportunities. Youth living with implications of socioeconomic complications and barriers also have little access to gifted and talented programs (Grissom, Redding, and Bleiberg 2019), community education after-school programs, summer camps, or sports clubs, all of which could be enriching. This underscores the need for any program that truly serves students—especially intervention programs—to include high-quality, substantial enrichment experiences.

Middle- and upper-middle-class youth are often registered for continuous pay-to-play activities. In some instances, scholarships can be lined up to cover the activity fees for families experiencing financial challenges. However, transportation is another barrier. Buses are often too expensive or simply not available due to driver shortages. And as poverty spreads beyond the urban core to suburbs, public transportation becomes less available.

We have observed these realities throughout the United States in service work and site visits, which leads us to assert the need for creative, cross-sector systems changes.

STEAM Enrichment and Our Partnership

The philosophy of The Gear Model approach is to weave together the math and/or reading intervention provided during the school day with after-school academic support time. This double dose of academics is what it takes to accelerate learning and end disparities. The teachers had sufficient training in, and could manage, the following gears: Attending to Emotions, Collaborative Movement and Play, Academic Intervention, and Communication Skills. Taking on the last gear, Enrichment Activities, was an option, but the teachers were already stretching their capacity. Plus, a partner with deeper expertise and passion in an enrichment area would be beneficial for students and teachers. This type of collaboration has the potential to benefit the partner as well if they are creating a new program or are new to working with youth. In addition, partnerships bring more of the extended community into the program.

We found that it helps to have a network of enrichment partners to draw from. In previous summers, in after-school and in-school intervention programs, Sue partnered with arts organizations, parks and recreation groups, boat builders, dance groups, and parents who were eager to share their unique cultural backgrounds and provide authentic, real-life enrichment activities. You will want to look around your community to find like-minded arts groups, nature programs, community service groups, or other parties offering real-world enrichment activities. Conducting internet searches, attending community networking events, and simply talking to neighbors can lead you to passionate and invested enrichment partners.

We found that it helps to have a network of enrichment partners to draw from.

Through networking, we learned of the University of Minnesota's budding Mechanical Engineering Ambassadors' desire to develop school enrichment programs to increase the pipeline of girls and racially diverse students into their program and profession. We introduced the Engineering Ambassador program in chapter 4. Here, we focus on that specific partnership and the work we did together.

Intentional Development of Activities

In chapter 4, we discussed the collaborative process of developing the STEAM modules (pages 68–69). Let's take a closer look at the modules. One module was developed for each week of the winter/spring session. Ambassadors working in partnerships chose a topic and engineering principle for each module, which would take place on two consecutive afternoons, during sixty-minute periods with the following time segments:

- 15–20 minutes: Presentation and demonstration that included background knowledge needed for the team challenge
- 15–20 minutes: Hands-on team challenge activity
- 7–10 minutes: Oral or written reflection questions to aid in summarizing the learning
- The remaining time was for expressing gratitude and getting ready to go home.

We wanted to see students deeply engaged in new learning, using the engineering design process and the scientific process, and working collaboratively and communicating with others.

Figures 6.1 and 6.2 show examples of the engineering modules.

Figure 6.1 How to Build a Ship Presentation and Demonstration

The presentation showed heavy ships and explained the principle of water displacement. Demonstrations included tubs of water and 3D-printed ships that ambassadors loaded with heavy "cargo bolts" while learners counted to see how many bolts the ship could hold before sinking to the bottom of the tub. Youth love sinking things. Sue had extra plastic tarps at the ready!

Essential vocabulary: *floating, sinking, water displacement, load*

Afternoon 1 Essential question for the team challenge:

- In what ways could you make a foil boat that displaces the most water?

Afternoon 2 Essential questions for the team challenge:

- How can half your team use craft sticks, foil, and tape to build a boat that displaces even more of the water and can manage a heavier load?

- How can half your team use foam balls, foil, and tape to build a boat that displaces even more of the water and can manage a heavier load?

Note: Essentially, the challenge on afternoon 2 was the same as on afternoon 1, but the options of materials provided more complexity of choice and greater challenge.

We watched with interest as students who had been frustrated and teary-eyed the first afternoon—when their boats sank—returned the next day with fresh determination and new design ideas. The iterative process of rethinking, rebuilding, and trying again with new materials brought out their persistence. Many students were jubilant as they left on the second evening.

Learning continued outside of the Club. Curious parents emailed asking why their children were using up all the aluminum foil at home and filling the bathtub with water to float foil boats. It was satisfying to hear that students' natural curiosity and critical thinking were extending beyond the program.

This activity was such a hit with the youth that we extended it with a third activity day. Students added propellers and small engines to model boats and explored the impact of the size and number of blades on a propeller by counting RPMs (revolutions per minute). This became a reference point for the next unit. We were responding to what motivated students.

Figure 6.2 Additional Examples of Modules

How Do Planes Stay in the Air? Presentation and Demonstration

Ambassadors gave a presentation focused on images of spiraling footballs (*push/thrust*), parachutes (*drag/pull*), and planes (*lift*). Demonstrations followed, and students were taught multiple ways to fold paper airplanes.

Essential vocabulary: *thrust, hang time, drag* (pull), *lift*

Afternoon 1 Essential questions for the team challenge:

- How will you design a paper airplane that flies far?

- How can you design a second paper airplane to fly high and stay in the air longer?

Afternoon 2 Essential questions for the team challenge:

- How can you design a plane to fly halfway across the gym?
- How can you design a plane to stay in the air for 30 seconds or more?

Lighting Up the World (Circuits) Presentation and Demonstration

Ambassadors discussed applications of electric energy. They displayed diagrams showing how circuits control the flow of energy to a light bulb through the use of basic open, closed, and parallel circuits. Learners designed circuits using wires, light bulbs, and homemade conductive play dough (for more on conductive play dough, see exploratorium.edu/tinkering/projects/squishy-circuits).

Essential vocabulary: *circuit, conductor, insulator, open circuit, closed circuit, parallel*

Afternoon 1 Essential question for the team challenge:

- How can you connect a playdough circuit to light up your tiny light bulbs?

Afternoon 2 Essential question for the team challenge:

- What are the differences between connecting lights in a series and in parallel?

Engineering a Solar Future Presentation and Demonstration

Ambassadors showed examples of power sources such as coal, fossil fuels, and kinetic energy while introducing the benefits and challenges of solar energy.

Essential vocabulary: *obstacles, angle, installation, location choice, capture* (sun's energy)

Afternoon 1 Essential question for the team challenge:

- How does the light (bulb) affect a solar panel?

Afternoon 2 Essential question for the team challenge:

- When given a diorama with a moveable toy house, a yard, a plastic solar-powered dancing flower, plastic or cardboard moveable trees, wires, and a mini solar panel, which place is best to install a solar panel to get the solar-powered plastic flower to dance the fastest? (The dancing flower represented the powering of household appliances.)

Team Challenges

Each week, the team challenge built from the first day to the second day. The students were placed in groups of four for the team challenge. Mixed-age groups worked remarkably well.

On any given afternoon, each team member had one of the following roles—leader, recorder, supply-getter, and spokesperson. The leader directed the design-thinking planning process. Once the team had brainstormed approaches to the essential question and developed an initial plan for tackling it, the supply-getter raised a hand for permission to get the materials needed. The recorder wrote the group's findings on a form the ambassadors prepared for the activity. If data or time trials were being compared, the recorder also documented that information. At the end, the spokesperson used what was recorded to verbally share with another team or the whole group what their small group learned and what they would do differently next time.

The whole-group reflections on the first evening allowed the Engineering Ambassadors to chime in with probing questions, lavish affirmations, brief clarifications of important engineering principles, and connections between the students' learning and what they do in their labs.

Results of the team challenges included the following benefits for students:
- Practice and growth in collaboration skills
- Increased understanding of their own abilities and intelligence, which is significant since intervention often makes students feel as if they are missing out on enrichment
- Engagement in critical thinking beyond the school day
- Practice applying content and real-world knowledge and skills to different situations

Figure 6.3 Anchor Charts Used as Part of the Enrichment Gear

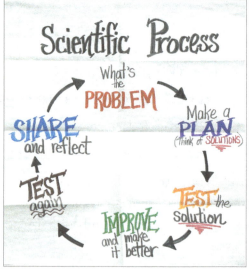

Managing the Enrichment Activities

You might assume that people interested in working with youth have knowledge and experience in managing large groups of them. This is rarely the case. As with volunteers, we provided training to the ambassadors on how to give directions and release responsibility to the students. The guidelines were as follows:

Basic Tips for Running Enrichment Activities

1. Start talking only after the entire room is quiet and looking in your direction.
2. Use an age-appropriate cue to bring students back together. Examples: a chime, a hand clapping pattern, a call-and-response, a hand up.
3. Be still and calm at the front when presenting.
4. Youth can sit for fifteen to twenty minutes maximum, especially after school.
5. Materials for activities must be prepped and easily accessible before you start.
6. Use a visual schedule or flow map; segmenting the time helps youth focus and stay on track.
7. Follow the same routine for passing out and collecting supplies and materials.
8. Leave time at the end for group reflections. These reflections deepen learning and inform future programming.

In addition, for every module they taught, we asked partners to use a specific template for the final slide displayed after their presentations/demonstrations. For partners with little to no experience working in schools, this slide supports desired student behaviors and time management, as well as effective connection to the activity. Key parts of the slide were as follows:

The goal (for that day's team challenge)
The real-world question for the afternoon, establishing the connection between the presentation/demonstration and the small-group team challenge or activity.

A list of materials
Provide a clear list of materials and encourage students to get the materials at the beginning to avoid unnecessary roaming around the room or wasting valuable production time.

A visual list of tips and reflection questions for easy reference
Volunteers should quietly point to the visual list to encourage learners to look up to remember what they are supposed to be working and reflecting on.

A visual countdown timer (or appoint a timekeeper) to keep engagement high
Students can monitor their own use of time (fifteen to twenty minutes for teamwork or partner sessions).

The Engineering Ambassadors' large-group presentations ended with this type of slide to support the transition to the small-group team challenges. Figure 6.4 shows an example of how this slide incorporated routines and group management.

Figure 6.4 Slide for Transition to the Small-Group Challenges

Tonight's Team Engineering Challenge:

Plan first: Discuss & brainstorm with your team . . .
How will you design a building to withstand wind or rain?

Then get supplies:
1. Dowels
2. Noodles
3. Marshmallows
4. Tape
5. Paper
6. Parchment
7. Plastic straw

We'll stop every 10 minutes to share thoughts.

Keep in mind for testing:
A. What shapes are strong?
B. How do materials act differently?
C. We can always make it better!

When groups were off task, confused, or frustrated, they were encouraged to look at the slide on display. This increased students' autonomy, self-directedness, and time on task as small groups completed the team challenge at tables around the room. Students could easily refer back to the directions and the key ideas. This approach reduced the need to answer the same questions multiple times. When inappropriate behavior erupted, it was usually because a student or students had missed directions. Behavior was redirected by an adult who took the student aside to reread the screen. Engagement followed.

Building Relationships and Assessing Prior Knowledge

We wanted the Engineering Ambassadors to feel welcomed to the program. The first afternoon of the eight-week winter/spring session was dedicated to community building. Since the elementary participants were in school together and had participated in the four-week fall session, they had already established relationships, but we needed to welcome the others to our microcommunity. On this special afternoon, the ambassadors and new volunteers did not have any responsibilities beyond attending and connecting. They were treated as guests being welcomed into our space. Instead of starting with academic tutoring and attending to emotions, the elementary students completed pre-assessment surveys of their current understanding of the world of engineering. Next, with great fanfare, the students and the adult and high school volunteers welcomed the college students and professors into the room with high fives and greetings. Instantly, something unexpected happened. Elementary students who spoke Portuguese or Spanish noticed that some of the college students had names similar to theirs and they realized they spoke the same languages. Wow! They made instant connections. The elementary students (and high school volunteers) were in awe of the cool college students and asked questions about college life. Then the elementary students shared the vision boards they had made in the fall session, enabling the ambassadors to learn about their unique identities, strengths, interests, and career aspirations.

Everyone went to the gym, where Sue and her co-teacher led parachute activities—a classic favorite from P.E. class. The whole group bounced rubber chickens and balls into the air by collectively following directions to "snap" and "pop" on command. Then, in small groups, elementary, high school, and college students designed and built "homes" for stuffed animals using recycled cups, egg cartons, boxes, and doodads. Sue and her co-teacher planned and directed this relationship-building encounter.

> Intentionally building hospitality into your program is a foundational step to forging developmental relationships. Time spent building community sets the stage for an environment where everyone can be vulnerable, take risks, and challenge each other's growth. Looking back, we are so thankful we kicked off the first year with a whole-group fun afternoon and a warm welcome to the college students and professors. In the second year, we skipped those activities. As a result, relationships during the second year weren't as strong, and the momentum suffered.

All twenty-five Engineering Ambassadors and all three professors attended, learning everyone's names and getting a sense of the culture of the school and the feel of the room. They stayed behind after the young learners left to reflect and ask questions, especially about specific participants who clearly had unique needs.

Pre-Assessment

One of the principles of the Enrichment Gear is to teach students to use the known to find the unknown. The goal of the first afternoon's pre-assessment was to learn the answers to this question: "What understandings about engineering do the participants have to build from, and what engineering knowledge do they need to collaborate and design_____?"

The questions, responses, and what we learned from them are shown here.

Question	What we learned from responses
What is engineering?	Responses told us students had limited background knowledge. Many wrote about building and fixing stuff. One learner thought it was someone who drove the train. This told us we need to explain that engineers work in teams using a process to make design mechanisms to improve people's lives: mechanical, electrical, chemical, environmental.

Question	What we learned from responses
What does an engineer do?	Student responses consisted of short two- and three-word answers including the words "building" and "stuff." Students said engineers were really smart. Some said they worked hard. The engineering students were happy to be associated with being hardworking and smart.

Responses to additional questions made clear that the engineering process, the scientific process, and language for scientific collaboration needed to be pre-taught and referred to frequently.

Post-Assessment

We saw substantial growth in all participants. At the beginning, the students generally knew engineers built or fixed "things." By the end, they associated the work engineers did with designing and building everything from bridges to hairdryers to ships to earbuds. At the beginning, only one student knew of an engineer in their life. By the end, when asked if they knew any engineers, they all wanted to list the name of every professor and college student they had met from the Engineering Ambassadors program. Some had come to know of relatives who knew engineers. Half reported in a school survey that they were considering going into engineering after high school. In the fall, when creating their vision boards with the art teacher, students had gained a vague idea of the design process. By the end of the winter/spring session, they could draw the collaborative iterative design process with fine detail and give specific examples of the steps.

Figure 6.5 Example of a Student's Pre- and Post-Engineering Survey

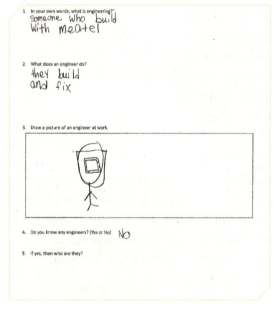
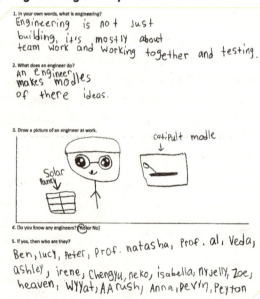

Celebration Showcase Highlighting Success

To celebrate the end of the intervention program and the success of students, we made ice cream and shared it with youth who were in the school-based childcare program. The ambassadors wanted to end in a fun and memorable way, and making ice cream allowed them to teach about molecular changes that occur when liquid dairy products become solid ice cream.

On the last afternoon, families and community members were invited to join the ambassadors and students for a Family Science Carnival. Students showed examples of what they made during the team challenges. We had art and STEAM activities for parents and siblings to try out. We ate cookies and watched a video highlighting pictures from the program. Every child had a family member there. The parents were so impressed by what their children were saying as they came home each night that they all found ways to adjust work schedules to attend the celebration. The school paid for a ride for a mother who did not have a car. Local police officers and firefighters were invited to attend to support any youth who did not have a family member able to come. They enjoyed getting to know the families. Upon seeing the video, officers and firefighters assumed this was a program for gifted and talented youth at the school.

What We Learned from Our Experience

As we reflect on what we learned, there are a few key things we want to highlight:
- The enrichment experiences must be based on the interests of the learners enrolled in the program. This interest will support increased academic motivation.
- We cannot overemphasize the need to train your partners (and volunteers). Partners can bring deep knowledge in an enrichment field that you do not have; you bring deep knowledge and understanding of youth and youth development. The ambassadors who were trained in our program learned a lot about youth and teaching.
- Students need to see community members of all ages, races, genders, and backgrounds as smart leaders, mentors, and role models.

Enrichment brings a range of benefits to youth:
- Learning the iterative process of engineering design and its application to real life will benefit this group throughout their lifetimes.
- Important content-knowledge growth in thinking strategies has long-term benefits for students. Figure 6.6 shows how one student drew and labeled the steps of the engineering process correctly.
- Enrichment helps raise students' aspirations. Almost all of the participants said they would go on to do something with engineering in the future, thus meeting the goal of the Engineering Ambassadors program.

Figure 6.6 Sample Student Response

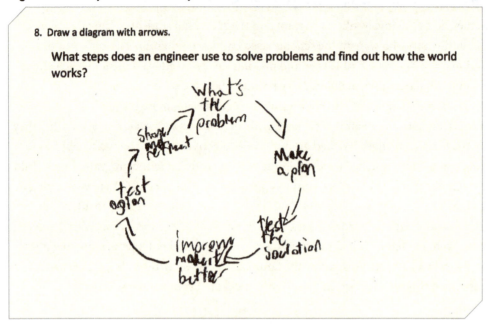

Enrichment brings benefits to volunteers and partners too. Notably, the high school volunteers and college students grew in self-awareness, leadership, and facilitation skills. One particularly quiet engineering student seemed self-conscious and struggled for words during her practice presentations, eventually shutting down. Later that spring, she was able to take command of a room full of budding elementary school engineers. One of the professors got tears in his eyes as he watched her working with the students. Those types of unexpected surprises motivated the teachers and professors to keep doing this extra work while also teaching full time.

Closing Thoughts

Upon reflection, we see how enrichment activated student voice. Enrichment is the glue that holds this whole model together. It is what keeps the students coming back each afternoon. It shows students the value of school, learning, and education. Students built important background knowledge while being highly motivated and engaged. The real-life learning was personalized based on students' interests and development, and it was contextualized. The lessons had a guiding framework, but student voice and choice were essential to engaging students in the learning. Enrichment is the key to meeting the "expand possibilities" element in the Developmental Relationships Framework (Search Institute, n.d.).

The extra energy it takes to set up highly engaging enrichment activities is worth the long-term transformative results. It takes courage to buck the current skills-oriented "Hurry up!" and "Did they pass the test?" vibes in education. It takes courage to ask funders, "What are the skills youth need to develop in the program that will give your company a great photo op?" Coming together around real-world projects, learning real-world skills, and conjuring strong relationship networks is what we are after.

Reflection Questions

- How can you discover students' interests for enrichment? What have students asked to read or learn about?
- How will you provide opportunities for learners to work independently on enrichment activities?
- When thinking about the youth you aim to impact, how could relationships become stronger as a result of art, culture, STEAM, and nature experiences?
- When (and where) do youth have dedicated time to explore who they might want to be someday and what they might want to contribute as independent young adults?
- How might an adult's view of youth be enhanced as a result of hands-on, real-world learning?
- How does the iterative process of learning a real-life skill offer opportunities for learners to be vulnerable?

CHAPTER 7

Communication

"Reading and writing float on a sea of talk."
—James Britton, educator and writer

Communication has an important role in The Gear Model. It is the grease that keeps all the other gears moving. We rely on it to share thinking about academic content, to identify and share emotions and express empathy, to read directions and other texts, to have conversations and support one another, and to learn about and record important enrichment ideas.

Throughout the program, we advance communication skills for learners through intentional, thoughtful use of several strategies. In this chapter, we examine these strategies and explain how we use them to ensure that students have ongoing opportunities to engage in meaningful communication and develop their skills.

The following questions are answered in this chapter:
- What role does the development of communication skills play in The Gear Model?
- What ways are there to integrate communication knowledge and skills into all parts of an intervention program?
- How does this gear influence or work with other gears?

What Is Communication?

Communication refers to all the verbal, nonverbal, written, and visual interactions that occur between people to share information, emotions, and ideas. These interactions range from meeting basic needs to building relationships for love and belonging. Communication involves the sender of the message, the message itself, and the receiver of that message. Relationships are built on communication, as it is essential to understanding others and

15% Verbal & Written
COMMUNICATION
- Reflections
- Self-Monitoring
- Journals
- Academic Language

sharing perspectives. Communication is the cornerstone of functioning communities. And of course, communication is the bedrock of learning.

Why Is Communication Important?

Communication is integral to academic success. Students must be able to communicate with others in order to understand and engage with academic content. Communication happens continually during the educational process, through asking questions, joining discussions, taking notes, recording projects, and sharing ideas. Communication, whether nonverbal, oral, or written, is how people interact with others and build relationships. Students use communication skills to build friendships, learn from each other, express care, resolve conflicts, and more. Collaboration, teamwork, and group work are built upon communication. Students need to be able to express their thinking and listen to others to contribute to the work at hand. Personal growth and learning happen through communication. Students must learn how to express themselves to expand their critical-thinking and problem-solving abilities.

Efficient, Intentional Communication Strategies

Every interaction youth have with adults contributes to the development of their communication skills. Youth are communicating, reflecting, and sharing feedback all the time. In our work, we created opportunities to build communication skills through informal and formal getting-to-know-one-another activities, as well as reflections, self-evaluations, and journals. The program volunteers modeled and encouraged high-level academic talk. We think of communication as the process of understanding and sharing meaning. This includes listening, speaking, reading, writing, and drawing to express understanding and expand thinking. As we worked to personalize learning, we intentionally provided opportunities for students who did not have strong reading skills to lean into other areas of communicating (e.g., auditory/artistic). We know that oral language comes before written language, so our goal was to help students articulate their thoughts through spoken words.

Verbal Communication Skills Development

Verbal communication skills are essential for future success. Our focus in this area is on learning the skills and applying them in context. Strong communication skills are intertwined with thinking, and the Habits of Mind are a valuable framework for thinking. These habits offer key concepts to focus on. Students need opportunities to learn and practice both thinking and communication skills.

Figure 7.1 Habits of Mind Related to Communication

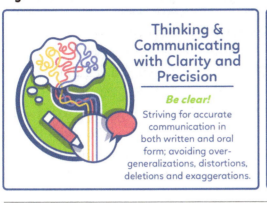
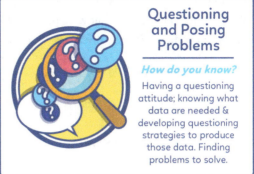

Thinking & Communicating with Clarity and Precision

Be clear! Striving for accurate communication in both written and oral form; avoiding over-generalizations, distortions, deletions and exaggerations.

Questioning and Posing Problems

How do you know? Having a questioning attitude; knowing what data are needed & developing questioning strategies to produce those data. Finding problems to solve.

Source: "What Are the Habits of Mind?" Institute for Habits of Mind. n.d.-a. Used with permission.

Asking Questions to Stir Conversation and Build Relationships

As a means of increasing empathy in learners, we thoughtfully infused listening and communication skills into all routines and rituals. At the beginning of each session, we left printed conversation starters on each table for volunteers to use to connect with individual students and establish supportive, caring relationships. During training, volunteers were taught to scan the room upon entering to find any learners who weren't yet included in conversation. Then, they were encouraged to be curious and attentive listeners, using the conversation starters to support that effort. Instead of the often unproductive "How is your day going?" or "How was your day?" we used questions that reflect the elements of the Developmental Relationships Framework (Search Institute, n.d.):

- Who made you smile or laugh today? (express care)
- I notice your body language might be _____. (express care)
- Perhaps something made you frustrated or angry today? I wonder what might have happened to you. (provide support)
- Where would it be most helpful to begin our work together for the next half hour? What supports will be helpful for you to complete the work and feel proud? (share power)
- How might we together learn to _____? [tie shoes, close your water bottle tightly, check your work, remember to turn your work in] (provide support)
- Tell me about your interest in _____. [a hobby known to be of interest] (expand possibilities)

Volunteers passed along information we might not otherwise have known, such as interests learners wanted to explore or social concerns they had. For example, one boy felt left out because he was not in an organized sport like everyone else. After learning this, we worked with sports partners to get paper registration forms and touched base with his parents to provide support and connection to other youth programs. Another student said she would focus better if she could work around the corner in a hallway during tutoring time. The volunteer helped her get set up during tutoring from then on. The two built a sweet friendship and the student was proud to be gaining a better understanding of math.

We cannot overemphasize how helpful it is to have readily available conversation starters. Samples and products abound if you search online for "getting to know you questions." These days, the art of conversation and truly listening to another person's stories often requires direct teaching. We choose to intentionally model and create space for conversation skills, rather than simply complain about the younger generation being on their phones or having earbuds in all the time, never talking to the person beside them. Cell phones were never out during our program, and warm verbal regard was expected everywhere.

> *We choose to intentionally model and create space for conversation skills.*

Nonverbal Academic Cues

Nonverbal cues helped keep volume in check during academic activities and team-based enrichment challenges. Here are some other ways we used nonverbal cues:

- To visit the restroom, students used a hand signal and a sign-out sheet.
- We established a signal to get everyone's attention.
- We played the same song every day to signal time to clean up after snack and tutoring time. Even teens love this if it's the right song.
- We pointed a lot at visual directions or the direction the group was moving.
- Volunteers were trained not to ask rhetorical questions that added nonproductive noise to the air space. For example, instead of asking, "Do you want to get your backpack?" they pointed to the backpacks and walked beside the child.

Jean Illsley Clarke, an internationally known parent educator, used her hand as a visual strategy to explicitly teach the five parts of doing any task or job. Sue further developed that concept by creating the hand visual shown in figure 7.2. This visual could be displayed in any learning space. During the After School Club, the hand visual was posted in the room and referred to often.

Think about how many times your partners, children, and the people you work with start a job without really understanding it. Think about the wasted words and frazzled nerves that result when nobody cleans up after a job. Instead of wasting words on repeating ourselves, at the beginning of each session, in a joking, cajoling way, we all used

Figure 7.2 Five Parts of Any Task

106 Academic Intervention Success

our hands (yes, even the fifth graders, whose eyes rolled only slightly) to go through the five steps of how we would tackle tasks individually and as teams.

A strength of this process and visual is its tie to problem-solving. Problem-solving has similar phases of work, and, as shown on the hand visual, there are times you must stop the process and back up in the work in order to move forward. Learners may begin a task and then realize they do not understand it. The hand visual supports backing up to revisit what the task is or what questions they have about it. In the problem-solving process, this happens as well. Learners might start solving a problem and then realize their plan (strategy) is not working and they need to back up in the process and make adjustments.

Journals

We started and ended each day by communicating through talking and writing. Journals were used at the beginning for self-awareness (using sentence frames) and at the end for academic and teamwork reflection.

The sentence frame "Today I am feeling _____ because I am thinking about _____" was a quick, standard writing prompt students used as they entered every day. We have found that when encountering a caring adult, youth like to verbally announce whether their day was awful or wonderful and explain why. We wanted to be responsive but were often busy. Our solution was to have students practice writing complete sentences describing their emotions and thoughts. When we had a free moment or two, we quickly scanned the journals to see if anyone needed emotional support or had a celebration to honor. We hoped learners would become aware of patterns or notice how emotions can change and shift. Being sad or angry one day does not mean you will feel that way every day. Students' journal samples are on page 118.

At the end of the sessions with the Engineering Ambassadors, students used journals to record new ideas related to the engineering enrichment activities (see chapter 6). This provided an opportunity to model for students how to use academic writing, which is different from personal writing. In their academic writing, we were specifically looking for content and vocabulary learning.

Figure 7.3 Sample Questions from the Challenge to Build a Strong Skyscraper

1. What materials worked well?
Some materials that worked well are _____ _____ because _____ _____

2. What did we learn about shapes?
We learned that _____ _____

3. What shape was your base?
The shape of my building's base was a _____ _____ because _____ _____

4. What would you do differently tomorrow when we build again?
Tomorrow, instead of _____ _____, I will _____ _____ _____

Figure 7.4 Sample Student Work from a Module on Solar Future

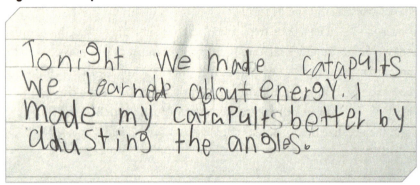

Sentence Frames

Sentence frames support learners' academic language development in writing and in speaking. The frames provide a prompt and keep students focused on the academic purpose. We were purposeful in how and when we used sentence frames. They are an efficient entry point into language. They are safe and doable, fostering success, which then builds confidence.

Sentence frames can be used in many different contexts. When it was time to tackle an engineering enrichment challenge, we encouraged teams to make a plan before getting their materials. We used sentence frames such as these:

- I agree with what _____ said because _____.
- Adding on to what _____ said, _____.
- I have a different perspective because _____.

Sentence frames were used following enrichment activities to provide feedback to the ambassadors and program leaders:

- What materials worked well? Some materials that worked well were _____ because _____.
- What did we learn about _____? We learned that _____.
- What would you do differently tomorrow when we build again? Tomorrow, instead of _____, I will _____.

Exit slip sentence frames were used to ask content questions and affective questions to get students' insights (sometimes humorous!) on that afternoon's topic:

- I like _____ today, because _____.
- Tomorrow, I want to _____.

Embedded Communication Opportunities

We looked for and found many places during the program to embed communication skills. The movement activities described in chapter 9 involved menus (lists of choices) for open-ended debate and brainstorming. They were designed with communication goals and growth in mind. Students need to be active listeners to follow directions for games and physical activities. These are learning skills we chose to focus on for movement:

- active listening
- understanding and following directions
- planning
- flexibility to be able to change plans
- collaboration and cooperation

Inevitably, there was downtime. To keep everyone engaged, we made sure all volunteers and program workers were ready with communication-building activities in the event of unexpected time with students. For example, we taught them the communication game Would You Rather? This silly game sparks conversation by posing two hypothetical situations and asking someone to choose which they would prefer and share why. Here are a few examples we have heard:

- Would you rather be Superman or Batman?
- Would you rather swim in pudding or maple syrup?
- Would you rather have a cleaner or a chef?
- Would you rather have an extra toe or an extra finger?

You can easily find more questions by searching the internet. We used this and other social games while walking to and from the gym, or when we had a few extra minutes.

Rituals for Greetings, Gratitude, and Goodbyes

Just as the art of conversation needs to be directly taught, so do the skills of saying hello, good-bye, and thank you. We taught students already seated to look up and greet their peers by name as they arrived at their tables to begin work. We formally introduced volunteers, and in subsequent sessions, a moment was taken between activities to recognize each volunteer with a choral, "Thank you for being here, [insert name]." The community volunteers were impressed, and the high school volunteers were validated and recognized as having an important role worthy of respect.

Just as the art of conversation needs to be directly taught, so do the skills of saying hello, good-bye, and thank you.

The Engineering Ambassadors realized how much they were appreciated when, at the end of enrichment time, one young participant prompted all her peers to line up to give them elbow bumps. This ritual, started by the quietest and youngest of the learners, became a beautiful part of the daily fabric.

These rituals are part of being in a community together and helped build the cohort's identity.

Academic Language

As we planned individualized tutoring activities for the Academic Intervention Gear, we noted the math vocabulary we wanted infused into conversations between volunteers and students. We created short lists of vocabulary related to each student's goal. Use of these lists increased students' exposure to and use of the terms and improved their verbal explanations of math processes. These are the same terms that are used on assessments. As it turned out, this practice also increased students' test scores, because they better understood what was being asked. Take, for example, the word *result*. Many times, during standardized testing, Sue has heard students ask, "What do they want to know? What is this word?" The word was *result*, which, in this context, means "answer." Sue believed that often the students understood the concepts but probably missed those test items because they did not understand what was being asked.

When developing the weekly enrichment modules (lessons/activities), we consulted with the University of Minnesota Mechanical Engineering Ambassadors about which scientific vocabulary was essential to include and directly teach during the presentations. The discussion focused on words that youth don't typically use with each other—words they need to know how to use to demonstrate understanding of the engineering principle being taught that week. The result was four essential vocabulary words per module, explicitly defined by visual, real-world representations. These words were embedded into everything the ambassadors presented, and the ambassadors modeled their use and coached students to use them during team challenge projects.

We listened for students to use the words orally in group reflections on the first afternoon and in written individual reflections on the second afternoon. If students did not use the vocabulary words on first afternoon, the ambassadors reemphasized them in their opening presentation the second afternoon. If students did not use all four vocabulary words in their written reflections on the second afternoon, the module was reworked, with increased explicit instruction in the use of those words. Our observations were essential in creating a responsive instructional feedback loop.

Here is an example of how this worked for a lesson on how planes stay in the air. The presentation focused on images of spiraling footballs (*push/thrust*), parachutes (*drag/pull*), and planes (*lift*). The presentation was followed by a team challenge activity. Teams were given directions and paper for folding various designs of paper airplanes. This was the essential question: "How can you design a plane to stay in the air for 30 seconds or more?"

At the end of the first afternoon, when team leaders shared their group findings, we heard students using the vocabulary in their explanations of what worked best. "The plane with the least *drag* had the most *lift*, and that may have helped it stay in the air longer."

The program leaders intentionally listened and looked for use of the key vocabulary in student reflections. This allowed them to measure whether learners were engaging in structured academic talk.

Cloze Procedure

The cloze procedure is a strategy we have used to support students' note-taking. For the cloze procedure, you create a passage of text with missing key words. The learner must supply the missing words based on a discussion or using context clues. This strategy supports learners in building meaning from a text. During enrichment time, when there was important information for students to remember, this was a useful tool. For example, in the Propellers and Boats module, students needed to know and understand Newton's laws of motion. Figure 7.5 shows a sample from an activity sheet students completed.

Figure 7.5 Cloze Procedure Sample

> What is Newton's Third Law of Motion?
>
> For every a_ _ _ _ _ there is an e_ _ _ _
>
> and o_ _ _ _ _ _ _ reac_ _ _ _.

Restorative Practices: Using Strengths to Build Community

Circle practice comes from the world of restorative justice. It draws from Indigenous traditions of talking circles, where everyone has the opportunity to speak and be heard equally. Participants sit in a circle with no distractions and pass a talking stick around. Only the person with the talking stick is allowed to speak, while everyone else listens. It is always acceptable to quietly pass if a participant does not want to share. This technique was already familiar to the third through fifth graders in our program, as many of their teachers used it during the school day.

Recall that during the fall session of the After School Club, each student engaged in strengths-finding self-surveys. For their final project, they each created an artistic vision board, essentially a visual representation of their own unique gifts and future aspirations. The first four weeks of the program in the fall were facilitated by Sue and her co-teacher with the support of the high school and community volunteers.

In February, when After School Club started back up, we used circle practice to welcome the University of Minnesota Mechanical Engineering Ambassadors and their professors to the program. We did not expect our elementary intervention students to be excited about the rigorous STEAM activities. The STEAM lessons and team challenge activities would not start until 4:00 p.m., after a full day of school for the learners. It was worth taking time upfront to get to know our new enrichment leaders personally. Circle practice helped us weave them into the club's growing microcommunity.

The Engineering Ambassadors and volunteers sat in small-group circles, listening as each learner explained their vision board and passed the talking stick. The ambassadors and their professors also shared as the talking stick arrived in their laps. After the small groups met, the whole group came together in a large circle. All participants—students, volunteers, ambassadors, and teachers—responded to these sentence frames as they passed the talking stick:

- Two or three strengths I bring to this club are _____.
- And I show these strengths when I _____.

This circle practice was a space where students shared their own strengths and began to notice and honor the strengths of others. Students felt safe enough to be vulnerable and their confidence began to grow—transforming the atmosphere in the room. Circle practice could be used as often as needed to strengthen bonds and uplift the self-esteem of the youth.

In hindsight, the circle practice reinforced our value in the power of reflection. We held small-group circles using these sentence frames occasionally when we had time throughout the program:

- I have noticed _____'s strength when they _____.
- I have noticed _____'s strength because that strength helps our group _____.

To learn more about building a restorative school community and circle practices, we recommend the book *Circle Forward* by Carolyn Boyes-Watson and Kay Pranis (2020).

Closing Thoughts

Communication will happen; the only question is whether or not it is used intentionally to promote growth and learning. We aimed to harness the collective power of common communication techniques to deliberately build a community focused on growth and cohesion. In every interaction with students, we focused on increasing their communication abilities. As a result, we saw both personal growth and growth in academic skills. Reviewing student data, we saw growth in writing, growth in use and understanding of academic vocabulary, and growth in the ability to confidently and politely communicate with adults in a direct and productive way (self-advocacy).

Reflection Questions

- What communication skills do your students need to be successful?
- What nonverbal cues could reduce the need for repeating information or directions?
- How can journals be used to develop self-awareness?
- How can journals be used to deepen use of academic language?
- What techniques or resources do you have access to, or know of, that could be used to increase reading, writing, and oral language development in your program?
- What practices are you aware of that get adults authentically talking with students and get students listening and writing to learn from one another?

CHAPTER 8

Attending to Emotions— Building Self-Awareness

"We need to attend to Maslow's needs before we can attend to children's instructional needs."
—Anne Gerrity, LICSW, adjunct lecturer, University of Minnesota

In this chapter, we discuss the Attending to Emotions Gear. We routinely teach self-awareness and self-regulation in brief snippets for this small but mighty gear. Five percent of program time is dedicated to attending to emotions in order to set a foundation of acceptance, connection, and trust. These are key components in belonging that must be consistently established and upheld over time to develop deep authentic relationships that impact student motivation and learning.

The following questions are answered in this chapter:
- What does naming your emotions have to do with moving on and getting to work?
- How can we prevent behavior challenges and increase self-awareness in youth?

- How are self-awareness and independence fostered?

In our program, we began and ended each session with three to ten minutes of self-awareness activities, setting the stage for psychological safety. According to the staff at the Boys & Girls Clubs of Metropolitan Baltimore, this step is often missing in intervention work, and yet it is vital, particularly for youth who have experienced trauma.

You may already be familiar with opening circle activities from organizations such as the Responsive Classroom. Regular, low-pressure ways to get students talking and comfortable with each other are important. Ice breakers, connecting activities, and "circling up" are fantastic ways to build community, but there is a deeper layer to authentic emotional work. When we offer youth a time and space to name their emotions and say a little bit about why they are feeling a certain way, they are able to connect matters of the heart to their conscious thoughts.

Belonging and Emotional Safety

According to Maslow's hierarchy of needs, as pictured in figure 8.1, a sense of love and belonging is ranked after the basic physiological and safety needs. Belonging has been established as a fundamental human need by social psychologists. Allen and colleagues summarize belonging in the school setting as "a student's feelings of being accepted, respected, and valued" (Allen et al. 2022, 1135).

We often hear "Maslow before Bloom." This is a way of saying belonging and security come before academics. But we believe this statement is slightly misleading. Students need both to happen at the same time. Educators need to combine relationships and belonging with academic pursuits. This approach allows more connections to develop in the brain and leads to deeper learning. From our experience, we know learners' sense of belonging directly correlates with their academic success.

Figure 8.1 Maslow's Hierarchy of Needs

During Sue's program research, she had the most memorable and deeply impactful conversation in 2021 with two youth workers who grew up attending the Boys & Girls Clubs of Metropolitan Baltimore and returned as managers. Reflecting on the importance of emotional needs, they said, "Our whole job currently, without a doubt, is almost completely to establish a foundation of psychological safety." To restore equilibrium, youth need constant clear and deliberate messaging: They are listened to, their needs are important, they can trust the space they are entering. Their gifts and strengths must be focused on.

Identifying Emotions

All emotions were acceptable at the After School Club. Everyone was allowed to have all their feelings. Being able to identify emotions is important for everyone—teachers, parents, caregivers, community members, and students. We all bring our emotions into the learning space. When strong emotions are not identified and addressed, they can disrupt the learning community. Identifying emotions lays the groundwork for being able to address emotions that could distract from learning. Being in touch with our emotions is closely tied with behavioral regulation. This means it helps to identify an emotion before attempting to address an emotionally driven behavior.

Identifying emotions is the groundwork for being able to address emotions that could distract from learning.

We highlighted all people in the program and their emotions due to the way emotions can influence our work. When the leader of a program or an educator or volunteer is dealing with their own strong emotions, this impacts the entire learning community. When a student is experiencing a heightened emotional state, this can impact the learning community in addition to their own learning. We all need to know our baseline emotional state so we can recognize when we are unfocused or unsettled. Being unsettled could be because of happiness or excitement, or it could be due to fear or anger. Emotions, no matter what they are, can and do influence the learning space.

Students often struggle to identify the emotion(s) driving a particular behavior. Third through fifth graders are still learning how to name and talk about their emotions. Setting aside a moment for reflection sets the stage for focus and flow. Daily reflective time to *focus* on and name specific feelings was helpful before starting small-group academic work. *Flow* refers to "a state of deep concentration" and is a part of emotional intelligence that leads to self-awareness. We need learners to be in the flow while working on challenging tasks.

The purpose of the Attending to Emotions Gear is to teach learners to recognize, name, and then (if possible) let go of unproductive emotions and thus behaviors that interfere with learning. Our goal was to have students identify their emotions so they could work on redirecting them. Emotions are often directed at people or groups of people instead of at actions or events. For example, when a student is frustrated with academic work, they need to be able to share their feeling of frustration, understand where it is coming from, and know who to share it with to work through it and let go of the distraction. We do not want students to be frustrated with teachers—this is harmful to the relationships we are trying to build.

Emotions and Learning

The Attending to Emotions Gear supports engagement in learning. Students who feel like they belong in a space are more motivated and engaged (Allen and Bowles 2012). Engagement is an antidote to the behavior challenges that sometimes derail success. When students learn to label and move past their emotions, they can more easily engage—or reengage—with the task at hand.

> The fastest way to move on from an emotion is to name the emotion.

This emotional awareness helps them express when they are frustrated with learning and their struggle is no longer productive. Attending to emotions allows them to communicate their learning needs.

Naming an emotion can help one move on from it. Naming the emotion reduces its intensity and helps the individual feel more in control. This practice, often called "name it to tame it," was popularized by psychologist Dan Siegel. When students begin to label their emotions, this step can become part of the process of defusing intense emotions, especially when working with peers. According to Jill Bolte Taylor (2008), a neuroscientist from Harvard, when we are reacting to something, we should pause for ninety seconds. The ninety seconds give us time to notice the emotion and allow it to dissipate in our brain; then we regain control. A person's reaction to an emotion can sometimes get stuck in a loop. The goal is to learn how to pause and regain control. This is not an easy task for an adult and is potentially even more challenging for youth. For additional reading in this area, we recommend Marc Brackett's book *Permission to Feel* (2019). Brackett shares five steps for managing emotions: recognizing, understanding, labeling, expressing, and regulating.

Tools for Attending to Emotions

For our program, we began with a simple assessment on identifying emotions. We gave the students a sheet of paper filled with emoji-like faces that showed different emotions. There were examples of more than thirty emotions, and there was no exact right or wrong way to label them. We gave the learners five minutes to write the names of as many emotions as they could under the faces. This seemed to us like a task an eight- to twelve-year old could do well. We were surprised that the students in the program were able to name an average of only three to four emotions. They most often wrote *sad*, *mad*, *happy*, or *tired*. This matched what we had seen kindergartners do when we were classroom teachers.

We knew that six to eight of the learners in the cohort were highly action-oriented and challenged with managing their emotions and engaging in academic work. Interestingly, peer relationships were a motivating strength for these students; however, their relationships with adults were few or fragile.

Emotions Through Emojis

To address the emotional needs of the participants, we established a routine at the start of each session. When learners arrived, they each received a new emoji face activity sheet and were asked to choose and color one image. Their work was to represent how they felt when they entered the room that day. After a few weeks, we told them to color five emotions they felt earlier in the day. Soon, learners were talking with each other about the different emotions they were experiencing during their days.

We used these emoji faces in two other ways:

1. Each student cut out the emoji face that matched their current state of mind, then taped it to a sheet of chart paper at the front of the room. Without prompting, learners started sorting the emojis, finding commonalities. They had rich conversations about what had happened just before they experienced each emotion. On their own, students started minimizing and letting go of small distracting frustrations from the day. They began to use more precise labels for the emojis—for example, replacing words like *mad* with terms like *frustrated* and *exhausted*—refining how they described their own emotions and responses to events.

2. Program volunteers also started coloring emojis, sharing how they felt and explaining why. Students were surprised that teens and community volunteers who otherwise looked calm and put-together had interior feelings of frustration, jealousy, and worry too. This process normalized all feelings so they could be accepted, honored, and, when needed, dealt with.

At the end of twelve weeks, on average, learners were able to label twelve to thirteen emotions on the same activity sheet. Importantly, students had fewer and fewer disruptions or emotional outbursts, and they spent more time collaborating about math, reading, and STEAM problem-solving. Coloring emojis took no more than two minutes at the start of each session and resulted in gains in instructional time since students spent more time on task.

Journaling About Emotions

Another strategy for attending to emotions was journaling at the start of each session. Students used their journals to write quick responses to the prompt at the right.

The sentence frame helped keep students' responses short and focused on attending to their emotions at the end of the school day. Providing a choice of words was a way to scaffold precision of expression and expand students' self-awareness.

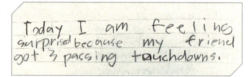

Below are example responses from students:

Today I am feeling smart because I am thinking about math.

Today I am feeling surprised because my friend got 3 passing touchdowns.

Today I am feeling happy because I am thinking of talking to my best friends.

The note below on the left is from Ben, one of the Engineering Ambassadors. When he heard Khloe share that she aspired to be a social justice advocate, he took a special interest. He selected a book that "touched his heart" when he was her age and left it for her along with this handwritten note. Khloe's journal response appears on the right.

Hi Khloe! It's Ben (The guy from ME Ambassadors! I think you'd really like the book "Chains" by Laurie Halse Anderson. It is just like the book you showed me on Tuesday. It is very mature, so read it when you feel ready! — Ben

Today I am feeling curious because I feel like reading the book "Chains" that Ben recomended to me.

Academic Intervention Success

We used the journal prompts in two ways.

1. Students were given two minutes to read their sentences to anyone in the room if they chose to. Within a few weeks, even the more introverted youth jumped at the chance to discuss their journal entries. They briefly connected and expressed themselves and then walked back to their tables, where they got out their tutoring or homework. This routine allowed students to label their emotions and move on to the academic work of the day.
2. Students left their journals upside down at their seats, signaling the journals could be read by the educators. If a student did not want their journal read, they could place it back in the bin in the center of the table where their personalized work was kept. The educators stayed in the media center when the rest of the group transitioned to the gym for movement and read any journals left out, using what they read to personalize their approach to relationship building. Educators informally and discreetly touched base with students to express care and availability to talk later if needed.

Reading student journal entries helped educators know who was in a tough place emotionally that evening and would benefit most from extra attention from a volunteer. It allowed educators to be purposefully attuned to student needs and build trusting, supportive relationships. For example, when Daniel appeared disengaged and angry upon arrival, it made sense later—he wrote in his journal that he lost his football game and got in a fight three hours prior. He was likely ruminating about this. In response, a trained adult could quietly recommend that Daniel's favorite volunteer, who was a high school football player, check in during the movement break and debrief. The idea of letting go of losses and aiming at the next win could help reframe Daniel's mood. We simply prompted the teen to ask Daniel how his day went and possibly fit in the topic of football. Sometimes, we gave them a football and five minutes to toss and talk. Sure enough, Daniel was able to happily engage in the enrichment activity that followed without dwelling on the football game loss and fight that occurred earlier in the day.

Reading the emotions reflection sentences also informed us when celebrations were needed. When a quiet fourth grader wrote that she was excited about a new baby sister, the adult community volunteer was excited with her and later brought two board books for the baby. The next week, the fourth grader bounced in proudly to tell the volunteer how much the baby liked *Chicka Chicka Boom Boom* and giggled when her big sister read it to her after dinner.

Developmental Affirmations

A third tool we used to attend to emotions is the Developmental Affirmations created by Jean Illsley Clarke. These affirmations are carefully crafted phrases that humans benefit from hearing at each stage of their development. They are based on Erik Erikson's stages of psychosocial development.

We knew that students in our program were at different stages of development. Our approach allowed us to attend to the stage each student was currently in. If, for instance, a youth had gone through a traumatic experience for an extended period, we could revisit the developmental messages they may have missed during that time—messages that are essential for building strong mental health.

Clarke was instrumental in our thinking on affirmations. Sue has used Clarke's work in her teaching for many years. In Clarke's own words:

> The Developmental Affirmation ovals are color-coded oval-shaped discs with a development affirmation printed on each one. Why oval? The oval is a symbol of constantly renewing life and of hope. The sequence of colors reflects the rainbow to remind us that moving through the developmental stages is a natural and sequential process. There is a different color associated with each set of development learning. (Illsley 2021, 10)

The affirmation resources are available at no charge through the University of Minnesota Extension website, and Clarke's 2021 book, *Words That Help: Affirmations for Any Age, Every Stage*, can be also downloaded at no cost. Several stages of Clarke's Developmental Affirmations are listed in figure 8.2; they are also available for download as oval-shaped discs (pressbooks.umn.edu/app/uploads/sites/75/2020/09/Affirmations-poster.pdf).

Figure 8.2 Clarke's Developmental Affirmations

Becoming, prenatal stage
- I celebrate that you are alive.
- Your needs and safety are important to me.
- We are connected and you are whole.
- You can make healthy decisions about your experiences.
- You can be born when you are ready.
- Your life is your own.
- I love you just as you are.

Being, Stage 1, 0 to 6 months
- I'm glad you are alive.
- You belong here.
- What you need is important to me.
- I'm glad you are you.
- You can grow at your own pace.
- You can feel all of your feelings.
- I love you and I care for you willingly.

Doing, Stage 2, 6 to 18 months
- You can explore and experiment and I will support and protect you.
- You can use all of your senses when you explore.
- You can do things as many times as you need to.
- You can know what you know.
- You can be interested in everything.
- I like to watch you initiate and grow and learn.
- I love you when you are active and when you are quiet.

Thinking, Stage 3, 18 months to 3 years
- I'm glad you are starting to think for yourself.
- It's okay for you to be angry, and I won't let you hurt yourself or others.
- You can say no and push and test limits as much as you need to.
- You can learn to think for yourself, and I will think for myself.
- You can think and feel at the same time.
- You can know what you need and ask for help.
- You can become separate from me, and I will continue to love you.

Identify and Power, Stage 4, 3 to 6 years
- You can explore who you are and find out who other people are.
- You can be powerful and ask for help at the same time.
- You can try out different roles and ways of being powerful.
- You can find out the results of your behavior.
- All of your feelings are okay with me.
- You can learn what is pretend and what is real.
- I love who you are.

Structure, Stage 5, 6 to 12 years
- You can think before you say yes or no and learn from your mistakes.
- You can trust your intuition to help you decide what to do.
- You can find a way of doing things that works for you.
- You can learn the rules that help you live with others.
- You can learn when and how to disagree.
- You can think for yourself and get help instead of staying in distress.
- I love you even when we differ; I love growing with you.

Note: Clarke's affirmations span developmental stages across a person's entire life; however we used the affirmations for birth to age twelve.

We used Clarke's ovals in the program. We cut them out and hid them around the room before the learners arrived. After they attended to their emotions, finished their tutoring or homework, and cleaned up their snack, one group at a time was released to walk around the room, find any five affirmation ovals, and return to their table. Students read the ovals aloud to one another or to a volunteer. We had two students who could not yet read, so we used a prompt that allowed them to feel safe and successful: "Would you like me to read the affirmations to you, have a friend read them, or would you like to read them to me?" Volunteers were discreetly cued to these students' unique needs. Everyone was hearing these powerful affirmations every day. After reading, another question was posed: "Which one will be most helpful to you for the rest of the day?"

Though the eight- to eleven-year-old participants were in the Structure stage (light blue ovals), when asked which affirmations helped them *most*, they often referred to the earlier developmental stages (peach, red, and orange ovals). At first, we guessed they liked those colors. So occasionally, we casually asked in passing, "How are those particular words helpful?" The answers were profound.

Diamond, a fifth grader with a passion for social justice, quietly and firmly stated, "I chose the oval that says, 'You belong here!' For me, walking around this mostly white community, I'm not sure I always feel like I belong." This was a year after the protests spurred by the murder of George Floyd, which happened just twenty minutes away. Her family had joined those protests. One of the Engineering Ambassadors, who had become a close ally to Diamond, quietly asked if she could say more about that statement. As a white male, he was curious to learn more about her perspectives. She shared more and, in the end, they both walked away with titles of books about historical social justice figures that they wanted to read. This interaction felt safe to both parties, and a strong, special connection was made that spanned this multi-year program.

Throughout the whole program, students used journals to name how they were feeling about their school day and to share what they were thinking about as they entered the media center.

As we reflect on our work related to this gear, analogies of walking or biking come to mind. These are two activities we personally enjoy in our free time. When doing them, we find the first few miles to be challenging. However, once we are past those first miles, the going becomes easier and we get into the flow. With students, the first weeks of attending to emotions are a challenge, but the routine of briefly pausing to honor our emotions pays off. Once the routine is established, there is a flow to students tapping into their emotions.

These three activities took only five minutes but were influential in students' relationship building and sense of belonging. For the first several weeks, we always used the emojis to help youth recognize emotions and expand their vocabulary for all the various emotions felt in a day.

That enhanced the specificity of their journal writing. Throughout the whole program, students used journals to name how they were feeling about their school day and to share what they were thinking about as they entered the media center. The affirmation ovals were a crowd favorite and were sprinkled in randomly whenever time was available.

Communicating with Parents

We involved parents from the beginning so they would understand our goals and be able to support our work as partners. Our communication included phone calls, connections at pickup, and notes home. The communication was concise but clearly explained that we were focused on learning about, talking about, identifying, expressing, and labeling emotions. We shared our goal of helping their children learn how to describe emotions and our hope that their children would develop a greater understanding of their own feelings and emotions, as well as the emotions of others. We offered parents suggestions for work at home and thanked them for their partnership.

Closing Thoughts

The activities described in this chapter allowed us to shift the focus from disruptive behaviors to learning behaviors. They supported our growing sense of community, increasing student collaboration and motivation. As you reflect on what you learned in this chapter, think about the rituals you are currently using to support students' identification and addressing of emotions.

Reflection Questions

- When do your students seem to have the hardest time working together or getting along with others?
- What are some tried-and-true activities you use to support students in recognizing and naming their emotions?
- Where can you fit five to seven minutes into your daily schedule for learners to pause and identify their emotions and build self-awareness?
- How will you engage with students when they share their emotions?

CHAPTER 9

Collaborative Movement and Play

"Coming together is a beginning; keeping together is progress; working together is success."
—Edward Everett Hale, author, historian, and minister

The Gear Model includes dedicating 15 percent of the time to focus on one or more movement activities that help students gain the benefits of physical exercise (outdoors, if possible), with a focus on collaboration with one another and a common goal. In this chapter, we consider why movement and play are important and explain how we approached collaborative movement and productive play to create a different way of thinking about movement in this work.

The following questions are answered in this chapter:
- How do students benefit from movement?
- Why is it important to include movement, given the limited program time?
- What is the state of play, and how can we use it to support our work?
- What essential skills are taught and learned during productive play?

- How are relationships and trust built during low-stakes productive play?
- How do low-stakes playful challenges create safety for vulnerability?

The Sounds of Productive and Collaborative Play

Giggling, brainstorming, and curious questions filled the space as learners and high school volunteers engaged in playful, productive movement time together. Envision each person solving math problems on paper slips in their hands, then trying to find three other people with the same answer. Next, picture these teams finding their starting spots, where a scooter and tongs await. Their job is to choose a leader to push and weave each team member between the street-cone obstacles as the rider uses the tongs to pick up a costume hat, tutu, or jersey. The goal is to get to the other side without bumping into anyone. Finally, the team members are on the other side of the gym. They have five minutes to use the costume pieces they collected to create a commercial they will present to another team of four. This was one of many activities the youth developed in collaboration with us and then led at After School Club.

Why Are Movement and Play Important?

Student mental health concerns are increasing, according to the National Center for Education Statistics (2022). We have seen this in our home state of Minnesota, where data from a recent survey of youth shows a continuing upward trend in mental health concerns (Minnesota Department of Health 2022). Depression and anxiety are the two most commonly seen mental health concerns. Studies have shown that exercise eases the symptoms of these two concerns (Mahindru, Patil, and Agrawal 2023).

You may be familiar with the concept of a runner's high, when the brain releases endorphins after a run. Endorphins released through exercise, fun, and laughter affect stress, pain, and mood, and improve overall brain function. They can have a powerful positive impact on mental well-being and academic success. The research on physical activity, which is one source of endorphins, includes these key points:

- Physical activity during the school day has a positive impact on academics.
- Some research shows that academic achievement correlates to increased physical fitness.
- Students are able to stay on task longer when they have physical activity in their day.
- Students should have frequent physical activity breaks.

(Kohl and Cooke 2013)

Play Supports Relationship Building

Movement and play are intentionally integrated into our program with the goal of increasing endorphin levels in participants. However, we take this a step further, using cross-age groups of youth and adults moving together to strengthen relationships. Best of all, movement and play are fun, which impacts motivation, excitement, and belonging, supporting the desire to attend the intervention sessions. All the more reason to get out and move together.

Play Supports Learning

When learners are sedentary for more than twenty minutes, their ability to concentrate, understand, and recall information decreases (Farraj 2018). Yet the structures of school often do not allow time or space for students to get the movement their bodies and minds need. With a heavy focus on academic outcomes, many schools have reduced their daily physical education requirement and their recess time. Young bodies have excess energy that needs to be released, especially if your program is during the later part or the end of the school day.

Two Kinds of Play

Play is important to the development of youth. Yet we have seen a dramatic decrease in play in childhood. The lack of playtime is having an impact on our students. Researchers are connecting the loss of playtime with an increase in anxiety and depression in youth (Gray, Lancy, and Bjorklund 2023). Youth have fewer and fewer opportunities to try things out and test ideas in a low-stakes environment. We must refocus on play.

There are two types of play to consider: open-ended free play and structured play. Youth benefit from both. We believe both open-ended and structured play should be incorporated into a program, with the goal of encouraging productive play. To us, *productive play* means activities that are purposefully designed to promote the identified learning goals through exploration or reinforcement of skills.

The five elements of developmental relationships (Search Institute, n.d.) shine through during low-stakes, collaborative playful movement. Participants *express care* and show each other they matter when they cheer each other on. *Growth is challenged* when they stretch each other and learn from mistakes. Team members *provide support* and navigate challenges since they want to accomplish a task. If competition is involved, they need to support each other to win. Over time, *power is shared* as they come to realize everyone in the group has unique skills that could be useful, sometimes at the least-expected moments. Finally, *possibilities are expanded* as the broader cohort of youth is connected with peers and adults they have grown to trust.

The State of Play: What We Have Observed

When visiting programs around the United States, we typically observed one style of play or the other: unstructured, open-ended play or highly structured play. Occasionally, we saw deliberately designed productive play with consistently high levels of movement. But it was rare. In our program, we strive for productive play within a semi-structured framework.

Unstructured Play

In our experience, in under-resourced, community-run programs, youth spent time outside in confined spaces with little structure and few options. While serving in severely under-resourced summer programs in Mississippi and Pennsylvania, we witnessed bored youth sitting around. They did not have agency to create anything or go anywhere. There were no gymnasiums or sports equipment. Playgrounds were unsafe or nonexistent. Where we have seen inadequate facilities, we have also seen nonproductive arguments escalate, distracting youth from the purpose of being together. Adults spent their time managing conflicts, because youth lacked physical outlets. The resulting fights and shouting matches ran counter to the development of mutually beneficial relationships within the microcommunity. Nobody was having fun.

In the school-run programs we have observed, it was common to see the gym opened after school with a minimal amount of P.E. equipment available. Sometimes this was effective, especially for action-oriented youth. However, youth who are less action-oriented were sitting along the walls, talking with friends. Of course, there is nothing wrong with hanging out with friends, but socializing needs can be addressed during other parts of a program. Getting youth involved in activities that release energy and get their blood flowing should be the goal of movement time. These open gym times also had little in the way of instruction or guidance in the language of how to collaborate.

Finally, in the scope of play, we have seen warm-hearted, enthusiastic leaders or teachers orchestrating large-group games such as Four Corners, Ships Across the Ocean, or variations of tag. These are excellent games that some consider structured play. Blood is flowing and energy is released. It was lovely to see youth having a choice of games on occasion, but still, in our observation, the adults held the authority, so disagreements between youth during the games were managed by the adults. Youth were more likely to be moving, but the locus of control resided almost exclusively with the adults.

Structured Play

The second kind of play, structured play, was present in some programs we visited. Many programs use activities and games from GoNoodle (a website that supports students' physical and mental health) or other interactive dance and workout videos. Watching adults and youth dance together was beautiful. Engagement was high for primary-age children, but upper-elementary and middle-school youth felt the activities were somewhat beneath their age level.

Another trend in structured play is seen in after-school programs set up around sports like basketball or soccer. Sports and the structure (rules) they provide are very valuable for youth. And while sports can challenge growth and expand possibilities, sports alone will not improve academic outcomes. We desired time for youth to move after school with a more direct throughline to the skills needed to persist and problem-solve in academics.

Sports-oriented after-school programs sometimes secured funding by naming math goals such as "Students will learn to find the difference between the scores of the final basketball games." That is an important math procedural skill. Presented correctly, with students solving for an unknown difference, it could be algebra. But only a few procedural math problems are solved a day this way.

For youth who are less motivated by competition or who have fewer skills or experience playing the given sport, frustration and comparison with others can cause them to shut down. Middle schoolers in one after-school volleyball and basketball program dropped out when they realized they did not have interest in those sports. Once they dropped out, the school lost its opportunity to provide the homework time and academic support these students also needed. The ultimate outcome was that the school was no longer serving all students who needed extended academic support, only the students who liked volleyball and basketball. We believe it is a mistake to over-focus on specific sports due to the possibility that students will be uninterested, either from the start or after giving them a try and discovering they don't enjoy them.

Preparing for Collaborative Movement

Based on our experiences and our research into successful programs, we believe youth need opportunities for collaborative movement. Yet student choice, sustained movement, and collaborative problem-solving are sometimes forgotten in overly open-ended or overly structured play. Collaborative movement is a foundational aspect of The Gear Model. Participants are invited to join games and tasks that include movement and a shared goal or outcome, making them low stakes. As the program progresses, the tasks shift toward being more open ended and student centered through a gradual release of responsibility.

We created a process to slowly release the ownership of collaborative productive play time to the learners and the high school leaders (volunteers). Adults modeled, trained, and increasingly had students develop and give instructions for the gym and outdoor activities. After a few weeks, we casually chatted with students who were less engaged, so they could help us plan the collaborative movement time for the coming week.

Youth are invited to join games and tasks that include movement and a shared goal or outcome, making them low stakes.

Essentially, we were folding in the learners who would otherwise be "wall talkers." This deliberate strategy helped increase engagement in cardio activity. We aimed to inspire the high school volunteers—potential future teachers—by encouraging them to lead highly engaging creative movement games. Their youth and vitality inspired everyone!

These are the skills we chose to focus on:
- active listening
- understanding and following directions

- planning
- flexibility to be able to change plans
- collaboration and cooperation

Our goal was for participants to spend 15 percent of program time with raised heart rates, learning the strengths of peers around them as they took on progressively more physical activities—such as relays, complicated obstacle courses, and team-building challenges. Because of our focus on relationships, youth felt safe to take action, try things, and fail. When it is just a game or task, it is easier for youth to practice accepting failure. "Oh well, that did not work out. How will we do it differently next time?"

Planning Based on Students' Needs

We gave careful thought and planning to the collaborative movement programming. We started by observing the youth at play, using a roster of participants and taking note of who played alone and who played together. We noticed what games they were drawn to. We looked for those who were using their imagination to play. We also connected with adults who worked with the students. We talked with the paraprofessionals who supervised recess and with the dean of students to learn their perspectives. We asked, "What are the strengths and interests of these students when they are in large spaces?" and "When are they in a state of flow and communicating with peers?" We also reached out to the P.E. teacher. She was ahead of us in relationship-building and already knew all the students. She also had equipment we wanted to borrow, so we needed her trust and partnership.

These conversations confirmed our observations. We had observed youth with a strong desire to win who would have meltdowns when they did not win. The meltdowns could last hours. We saw many youth who were challenged when asked to follow verbal directions. They needed either explicit small-group verbal pre-teaching of the game or written instructions available to refer back to. Some youth were introverted and hesitant participants in large-motor and large-group physical activities. Many were sensitive about their weight or physical abilities.

Selecting Movement Activities

After our observations and conversations, we were ready to select movement activities that would release energy and nourish developmental relationships based on our participants' needs and personalities. We searched websites and our bookshelves for cooperative movement (see appendix A). These are three of our sources for activity ideas:

1. Playworks (playworks.org)
2. Beetles Science and Teaching for Field Instructors (beetlesproject.org)
3. "45 Best Cooperative Games to Promote Comradery and Healthy Competition" (weareteachers.com/cooperative-games-for-kids)

When reviewing potential activities, consider the following:
- How many students can be involved? *The more, the better.*
- How competitive is the activity? *Balance activities throughout the program.*
- Will heart rates be raised for an adequate amount of time? *Higher heart rates are better!*
- Will all participants be able to access the activity? *Students must understand how to play the game.*
- What specialized skills are needed? *Are these skills your students have, or could you teach them in physical education class?*
- Are there opportunities for language development? *Vocabulary development in this context is powerful.*
- Can number sense be integrated into the activity? *This is a foundational skill in math that supports all students.*
- How do participants need to rely on each other to meet the shared goal? *Interdependence is important for this work!*
- How will relationships be strengthened? *Consider the types of interactions required by the participants.*
- Does this activity vary from others we have done? *Activities that are similar but different allow students to build on experiences.*

Getting Student Buy-In

This next piece was a game changer in getting all participants moving. During school lunchtime, we met with three hesitant and introverted students to ask their opinions about the activities being planned. The fact that we were seeking their opinions empowered them to feel confident. In the safety of Sue's office, we learned that these individuals were self-conscious about their P.E. skills in areas they considered weaknesses. One fifth grade girl said she would participate in movement if there were no basketballs. She was embarrassed by her dribbling skills, which made her feel decidedly "uncool." So, we used balloons instead.

One introverted student became a constant source of ideas for future activities and begged to help us type up the directions for the activities. She asked, "Can I make a poster explaining how to line up for the balloon toss challenges?" Then she held her poster up while volunteers started those activities. This student usually sat on a bench during recess. By giving input, she became invested and wanted to participate. Her attendance was initially spotty, but soon she started coming to every session. Her regular school attendance improved as well. She felt like she mattered, something we had not always observed before.

The trusting relationships we built with each learner led to 100 percent participation in healthy collaborative movement.

Securing a Space for Movement

We needed a large space for twenty minutes two afternoons each week. The school had a gym, but it was being used by the after-school childcare program. However, the childcare program supported the work we were doing and found another space for their participants during this twenty-minute block, freeing up the gym for our program. This was an important collaboration. There are limited resources, and opportunities to share them are often a matter of communication and understanding. We were also able to use the school's playground when weather allowed. You will need to find a space where participants can engage in collaborative movement.

Getting Started with Partner Activities

We intentionally designed movement activities for the first few sessions for pairs of youth to learn to work as partners. There is safety and comfort in small numbers, and this method helped participants get to know one another. Beginning with pairs allowed the introverts to feel connected. Of course, all students need to be connected and feel successful. But for some, this begins in small groups and then extends to larger groups. We have also known students who needed an anchor (a known, trusted peer) to help them feel comfortable and navigate new spaces.

One way of forming pairs used the color-coded affirmation ovals described in chapter 8. We prepared twelve pairs of affirmation ovals. Volunteers randomly passed out one oval to each student. Students found the person with the same affirmation oval, and they became partners and walked to the gym or playground together. This supported our ongoing focus on the whole child and meeting developmental needs.

A nonthreatening, inclusive way we paired students is known as Mix, Freeze, and Pair Up. Students walked or danced around the room while music played, touching nothing and no one. When the music stopped, they found the person closest to them. The students gave each other high fives. We played the music again. When the music stopped, they gave the closest person a fist bump. Repeating this several times (with different greeting actions each time) mixes the group up and gets everyone connected. Eventually we would announce that the person nearest them was their partner for the activities to follow in the gym. Each partner grabbed a copy of the written directions for the movement activity (placed by the door), and they read them while walking together to the gym or playground.

Another way we paired youth was by using math equation cards. Figure 9.1 shows an example of math problems we used. Notice that the math equations across from one another have the same solution. The equations were cut apart and passed out to students to solve during snack and tutoring time. When the room was cleaned up and everyone was ready for collaborative movement, learners walked around and found the person who had the same answer but a different equation. A written prompt posted at the front of the room asked students to discuss the steps they took to solve their equations. And again, they picked up the written directions for the movement activity and read them on their way to the gym or playground. As you see, math can be interwoven into all aspects of the program!

Sue got creative and even had the students in school-day math intervention groups help create sets of equations on cards to use in the After School Club. Each of her students, many of whom were also in the After School Club, was assigned one number and given two index cards. Each student wrote two different equations equaling their assigned number, one on each index card. Sue checked their work and collected the cards. Voilà! A deck of partner cards was ready for use.

Figure 9.1 Sample of Math Equations to Match Up Partners

PARTNER MATCH UP

$(10 \times 10) =$ $90 + 10 =$
Result is _____

$101 - 1$
Result is _____

24×2
Result is _____

$12 + 12 + 12 + 12$
Result is _____

$17 - 2$
Result is _____

$1 + (5 \times 3) - 1$
Result is _____

Collaborative Movement Activities

The gym and playground activities changed each day. The first day, we explicitly taught the routine of getting to and from the gym and playground. We played a whole-group running game. The students ran around the space to music (without touching anyone or anything), stopping in a controlled way when the music stopped. We practiced using self-control while running and stopping. We role-played and modeled what it looked like and sounded like when we were kind to each other. High school volunteers demonstrated what quick, efficient movement between tasks looked like, and they got the students laughing when they also modeled undesired behavior such as pushing, dragging feet, or sitting against the wall. We reviewed these processes the next afternoon and again whenever there was a breakdown in behavior. Students were explicitly taught expectations through words and modeling. We established processes and set boundaries and expected students to respect them.

After the first week, we used a variety of activities. Three of them are presented below.

Partner Walk, Run, and Play

This activity (figure 9.2) requires twelve scooters, but hula hoops or balls could be used instead. It takes seven minutes, and then

Figure 9.2 Partner Walk, Run, and Play

LET'S GET ACTION ORIENTED! STAY WITH YOUR PARTNER!

While You Walk:
Where do you like to read books at home?
What's your favorite healthy snack?
What's your favorite not-so-healthy snack?

Around the perimeter of the gym:
____4 laps walking
____1 lap running
____1 lap shortest person being pushed on the scooter
____1 lap tallest person being pushed on a scooter

Go to the center:
____ Plank for 30 seconds

TOGETHER, you pick 2:
20 jumping jacks   OR   5 burpees   OR   10 push-ups
Give your partner a high five and tell them something they did well!

FINALLY: Shoot hoops or jump rope on the other side of the gym.

students get five minutes for open gym. We knew many would want that free time since it was the first afternoon of the week. The activity gives students choice midway through.

Team-Building Relay

The next activity (figure 9.3) marks the beginning of the group becoming team oriented. Notice this activity starts with easy, relaxed running, walking, and verbal connection, followed by a relay race. Any kind of relay race works once students have been taught how to be part of a relay team. We used scooters and balloons.

Figure 9.3 Team-Building Relay

> **LET'S GET ACTION ORIENTED!**
> **With people from your team:** College ambassadors and high school students join a team.
> - First: 2 laps running
> - Second: 2 laps walking (four walls) "What are your five favorite parts of school this year?"
> - Third: Give each other a high five and a compliment!
> - Fourth: Line up behind a cone to learn about your relay race.

A Skit Challenge

This activity (figure 9.4) is open ended and student driven. Three students who had a passion for art picked this for one of the final weeks. They said, "We haven't done enough art, and we like art!"

Figure 9.4 A Skit Challenge

> **GET SILLY AND CREATE A SKIT**
>
> **A Team Challenge**
> The person whose birthday is closest to today reads directions to the team!
> Time: 10-20 minutes
>
> **Materials Needed:**
> - These directions, one for each team
> - Large space inside or out
> - Salad tongs for each group of 4
> - A scooter for each group of 4 [If scooters are not available, have kids hop or crab walk.]
> - A line or cones for each team to line up behind
> - Hats, gadgets, balloons [and/or anything kids could use to make a skit]
>
> You'll need one or more objects for each participant.
>
> **Part 1**
> - Arrive at a plan for who is first, second, third, and fourth.
> - The first person scooters out and chooses any object across the space that intrigues them.
> - The first person scoots back to the team and tags the second person, who then scoots out to choose an object in the large space that interests them.
> - The second, third, and fourth persons continue the relay process.
>
> **Part 2**
> - The person with the biggest feet is your leader and reader. They can choose a co-leader if that is helpful.
> - Circle up with the objects: Sit in a circle knee to knee.
>
> *(If you have a teen or adult volunteer, include them in your circle.)*
>
> **Directions:**
> Use all the objects and every member of your team to either:
>
> **RETEACH** a concept you have learned in this class:
> - Principles of building
> - Ways to use a paintbrush
> - What to do when there is a group conflict
>
> **OR**
>
> Use all the objects to **MAKE A COMMERCIAL** for:
> - Shampoo
> - An art museum
> - Your favorite park or shopping mall

We listened and helped them choose and adapt an activity from a website. When students step up with their voices, we need to listen and engage them in the work.

As you think about these examples, notice that students will use oral language and active listening when they read directions to each other. The language in the directions is intentional, to support students' developing vocabularies. Math (number sense) is also integrated by comparing and sequencing birthdays and comparing shoe sizes. We wanted students to have opportunities to apply what they were learning in the program and in their classrooms. You can also see skills such as leadership, flexibility, and creativity, plus many of the Habits of Mind, embedded in these tasks. Finally, as with all the work in the program, the activities were grounded in creating relationships.

Benefits for Participants

Over time, learners were raising their heart rates and engaging in the fun while applying academic skills. They were arriving at empathetic, fair-minded ways to separate and mix up teams. Strong new relationships developed when learners' voices were activated. Decision-making was increasingly given to participants. Adults were following in the paths of the youth as they developed their own ways to play and move. Power was shared.

Teamwork Emerged After a Few Weeks

After two weeks, it was no surprise when our action-oriented, competition-loving learners spoke up saying they wanted to be with their chosen friends, not just random partners. They wanted to race and compete in games. We listened. With their input and the help of high school volunteers, we added relays with embedded physical challenges.

As is our style, we asked learners questions about the design and structure of the new activities:

- "How will we decide on these teams?"
- "How will our community respond when there are winners and losers?"
- "Do there need to be winners and losers?"

Students gave us many ideas on how to help everyone feel included. Sue pulled some students from their school classrooms five minutes early so they could help make team cards. These cards were randomly passed out to participants before the movement time. What we found is that even the competitive extroverts did not really care who won a relay. They were too busy giggling with new friends over their failed attempts to keep their scooters from rolling in the wrong direction. Friendships were trumping competition. Low-stakes, high-context movement challenges created the conditions for youth to take responsibility for their actions and failures and guide each other through.

All this to say, avoid being too loose or too tight with plans. Ultimately, activities must be responsive to learners. Collaborative movement activities can be as simple or complex as you would like. You can use collaborative movement to mix up the group so they get to know each other. You can use simple activities like relays, or you can create more complex activities like obstacle courses or scavenger hunts. High school volunteers might be interested in having a role in the creation of these activities.

Closing Thoughts

Our hope was that thoughtfully crafted, simple activities would have a positive impact on academic skills. We were especially mindful of inquiry and problem-solving skills. The work of coming together for these low-stakes activities was foundational to establishing a microcommunity where students were willing to take academic risks. They would attempt new things and be comfortable failing, recovering, and moving forward for deeper understanding.

Reflection Questions

- When you listen to participants play, what cooperative language skills do you hear or not hear?
- Are your participants more action oriented or less action oriented? (You may have some of both.)
- Are your participants competition oriented or more collaborative team players? (You may have some of both.)
- What collaborative learning skills will need to be taught that will hopefully carry over to academic aspects of the program?
- Do you have a separate space for the participants to engage in movement?
- What P.E. materials and equipment do you have?
- Who could help you create or lead this part of the program?

PART 3

IMPACT OF THE GEAR MODEL AND INSIGHTS

CHAPTER 10

Evaluation of the Two-Year Program Implementation

"Continuous improvement is better than delayed perfection."
—Anonymous

Implementing a new intervention model that leveraged partnerships and multi-age volunteers was an ambitious undertaking. Our goal was to use developmental relationships to build on each youth's unique talents while addressing their individual academic and social challenges. From the start, we recognized the critical role of data in informing our approach and evaluating our success.

Given the multi-layered philosophy of our program, we needed a similarly nuanced evaluation model. Traditional measures, such as standardized test scores, could not fully capture the impact of our work. Instead, we developed a broader framework to assess progress and outcomes.

This chapter explores these key questions:
- How did we evaluate progress toward our goals?
- What data did we collect, and from whom?

- What were the outcomes for all participants?
- What unexpected insights emerged from our data and evaluation?

We gathered data on every aspect of the program, reflecting our tailored approach to individual needs. We invited ongoing, informal feedback from all participants—students, volunteers, educators, and families. This feedback helped us refine our methods and maximize every moment of implementation.

Remember that relationship development drove the implementation of The Gear Model. The connections between teachers, youth, volunteers, partners, and families were the foundation for academic growth. We embraced a mindset of continuous improvement, using data not only to measure success but also to drive meaningful, real-time adjustments to the program.

Evaluating The Gear Model After School Club

The Gear Model approach was developed through incremental, data-informed changes that took place over a decade while working with trial-and-error interventions and curriculum for students performing below their ability. During our most recent implementation of the model at two elementary schools (twice a week for twelve weeks a year for two years), we intentionally gathered a variety of tangible assessments for several reasons. First, data informed continuous improvement. Second, we were aware that future funders, district leaders, and parents would want to see evidence of success. Third, data informed planning for future programs. We were focused on rigorous personalized academics, relevant learning, and developmental relationships across multiple learning environments (where possible) (see figure 10.1).

Figure 10.1 Focuses of The Gear Model Program

Rigorous Personalized Academics (Challenge)
- Math (five identified skill areas)
- Literacy (journals, affirmation ovals, dialogue protocols, reading STEAM directions)
- Engineering/Science (enrichment area, based on science standards at and above grade level)

Relevant Learning
- Real-world skills (enrichment)
- 21st century skills and Habits of Mind
- Student agency (student voice/developing leadership skills)
- Responsive to individual strengths and needs

Developmental Relationships
- Safe place to belong
- Routines and protocols
- Intergenerational
- Social resiliency

Assessment of the Academic Intervention Gear

In chapter 4, we shared the pre-assessment tools we used to understand where to start our work with individual or small groups of learners. We had access to broad standardized academic test data and classroom academic benchmark assessment (math unit tests). Throughout the program, we collected student work samples to consider how to modify the math games and materials we put into each learner's individual work folder.

The primary goal of intervention programs is to support students in closing learning gaps. Assessing students' growth gives us additional information on student learning and helps us determine what each student needs next in their learning.

Did Learners Meet Their Academic Goals?

As a brief review, our academic goals were to improve students' number sense and their academic persistence through problem-solving. Number sense is the conduit to future mathematics success. We also concentrated on problem-solving, as it is key for applying mathematical ideas in real-world work, in this case via STEAM. Problem-solving skills are foundational to developing human agency.

The goal to improve students' number sense is directly tied to the Academic Intervention Gear. We purposefully did not use state standardized test data to evaluate academic math or reading growth for the Academic Intervention Gear. Our state standardized test results are not designed to measure individual growth. In addition, many students were receiving additional interventions and supports in and possibly out of school for reading or math. We would not be able to definitively attribute changes on standardized tests to The Gear Model.

Remember that early in the fall session, students self-selected math goals from a list of grade-band standards related to number sense (see figure 5.4 on page 84).

Figure 10.2 Students' Self-Assessment

Name _____

1. Look in your journal. Find out what math goal or goals you chose.
2. Write down the goal or goals you chose.
_____
_____

Did you improve?
____ yes ____ no ____ somewhat
If you did not improve, what will help you going forward?
_____
_____

They recorded their goals in their journals. At the end of the program, we asked learners to reflect on their self-selected math goals (figure 10.2).

Ninety percent of the learners felt more confident in math and reported that they improved in their math goal area. In future years, we hope to gather additional data from multiple sources that would reflect changes in learners' math understanding.

Did Learners Increase Persistence in Problem-Solving?

Our second goal was to increase the learners' academic disposition for persistence (stamina) and develop strategies for precision in problem-solving. The final learner poll showed we met this goal with 72 percent of the participants.

Figure 10.3 Self-Assessment Poll: "Does being in After School Club make you more persistent when facing challenges?"

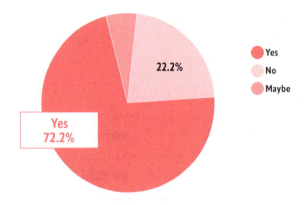

Assessment of the Enrichment Gear

Assessment of the Enrichment Gear gives us and our partners important information and insights. Time is valuable in education, and the evaluation of this gear reveals whether the enrichment time had an impact on students and their future success. This assessment also helps enrichment partners continually improve their programs.

The State Standardized Science Test

During the Enrichment Gear, time and focus were dedicated to understanding and applying the scientific process and design thinking language, since we wanted to instill habits of wonderment and constant inquiry about how the world works. The iterative process of improvement was intentionally taught and assessed throughout the program.

Scientific process language is used repeatedly in the Science Minnesota Comprehensive Assessment (MCA). The first time Minnesota students take the Science MCA is in fifth grade. This test evaluates understanding of process more than science facts. It is difficult for classroom teachers to make time for in-depth, hands-on science experiments where the scientific process is practiced to the degree we were able to after school with assistance from the Engineering Ambassadors. We believe our program filled that background knowledge void. As mentioned in chapter 6, anchor charts of our version of the scientific process and design thinking language were always on display (figure 6.3, page 94). They were constantly referenced and became part of the learners' working vocabularies.

Possible Improvement on Standardized Science Tests

Most participants met standards (passed the Science MCA). Three of the seven who had been in the After School Club scored in the top quartile. Classroom teachers were surprised. These students, many of whom were in math and reading intervention, did not typically perform well on the science test. Sue, the co-teachers, and the Engineering Ambassadors were not surprised at all. Enrichment activities created an opportunity for each child to develop and display skills and talents.

From day one, when given hard, real-world challenges, students demonstrated natural curiosity and determination to figure things out. We believe that this enthusiasm, combined with regular opportunities to participate in the iterative scientific process in small groups alongside actual engineers, strengthened learners' standardized test scores. We cannot draw a direct line from the experiences in The Gear Model After School Club to the results on the Science MCA; however, parents and teachers saw a likely relationship.

A few parents were especially proud, announcing their children's Science MCA test results at a neighborhood picnic that summer. The test results were a remarkable improvement over previous results for children from the same neighborhoods.

Informal Evaluation of the Emotions and Communication Gears

As described in chapter 4, students wrote one sentence at the beginning of each session. "Today I am feeling _____ because I am thinking about _____." Over time, these simple and quick daily journal entries showed less and less evidence of emotions involving distress or exhaustion. By the end of the program, students expressed feelings of confidence, excitement, and belonging the majority of the time.

Here is an example from later in the program by a third grader who started the program rarely ever talking. Her HSA showed that relationships with peers would be a helpful place to focus. This matched observations in school, where she often sat alone with few friends. Her living situation was isolating, and her parents didn't have time or transportation to bring her to extracurricular programs.

The example at the right is from a fifth grader whose mother reported he was building foil boats at home instead of playing video games all the time.

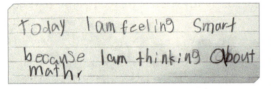

This example is from a fourth grader in week four of the twelve-week program. He grew to love the math games and was completing homework and personalized math practice more efficiently and accurately. His parents raved about the program because their child started enjoying school. They had always seen his engineering skills, but those skills had not yet been connected to academic schoolwork.

Classroom teachers confirmed students' increased confidence during math tasks. They reported that participants from the program contributed more often to mathematical discussions in the classroom and completed more work in class. Students were turning in homework consistently. Parents echoed the teachers' findings. The end-of-program parent survey showed that 100 percent of parents felt their child was more academically motivated to learn and do well in school. Parents believed their children's dispositions for learning were stronger in part because of participation in the program.

The Engineering Ambassadors noted the same positive responses in the small-group reflections and individual written reflections that concluded the enrichment activities. At the beginning, it was hard to even read what many of the learners had written. Over time, their reflections grew longer and more detailed. By the end, legibility and clarity of thought were evident in all but one participant. We asked a high school student to work alongside that child, recording their reflections.

We also know learners were reading more books for pleasure, as evidenced in this journal entry:

Assessment of Overall Well-Being and Resilience

As discussed in chapter 4, we administered the HSA from PEAR in January. The primary purpose of the HSA is to assess a student's social-emotional development. This measure has three domains: resiliency, adult and peer relationships, and academic engagement in school and life.

The pre-assessment showed three strengths areas for the overall cohort: empathy, emotional control, and school bonding. The cohort had four areas as a whole that tended to be challenging:

learning interest, academic motivation, perseverance, and reflection. Three subsets appeared; they are shown as groups A, B, and C in figure 10.4.

We used PEAR's Toolbox of recommendations with participants during the program. In May, at the end of the program, we administered the HSA post-assessment. Inadvertently, rather than using a format that gave students an opportunity to reflect specifically on the program, we used a format that provided a snapshot of each child's overall experience during the weeks and months between the pre-assessment and post-assessment.

The post-assessment broad-cohort summary showed the following:
- All but two learners had increased persistence. This was supported by observations of students' work habits by teachers and families.
- Net gains in reflection were seen on students' individual HSA results. Students' inner thought processes showed increased self-awareness. We saw this in journal entries as well, where students used more precise academic language when reflecting on subject matter—in this case, the engineering challenge activities.

Figure 10.4 Data from Students' Pre- and Post-Assessments

	Pre-Assessment	Post-Assessment
Group A	Five students high in action orientation and peer relationships were low in learning interest and critical thinking. Four were exceptionally low in persistence. These highly social youth had a hard time with directions and getting started with schoolwork.	Learners in this group increased in their learning interest, but academic motivation continued to lag. To ensure their interests are reflected, we would want these students to help plan future programming. More is yet to be learned from them.
Group B	Four students were high in empathy, and had many peer relationships, but low were in self-control, persistence, and maintaining trusting relationships with adults. Finishing work was hard.	Learners in these groups made marked gains, sometimes more than 1.0 standard deviation in assertiveness, peer relationships, and optimism.
Group C	Four students were high in empathy, learning interest, and emotional control. Peer relationships were challenging. They needed friends. Optimism and assertiveness were growth areas too. Engagement in academics came easily, but social situations were harder.	

Parents' Feedback: Evaluations and Anecdotes

Relationships with some families had been established long before the After School Club began. This resulted in immediate feedback from those families. At registration, they expressed gratitude that we were providing what they had been requesting for years: tutoring. We leveraged their enthusiasm and positive energy and connected them to parents we did not know yet. The simple act of chatting with parents when they signed their children out each evening encouraged them to give us feedback and insights. At school parent conferences in the spring, we sought out families whose children were participating in the program to say hello and ask what they thought about the program. Spending casual friendly time with the students' families was immensely fruitful and informative, as well as fun.

On surveys mid-program and at the conclusion of the program, respondents reported that their children's academic motivation increased and their children stuck with tasks for longer periods of time. Students completed more homework and complained about it less. In interviews, more parents said their child voluntarily took homework out at home to finish what they had started at the After School Club.

At the Family Science Carnival held on the final session, and after seeing the movie showing various activities the children had experienced, one mom approached Sue and said, "Oh my gosh! Now I know why all our aluminum foil kept disappearing and why the toolbox had been out. He was making foil boats and testing to see how many metal bolts the boat could hold!" The smile on this mom's face as she shared this story was new to us. In past years, the family had exhibited low energy for learning, often appearing worn down when the topic of assignments came up. The more we connected learning to real-world science principles, the more her child was extending his learning outside of school. In school, he started being seen as a helpful leader. General relations between the school and mom became more positive too. Other parents' reports that learning continued at home confirmed that the many afternoons of work put in by the Engineering Ambassadors, teachers, and volunteers were indeed worth the effort.

The input and feedback from families was essential. Our evaluation plan included short parent surveys (three questions—see chapter 11, page 160) at the beginning, middle, and end of the program. We purposefully kept the surveys short to increase return rates. Whenever possible, we called or visited families who did not respond.

Evaluation from Partners and Volunteers

Building, maintaining, and leveraging relationships with staff at the school district and in the community and utilizing the support of friends at universities appeared to pay off. A microcommunity of supporters with diverse experiences and backgrounds helped us empower a cohort of youth to step toward their future aspirations. Gathering feedback from everyone involved was important. We found that the high school volunteers, co-teachers, and partners learned as much as the youth participants.

Partner Feedback

The University of Minnesota professors who directed and supervised the Engineering Ambassadors learned that K–12 teaching is exhausting work and gained greater respect for elementary teachers. The Engineering Ambassadors said they had strengthened their own civic leadership skills (communication, collaboration, learning interest, optimism, and action orientation) while learning to instruct and coach the third to fifth graders. The Engineering Ambassadors wanted to continue working in some capacity with young people or do outreach work in the future.

Volunteer Feedback

The community volunteers and high school students gained a larger sense of community that kept them coming back week after week. We believe the volunteer training we provided in advance led to authentic reciprocal admiration and repeated moments of joy and laughter. "I feel so connected to [learner's name]." We heard it over and over. The high school volunteers learned about themselves as they reflected on their growing leadership skills. Hopefully some of them will consider teaching as a profession.

The focus on relationships was transformative to all parties and aided in building a pipeline of volunteer support, strengthening the sustainability and stability of the program. We have witnessed many programs, yet rarely have we seen the level of bonding we saw in this program. The energy each afternoon was so positive that it was hard to tell who was being served. Ultimately, we believe the cross-generational sharing of power created that positivity. We expect youth to learn from adults. But having elementary, high school, and college students; middle-aged teachers; and retired folks all coexisting and thinking together was unique and beautiful. "It is the best part of my week," high schoolers and retirees said.

Ongoing Conversations Everywhere

If educators or volunteers involved in the program reported that a learner was struggling in any way, Sue or her co-teacher always made a brief follow-up call to the parents, couched in curiosity and always including mention of the child's strengths. Insights from parents helped the team develop actionable new approaches for the learner. Parents appreciated being asked about the logistics of the program and its impact on their child. We were more pleased than surprised when every youth participant had someone from their family at the final night's Family Science Carnival.

We sought and valued every person's voice, including bus drivers, who we talked with to gather ongoing anecdotal feedback. We were always asking learners what could be better. Our ability to immediately respond, often in small ways, led to increased momentum, more time on task, increased critical thinking, and stronger human bonding.

Not only had we created a safe place for youth to be after school, but transformative relationships built a thriving microcommunity of happy problem-solvers. The experience left us wanting to foster that energy in more learning environments for youth and led us to write this book.

Improving Feedback Collection and Evaluation

The one group we did not formally seek evaluative information from was classroom teachers. Going forward, we plan to survey them in the middle and at the end of the program in a more formal way. Sue and her co-teacher worked in the school the participants attended, so they heard positive stories and enthusiastic questions about the program. However, in the future, we will seek more specific quantitative feedback from these teachers to document student growth and make ongoing program improvements.

Similarly, but at a broader level, we wish we had done more peer review with administrators and district leaders who were also accessing Targeted Services (state-funded before school, after school, and summer programs), to garner their thoughts and get the word out in our state about how The Gear Model program was meeting whole-child needs in intentional and creative ways.

As alluded to earlier, we also wish we had worked with the district testing coordinator in advance to compile the state standardized test data and classroom unit assessments for math and reading across the years the students were involved in the program. Collecting and reviewing this data would have given us longitudinal data on impact.

After working with the After School Club, the Engineering Ambassadors started working to improve their pre- and post-assessment of attitudinal shifts and understanding of engineering principles.

When working with youth, much of the assessment work is qualitative. Individual stories give insight into the impact of our work. In the future, we plan to do more to document individual growth in qualitative ways.

To close this chapter, we share the following story, which demonstrates how long-term relationships and all the gears of intervention worked together across the ecosystem for a learner to flourish the way her parents and others who worked with her knew she could.

Kayla's Success Story

> This is a story of how the gears came together to accelerate success for one student. Kayla was a fifth grade participant who could have fallen behind, particularly during the pandemic. Throughout her elementary years, she had a very hard time paying attention in school and staying focused on academic lessons. She was often fidgeting with something in her hands or daydreaming. Kayla received wraparound interventions both in and out of school in primary grades. And from 2017 to 2020, when she

was in first through third grades, she consistently attended the Homework Club in her neighborhood. There, she was full of personality, busy building structures, completing puzzles, and competitively racing through math games with her brother and friends. In terms of Habits of Mind, Kayla showed "Responding with Wonderment and Awe" and "Finding Humor" in her learning in the neighborhood outside the school, but not within the school walls.

Kayla's parents, recent immigrants and new speakers of the English language, valued education as a pathway to success and wanted to learn about the U.S. school system. They were among the first to participate in a parent university where they gained knowledge of how to use the district's online systems to access Kayla's report card and standardized test scores. They learned what to ask at parent conferences. "We get it now! We must ask questions and watch Kayla's progress on the district website! In Mexico City, parents just sent kids to school, but here, parents watch and help." They were particularly concerned about Kayla's standardized math tests.

From 2020 to 2021, Kayla's parents chose an online option for her fourth grade year. They were worried about her health and safety during the pandemic. However, they worked multiple jobs, so they were not always home during the school day. Sue was Kayla's intervention teacher. Sue checked in with the classroom teacher weekly and observed in class via Zoom. Sue stayed on Zoom with Kayla for half an hour after school until Kayla's dad arrived home, since the neighborhood Homework Club was shut down. Together, Kayla, her dad, and Sue made a plan for any work she missed or needed to finish up from the school day. Kayla's parents ensured she completed the assignments after dinner. All this to say, Kayla was one of the fortunate children who had in-school and out-of-school interventions prior to and during the pandemic.

When Kayla returned to school in person for fifth grade in fall of 2021, she joined The Gear Model After School Club. Her classroom teacher, Mrs. Gasch, was one of the program's co-teachers. On Tuesdays, Mrs. Gasch sat with Kayla and a few other fifth graders, fine-tuning their understanding of math concepts taught earlier in the day. The teacher modified the homework to match essential skills. Though Kayla was quiet in class, at the After School Club, Mrs. Gasch witnessed strengths not always seen in school: Kayla's determination, drive, and creativity during STEAM enrichment activities. Mrs. Gasch encouraged Kayla's peer collaboration skills and problem-solving strengths back in the classroom and Kayla's voice grew strong and confident for the first time in her school experience. Her circle of friends even grew. Kayla's focus improved, and her symptoms of ADHD diminished. The cycle of success accelerated her learning. Kayla was invited to visit the University of Minnesota Mechanical Engineering Department. While viewing one of the laboratories with her family, Kayla said, "I could be here one day!"

Kayla's standardized test scores at the end of fifth grade showed exceptional growth too. In third and fourth grade, her end-of-year standardized math and reading scores were in the "does not meet standards" and "partially meets standards" categories. In fifth grade, her scores advanced to "meets standards" (passing) on the math, reading, and science tests. Kayla's trajectory was up sharply because she had the benefit of full-service, whole-child interventions, partnerships, and strong relationships inside and outside of school. Rigorous personalized intervention from her teacher and relevant real-world experiences from the Engineering Ambassadors gave her a vision of her future self. As a bonus, the test data was evidence of the "success" that many administrators, policy makers, and funders are seeking.

Reflection Questions

- How does the thinking around relationships, rigor, and relevance influence your development or refinement of an evaluation plan?
- In what unique ways did the balance of gears in The Gear Model create conditions to improve intervention success for every learner?
- What additional data (academic and social) could be collected to personalize or tailor a whole-child approach to intervention success?
- Which of the five main gears might you consider starting or enhancing? (Academic Intervention, Enrichment, Communication, Attending to Emotions, Collaborative Movement and Play) Who will you seek program feedback from to help you evaluate and improve?
- How could data be shared to garner more support and funding from school and community leaders and partnerships? What parent releases would be needed to share this data?

CHAPTER 11

Next Steps—You Can't Do This Alone

"Almost always, the creative dedicated minority has made the world better."
—Martin Luther King Jr., minister, activist, and political philosopher

In this chapter, we help you think about your next steps in developing academic intervention and enrichment approaches that are focused on the whole child. Our goal is to help you incorporate everything you've read and consider your broader ecosystem and potential partnerships, while at the same time remaining focused on the learning strengths and needs of individual youth and families. You will need to consider what is best for the youth you are working beside first, foremost, and always. To that end, we offer questions to support your thinking as you move forward.

These open-ended questions must be answered based on your specific school, organization, or partnerships. Every microcommunity has its own unique culture and ways of operating. We think it's unlikely that anyone would take on all gears at once in the beginning. As we have shared, The Gear Model itself was developed over a decade, with gears added over time.

Consider these questions as you take next steps toward success for all learners:

- Why are you starting this work or changing your current intervention approach? What do you hope to achieve for and with learners?
- Who are the learners you seek to support? What do you already know about their strengths, needs, and aspirations?
- What do families say when you talk with them? What are the families' hopes and dreams for their children? What do they need to attain those dreams?
- What do the schools say they can provide for intervention and what are they struggling to

do to meet the whole child's learning and social-emotional needs?
- What and who are in your ecosystem to support learning and health outcomes?
- What conditions and circumstances need to grow or be enhanced in your ecosystem to increase learning outcomes?
- What are your ultimate aspirations in five years? Ten years? Beyond?

Start with the End in Mind

As you launch or refine your own intervention program, be mindful of your capacity. What do you dream of? Dream big, but balance those dreams with a realistic understanding of what is possible to do this year, in the next two years, and in the next ten. Start small and grow. Have a plan to celebrate the little wins for learners and adults. Maybe you'll ring a bell every time a learner reaches a goal. Maybe you'll have an extra cookie because learners persisted on a difficult problem. We remember when we stopped the entire group and gave Zeke three claps after he slapped his hands on the table and announced, "Hey! I read the directions wrong! I gotta fix this!"

Keep in mind that building a program that involves people is not a quick, linear process. Like the problem-solving process, the scientific process, and the design thinking process, you will move back and forth between the following tasks:

1. With the Relationships Gear in mind, build honest developmental relationships that are strong enough to challenge growth, walking beside the youth and families in school and out of school. Have lunch with some students. You'll learn a lot!
2. Identify and initiate conversations with fellow passionate believers in schools and in the community. Give thought to many different ideas and perspectives. This is a complex process that requires people with different areas of expertise.
3. Create a vision board. We used sticky notes on chart paper. (See figure 5.2.) Dream big, but also be ready to step back and start with the parts your ecosystem is ready for.
4. Choose just two or three main gears to work on in addition to the Relationships Gear: Academic Intervention, Enrichment, Communication, Attending to Emotions, and/or Collaborative Movement and Play. Tackle a few parts of the model and do them well. Then add more pieces if the work is manageable for you and your partners.
5. Ask what the school says it can provide for intervention and what it is struggling to do to meet learners' needs. We hear time and again that more kids need Tier 2 intervention than there are interventionists. Schools are an essential part of the learning ecosystem, but they can't do it all alone.
6. Draft a working plan for attending to different pieces of the program. Spreadsheets are helpful. You will want to revisit and update them often.

The Importance of Outreach and Relationships

Sue's site visits and discussions with proven, sustainable program leaders revealed that the best programs prioritize outreach over in-reach. Rather than waiting for families to seek help, teachers and program managers proactively engage with them.

Before starting, familiarize yourself with the Search Institute's Developmental Relationships Framework and the support materials on its website (see appendix A). This work is foundational to achieving success in intervention. You will want to develop specific relationship goals for everyone involved. As we have emphasized, the most important part of the work is building and maintaining authentic relationships.

Youth Perspectives

Start by listening to the youth you seek to help. Know who you are serving. What are their specific needs and desires? What are their interests, passions, and strengths? What motivates them? What has been their experience in school and out of school? What do they need most from the program? Finding this out requires many conversations with students and the adults in their families before and during the program. In appendix B, you'll find student interview questions to help you know who you are aiming to support and what needs they have.

Family Perspectives

To teach the whole child, you first need to know the whole child. The easiest way to gain perspective on the whole child's life is to have a working relationship with their family. Recall that Martha (the Neighborhood Homework Club manager) and Sue invited the families for ice pops and conversation the first month of their new program. The purpose was to informally talk and listen, and enjoy a treat. Martha and Sue gained invaluable insights about strengths, struggles and future dreams, and unknown skills and talents. Misconceptions about families' circumstances were cleared up. The conversations shed light on the realities of the barriers families faced as well as on cultural strengths and assets that were previously unknown to the school staff.

Parents can be your greatest allies. Welcome them onboard and make them your learning partners. Find ways to spend five to fifteen minutes asking them about their children.

The Broader Ecosystem: Partnerships

To think deeply about your ecosystem, go out into it. When learning about and evaluating your learning ecosystem, examine in-school and out-of-school time: curriculums, programs, and activities. Youth development *is* intervention, so intervention is already happening both in and out of school. Do all youth have access to all of that intervention?

Travel to spaces you have not yet visited. Talk to people you have not previously thought about talking to: teachers, paraprofessionals, caregivers, bus drivers, sports coaches, tutors, scout leaders, youth directors, piano teachers, and anyone else working with youth during their waking hours. As you develop or improve your program, always consider the link between regular classroom instruction (Tier 1 instruction) and what is provided by the schools and community to supplement and support the learning of youth.

You may work in a school, a community youth organization, a faith-based organization, a public safety office, city government, or another entity. What is the mission of your institution? How do your goals align with and/or support whole-child intervention success? What limitations does your institution have? What can't your organization do that others can? What partnerships already exist within your organization?

Building a cohesive, full-service team is essential; you cannot do the work alone. Sue knew this early on and reached out to Lucy for collaboration, then to the Engineering Ambassadors. You need thought partners, like Lucy, *and* implementation partners. You will need to access new parts of your own organization or harness the goodwill and talents of people in other institutions across the broader community to improve the effectiveness of your whole-child intervention program and increase access to it.

The next step is to find or inspire passionate, action-oriented supporters and identify potential barriers. Develop a contact list of friends and allies who will be dependable, go-to people for questions, support, and guidance. You also need to know what might get in the way so you can find a way around those barriers prior to launching the work. As you think about barriers, you may want to revisit figure 3.1.

Obtaining Funding: Do Not Let Money Stop You

Determine what funding is available to you. This varies based on the organization that hosts the program. School funding is complex, but it is worth taking the time to learn about it to understand potential funding sources. Our program was funded in different ways at different times. The latest iteration was mainly funded through the school district with revenue from Minnesota's Targeted Services program. In addition, we used Elementary and Secondary School Emergency Relief (ESSER) money allocated during the pandemic. The remainder of the funding—for the enrichment part of the program—was covered by a donor, making the program cost-neutral. As you consider funding, think about the type of program you want to offer, how many participants you will serve, and what supplies you will need, from healthy snacks to pencils to movement equipment. Work with your local community and businesses for funds or grants to support the program.

You might need to get creative and join forces with groups that already work in youth development! Seek out foundations, state funding, and faith and civic groups funding, or start a fundraising effort with your own network of family, friends, and community. Start anywhere you can. Your passion, mission, and plan will eventually be seen and recognized by people with access to financial and other supports.

The size and scope of your work will greatly influence your funding model. Develop a total budget so you can advocate for the resources needed to make your full vision come to life. This total budget amount will be helpful when talking with funders. Think about a short-term (first-year) budget and a long-term budget for sustainability and growth. The budget will also help answer the question of whether registrants will need to pay a fee to participate. Keep in mind, though, that it is important to break the pay-to-play cycle. The students who are not able to pay are often the ones who need the program the most.

Along with a budget, think about the number of students you will be able to serve and the outcomes you are aiming for. We caution you to begin small and grow. You want to create a program where all learners can thrive. And you will need time to develop those essential authentic relationships needed to build your microcommunity of learners and supporters.

> *We caution you to begin small and grow. You want to create a program where all youth can thrive.*

Most importantly, hold fast to your mission and purpose, the one that makes your budding initiative unique. This will help protect you from special-interest and political pendulum swings. Do not be shy about asking for funds from anyone who is interested in the success of students. Even if they cannot fund your program, they may have suggestions for you.

Designing Your Own Gear Model

Remember, you do not need to build the entire Gear Model all at once. Choose two or three gears to focus on, along with the central Relationships Gear. Whatever gears you choose, make sure your work is aligned to classroom instruction and has a strong focus on personalized learning throughout. Below are important ideas and logistics related to each gear.

Academic Intervention

- How will you decide what academic area to focus on during your program's academic intervention (tutoring) time? Math? Reading? Other?
- How will you learn about each student's current level of understanding for the selected academic focus area?
- Can you get current test scores from the school? Are you able to talk directly to students' classroom teachers? Are parent releases necessary to gain access to information about students' academic needs?
- If releases cannot be obtained, how can you use academic interviews or pretests to determine students' academic strengths and needs?
- What specific academic standard or skill does each student need to learn next? How will you know when they know? What will the student know and be able to do?
- What training for program staff is available within the school district or online? This will help determine what training you need to add.
- What existing materials are available to you? Are there intervention materials? Can you use materials from an existing curriculum?
- What materials can you find for free (online, etc.)? What materials do you need to invest in?
- How might you learn about the skills students are being taught at school during the weeks

and months of the program? Can teachers send you the classroom newsletters? Can you access a district scope and sequence online or in print? Does your state have academic standards you should review?

Enrichment

- Is there a student interest survey you have access to, or will you create one?
- What areas of enrichment are of interest to your students? Visual arts? Performing arts? STEAM? Environment? Outdoor education?
- What resources are available in your local and wider community?
- Who are your potential allies and partners? Art museums? Community theatre? A history center? Nature centers? Colleges or universities? Businesses? Libraries? Public safety departments? Churches, synagogues, mosques, and temples? Nonprofits? Junior Achievement? Youth sports leagues? Community parks and recreation departments? Boys & Girls Clubs? Scouts?
- How do your mission and desired outcome align with potential partners' desired outcomes? Do you have a shared philosophy or mission? Recall that the Engineering Ambassadors' key goal was to "improve diversity, equity, and inclusion in undergraduate and graduate programs in mechanical engineering by increasing the diversity of those in the pipeline." This aligned to our program goal of developing independent, contributing, healthy adults.
- What do you need a partner to bring? People? Materials? Expertise?
- After selecting partners, how will you efficiently and routinely reflect together about shared goals? This is essential so you can make continual adjustments to the instruction and to student behavior/management needs.

Communication

- What important outcomes in this area are you aiming for?
- What language(s) are spoken in students' homes?
- How will you know the students' writing abilities and levels of interest in writing?
- How might you learn if any students have exceptional reading challenges?
- How can you create journals for each participant?
- Who will read the journals to provide ongoing feedback to the program?

Attending to Emotions

- What philosophy or resources will you use as your foundation? We recommend using Developmental Affirmations (Clarke 2021) or something similar.
- Do participants have one or more shared traumas (natural disasters, community struggle, family changes, currently unhoused, and so on)?
- How will you build quick rituals into your routine for students to identify and make

connections to all their varied emotions orally or in writing? Remember, three to five minutes can be enough if done consistently.

Collaborative Movement and Play

- What do you hope to accomplish during movement time beyond getting the wiggles out? Our goals were to reinforce math skills, build communication, and develop new relationships.
- What spaces are available to you? Keep in mind the amount of time you need. See chapter 9 for more about how to structure time.
- Think about movement in the space you have. Does the space allow for large-motor activities? Is the space smaller, meaning you need to think about movement in different ways?
- What movement and game resources do you have access to?
- What materials can you borrow? Do you need to invest in materials?
- How will you keep the focus on collaboration more than competition?
- How will you teach teamwork?
- How will you ensure that everyone gets their heart rate up and releases energy?

Data to Inform Improvements and Demonstrate Success

The key to continuous improvement is having an evaluation plan that includes two components: frequent feedback loops and final program evaluation methods. We recommend you develop these before you begin the program. Start with the end in mind. The mere act of asking everyone involved if you're meeting your goals will help you achieve your goals.

Feedback surveys or questionnaires should be short and frequent. Choose daily, weekly, monthly, or quarterly feedback survey cycles.

Mid-program and end-of-program evaluations are extremely important to have in place. You will need to show growth and demonstrate accomplishment towards your goals.

Collaborate on Goals and an Evaluation Plan

To keep your new approach or program growing, you will need evidence of its viability. Sustainability is proof of success. Success is built on the buy-in of everyone in the microcommunity.

The first step in creating your evaluation plan is to think deeply with your partners from the start about key outcomes. You will need to evaluate the growth of each participant *and* the program overall. You will need to determine and agree upon a clear vision of what success looks like for you, for the learners, for the families, for the partners, and even for the volunteers.

Seeking the input and perspectives of everyone in the room teaches the community the habits required in the 21st century: the art of reflection, communicating with precision, responsiveness, learning continuously, applying past knowledge to new situations, innovating, and improving. Seeking input from everyone helps you truly reach your goal of responding to personalization:

- Where and how will you seek and receive feedback along the way?
- How will you celebrate the little successes day by day? Having ways to celebrate the small wins is essential in this work!
- How will you prioritize and focus the program evaluation? What are the key outcomes you want to know more about?
- How will you be sure you are collecting useful, actionable data?
- Who has the data you will need? When and how will you collect it?
- Do you have expertise in assessment and evaluation that you can lean into? If you are not a school employee, you might want to partner with a current or retired school staff member who has expertise in this area. It can be simple!

As discussed in chapter 10, we used a variety of sources for informal and formal data collection. Below we share sample questions you can use or build from. You will need to create your own surveys and feedback loops based on the specifics of your program.

Youth Feedback and Evaluation

Youth reactions and evaluative feedback are vital. Plan a way to gather and record information from the participants. This could be surveys, interviews, focus groups, or more informal means such as conversations and observations during program time. Using questions such as the ones below creates agency and buy-in. If you are using informal data, be sure you have a consistent way to collect and record it.

Daily or Weekly Questions

On a weekly and monthly basis, we sought students' suggestions, ideas, and questions. This helped us refine and personalize the program. It also helped us connect individual learners with peers and adults they were bonding with to further their developmental relationships.

These three questions were asked daily:

- Who did you connect with today?
- Who, if anyone, was challenging to work with today?
- Is there anything helpful for us to know?

Mid-Program and Final Evaluation Survey

Below are questions we used to make our own online and one-on-one in-person surveys. Edit these or write your own, depending on what you are trying to evaluate. The sample questions use different formats (select a choice, Likert scale 1 to 5, short answer). Decide what format is best to use with your audience *and* to gather the data you seek.

The Relationships Gear
- Tell me about your interactions with adults/other students.
- What new friends have you made?
- What volunteers do you enjoy working with and why?
- What else would you like us to know about relationships at our [After School Club]?
- When are the moments you find yourself feeling happy during [After School Club]? Who were you with? What were you doing exactly?
- What makes you feel supported or like you belong at [After School Club]?

The Academic Intervention Gear
- How has your engagement in learning changed in the [After School Club]? In your classroom?
- How have your [math] skills changed?
- Do you think you have improved? In what ways?
- On a scale of 1 to 5, have you mastered the academic goal you set for yourself?

The Enrichment Gear
- How do you see yourself in the future?
- How will you use what you learned during our [STEAM] enrichment time in the future?
- What new interests have you gained?
- What are you doing or learning about when you're really engaged and forget about time?

Overall Social and Emotional Experience
- What is/was the best thing about this experience for you?
- Alternate question: What do you think about this experience? Check all that apply. (Or, rate these statements using a scale of 1 to 5.)

    _____ I am learning here.
    _____ I can be with friends.
    _____ I am feeling confident.

- How did being here make you feel? Circle emotions words or emojis that apply. (Or, rate these statements using a scale of 1 to 5.)

    _____ I am more confident about academics.
    _____ I feel like I have an adult who cares about me.
    _____ I feel like I have friends.
    _____ I feel like I belong.

- How did this experience affect other areas of your life in school and out of school?

- What are you getting even better at? Check all that apply.

    _____ academics
    _____ trying harder
    _____ having fun learning
    _____ making friends

Parent Feedback and Evaluation

From parents, we gathered feedback at the beginning, middle, and end of the program. We kept the questions short and to the point. We aimed for three questions at a time. If parents were not proficient in reading and writing in English, we interviewed them, as most could speak English.

Sample Questions

- What impact has this experience had on your child (academically, socially, other)?
- Alternate question: Participating in this experience has helped my child grow in the following ways: (Check all that apply.)

    _____ academically
    _____ socially
    _____ emotionally
    _____ self-confidence
    _____ relationships

- Do you have suggestions [to inform the rest of the program this year?] or [for next year?] (Be sure to include questions about logistics of the program and the program itself. For example, we asked if parents who picked their child up would be able to pick them up at 4:30 p.m. instead of 5:00 p.m.)
- Would you (your child) return to the program?
- What area/s of enrichment would your child enjoy?
- What has your child shared with you about this experience? What have you seen?
- Alternate question: My child shared the following with me as part of the experience: (Check all that apply.)

    _____ made new friends
    _____ met supportive adults
    _____ became more confident in academics
    _____ experienced joy in learning

- How does being in the [After School Club] impact your child's motivation to learn and do well in school? Circle one.

    My child is more motivated.
    My child is less motivated.
    My child's motivation has not changed.

- Is your child more curious about [enrichment topic]?
- What else would you like us to know so that we can continue to improve?

Volunteer and Partner Feedback and Evaluation

We recommend preparing simple forms to gather information and feedback from all volunteers and partners. QR codes that linked to online surveys were preferred by volunteers with cell phones because they could scan the code and answer at a time convenient for them. Paper surveys are also efficient.

Daily Formative Feedback

To verify that all participants felt a sense of belonging, we asked volunteers to complete a short survey daily. This helped us ensure that every learner and every volunteer was connecting with someone in meaningful ways. The questions also allowed us to be proactive in developing a healthy microcommunity centered on learning. Volunteers could use the form anonymously to provide insights into things they learned about individual students and to report sensitive information. Most importantly the responses helped us connect individual volunteers with students in more intentional ways when making groups and seating arrangements. The purposeful groups deepened relationships. These were the daily questions:

- Who did you connect with today?
- Who, if anyone, was challenging to work with today?
- Is there anything helpful for us to know?

At the end of each day, to collect information on the program and consider changes for the next day, we held a ten-minute round robin chat session immediately after the students went home. We were seeking feedback to improve the activities and to increase student engagement. These debriefings were facilitated by the teachers and included the enrichment partner(s) and interested community volunteers. We typically used questions like the following:

- On a scale of 1 to 5, where 1 is the least productive and 5 is most productive, how productive was the group this afternoon?
- What students were you able to help get engaged with the homework/tutoring work?
- Which students do we need to continue to help get more engaged during tutoring time?
- Did your group make a plan before tackling today's STEAM challenge?
- What good questions did you ask, or did you hear, today?
- What students are you connecting with most?
- What else is helpful for us as the leaders to know?

We also continued to seek volunteers' suggestions, ideas, and questions informally throughout the program.

Summative Program Evaluation

As each year wrapped up, we used Google forms to gather continuous improvement data for the program. These questions can be customized to your partners, your volunteers, and your desired outcomes. We used questions like the following:

Recommendations for the program:
- What problems have you encountered?
- What changes might you recommend?
- What part of training was most helpful?
- What further training would help you and other volunteers improve your work and relationships with participants?
- Would you participate in future years if it fit your schedule?
- Would you recommend the experience to your peers?
- What is your biggest takeaway thought or piece of wisdom?

Benefits for you personally:
- What have you learned about yourself and our community?
- What new insights do you have about interacting with youth?
- What was helpful in building positive relationships with youth?
- What action steps might you now take as a result of having been a part of this program?

This helped us identify ways to improve and strengthen the program. The simple act of asking for their thoughts and opinions made ambassadors and volunteers feel valued. Being valued brought people back for multiple years, and they became some of the students' biggest advocates.

Developing a Team

As you build your program, think about sustainability. Programs rely on people and often end due to changes in personnel or because key leaders leave. Planning, goal setting, and putting the pieces of a program together takes collaboration. Develop a pipeline to attract and retain staff. Lean into intergenerational relationships to strengthen your community. Tap into any existing grassroots expertise and experience of teachers and other educators.

People make a program work, struggle, or fail. You need to consider the purpose of each role in the program and share that when recruiting your team. You want volunteers who are aligned with the program outcomes. As you recruit volunteers, you are also building buy-in for the program. The roles and responsibilities of each individual should be clearly documented in writing. Give these descriptions to people when they join your team. In addition, make copies available to volunteers as they enter each day; this will prevent unnecessary interruptions and allow you to remain in the flow with participants.

When recruiting, be mindful of the strengths each person brings and the roles they hope to play. For example, you need a nurturing person to help gather and serve the snack. You need an extrovert with a welcoming warmth who routinely makes sure everyone is seen and connected. You need volunteers who are timekeepers or taskmasters to ensure the program stays on schedule. You need calm voices of reason to step in during tense moments when the tone or energy is shifting away from the purpose of the work. You need volunteers who are organized to help keep all the parts moving and connected.

As you think about the volunteers, consider the following:
- What special skills and talents do you need in your team?
- Where will you find the leadership for the program?
- Who will be eligible to be a volunteer?
- Where can you recruit volunteers?
- How can high school students be involved?
- Do volunteers need a background screenings/checks?
- What do the volunteers hope to gain from the experience?
- How and when will you train people to support the program?
- How will you debrief with volunteers after tough days?

Recruiting Participants

Once you have identified and learned about the students and planned a program specifically for their needs, you will need to recruit them to the program. You must develop communication and registration processes. There are many details to consider here. If you have little or no experience with this, talking to someone in the community education department of the school district is beneficial. Be sure to ask a lot of "why" questions to understand the processes.

As you register participants, be clear about the date the program will begin. Be explicit about arrival and departure times. On the registration form, include a place for parents to provide emergency phone contacts and a photo release (with options to accept or decline). Also include a statement about behavior expectations in case behavior becomes a challenge. You may need to lean into or build relationships with families to get all students registered. We recommend holding 10 percent of your spots for new students or late registrations.

Handling Logistical Details

We encourage you to think about the logistics as you think about each of the gears. Decisions you make about the gears will influence the logistics, and the logistics might influence how you can implement the gears.

Be aware of the liability coverage for whoever is hosting. Think through the business processes if you hire staff. Some religious organizations and nonprofits offer human resources and legal assistance. Leverage relationships across sectors to explore payroll practices, legal liability, and training needs.

Finding a Location

Finding a location for a program can be a challenge. You could host it at a school, a community center, a religious facility, a community room in an apartment building, or another option in your community. Below are some questions to guide your thinking when securing a location:

- What are the rules or requirements for using the space?
- Is the space secure?
- What access do you have to a movement space?
- Will you need to move students to a different area for movement or certain activities?
- How close are bathrooms? A drinking fountain?
- Can participants eat snacks and have drinks in the space? (Some spaces limit the type of drink.)
- Are there tables for tutoring?
- How flexible is the furniture arrangement? Are the pieces easy to move?
- What space, furniture, and technology will be needed by your enrichment partner?
- Can you securely store materials and snacks at the location?
- How will students get to the program and get home from it?
- How will the volunteers arrive at and leave the space? Is there sufficient parking?
- Do you need to offer transportation for participants or volunteers?
- Will all feel welcome in the space? Be sure to consider the mission and purpose of the hosting organization and whether there is a conflict of interest that would eliminate some participants.

Obtaining Materials

The materials needed for a program vary based on age, goals, and enrichment partners. Identifying all the materials you'll need up front will help you build a budget and seek donations.

- What materials will you need for the program?
    - For academic work?
    - For movement?
    - For enrichment?
    - For attending to emotions?
- Can materials be donated? Will you be able to offer a tax receipt for donations?
- Where will you store the materials? Who will have access to the materials?
- Are the materials culturally responsive and bias-free?
- Will you offer snacks? Will they be donated or will you need to purchase them?

Developing a Daily Structure and Routines

Establishing a structure and routines helps the program run smoothly. You need to consider every minute of the program. Plan your transitions between each part of the program. Develop signals or ways for bringing the group back together. If you aren't a classroom teacher, include a teacher in your planning to tap into their experience with students, structures, and routines.

- How will you get students to the program?
- How will volunteers access the space?
- How will you communicate with participants, families, and volunteers?
- How much time will you have each day? How will you allocate that time?

Closing Thoughts

In this chapter, we provided questions to help you think about and plan how you will develop and improve your own intervention program. We believe The Gear Model will aid in the development of effective, comprehensive, sustainable, decades-long programs. The Relationships Gear is what keeps the model working. We want you to take our model to scale up and enhance the learning everywhere for more and more learners. Of course, how the gears come together will be based on your own microcommunity of volunteers, partners, participants, and families.

CHAPTER 12

Final Thoughts

"Educating the mind without educating the heart is no education at all."
—Common saying in education circles

So, when it is all said and done, what does it take to truly lift the trajectory for youth so they reach their fullest potential? Can we come together and create conditions where all youth have what is needed to grow into independent, contributing, healthy adults? How can we come together as a greater ecosystem to support learning everywhere it happens? How do we increase access to more learning time for children who need it most?

Key Thinking

We each bring our own backgrounds, professional experiences, and analysis of current research when we consider how to meet the needs of youth today. Needs have shifted, but our systems haven't. We encourage you to join forces with the leaders and thinkers in your corner of the world to intervene differently. In conversations where people are discussing the need for updating the approaches to education and learning, we circle back to these concepts. We hope you will revisit the five foundational concepts outlined in chapter 1 and promote a collective focus on these ideas going forward:

1. Be child centered and learning focused.
2. Developmental relationships are more than caring relationships or compliance.
3. Start with asset-based framing. Identify and utilize strengths of individuals and cohorts.
4. Focus on academics and beyond—Habits of Mind and 21st century skills.
5. Develop a systems orientation that aims to connect all the parts of the broader ecosystem of learning in your community.

Sue's travel to interview leaders and workers at longstanding effective programs informed the creation of The Gear Model as discussed in chapter 3. In figure 12.1, we revisit key commonalities of those programs and their impact on The Gear Model.

Figure 12.1 Key Findings from Site Visits

What's Needed? (for the 10–20% needing it)

1. Consistent intervention leadership and teachers. *Continue to scale up The Gear Model.*

2. A whole-child assessment showing individual child's strengths and needs. *Try Holistic Student Assessment (HSA) or Thrively.*

3. Our own pipeline of future "teachers." *Find academic mentors from the local high school.*

4. Time to develop personalized math or reading activities. *Design them to match classroom instruction.*

5. Partnerships for enrichment. *Connect enrichment to concepts taught during classroom instruction.*

New Initiatives and Change Fatigue

Over our many years as teachers in school districts of various sizes and in the education department of a university, we have seen more and more curriculum and philosophical trends coming to schools and educators at a faster pace. Of course, this speed of change is not unique to education. It is a reality for everyone living in the 21st century.

That said, new initiatives in STEAM, Science of Reading, standards-based math, and restorative practices (to name a few recent swings) occupy more time, energy, and human power than can be managed effectively. The systems are breaking. The people who work within them are stretched beyond what is sustainable for them alone to handle.

For school and youth workers in direct service of children and youth, we fear that the current speed of change and the demand load might break the school systems altogether. When we speak to groups of teachers and youth workers, they say that the needs of youth and the level of mental dissonance and physical exhaustion they are experiencing leave them wondering how much longer they can stay with the work. They alone cannot respond to all these pulls and pushes and maintain the day-to-day operations and relationship building required in human-facing caregiving and nurturing jobs.

Change is difficult at the best of times, especially large-systems changes. Changing American education as we know it is daunting. That is why we are proposing the development of microcommunities of supporters that wrap a balanced blend of relationship-rich and personalized support around our youth today. We must change our approach to intervene before students fail and before the system crumbles. For the sake of adults who work with children, and more importantly, for the next generation themselves, we do not have the luxury to wait to make changes.

Rethinking School Structures

We believe it is past time to rethink school structures. To us, this includes all the parts of the system. Our current systems are outdated and lack the responsiveness required to meet students' learning needs and support teacher retention.

Personalized Learning

Many schools are trying to meet individual needs, though others still approach instruction as if all students need the same thing, at the same time, for the same amount of time. To better serve students, many schools are utilizing the multi-tiered system of supports (MTSS), but they often struggle to serve all the children who qualify for Tier 2 and Tier 3 intervention. Classroom teachers are stepping up to meet students' needs, but they too struggle to personalize instruction for each individual. The balance of types of learning offered in The Gear Model could become the foundation for pop-up microcommunities of learning outside the school day. Ideally, school systems would be part of developing or partnering directly with these microcommunities that can offer the personalization students need.

Time and Calendar Limitations

It's not possible to address all the academic, resiliency, and 21st century skills youth need in a traditional school year and a traditional school day. Yet it's unrealistic to think that governments will fund expansion of that calendar or school day in the near future. Could a few teachers and trained paraprofessionals or retired teachers work flexible hours and days to provide the double dose of support that so many children need, outside the traditional school schedule? Could we provide more than just academic support, since it is plainly known our children are experiencing mental health challenges like never before? Engagement will increase and behavior challenges will decrease when we structure learning based on a balanced blend of the main gears: Academic Intervention, Enrichment, Communication, Attending to Emotions, and Collaborative Movement and Play.

Focus on Academics Alone Isn't Working

Schools are for learning. That is for certain. Since the beginning of the testing era, we have been hyper focused on academic learning, specifically, reading, math, and (sometimes) science. But there is more for youth to learn than just academics (for example, Habits of Mind and 21st century skills). Academics by themselves are not enough.

When it comes to The Gear Model, we know the importance of the gears working together. If all gears are separate and not working together, their impact is greatly

reduced. If the focus in schools is only on the Academic Intervention Gear, that gear will spin, but by itself it will not create the conditions to ensure the whole child is learning and developing. All youth need access to every gear working in tandem. Meaningful results occur when the gears turn together.

What If We Provided Whole-Child-Focused, Personalized Learning?

Without a doubt, the successful outcomes of the twelve-week After School Club validate our decision to put the Relationships Gear at the center of the model. The Developmental Relationships Framework (Search Institute, n.d.) kept the program in perpetual and productive motion. Following a full day at school, learners engaged in relevant and rigorous critical thinking, because the five pillars of developmental relationships created the conditions for persistence. The older generations expressed care, provided support, expanded possibilities, shared power, and challenged growth. This created a learning environment where students felt a sense of belonging and where their growth was supported. Learners developed two important Habits of Mind: taking learning risks and persisting when work was challenging. Developmental relationships and Habits of Mind allowed learners to become their best selves.

More Learning, More Often, and Everywhere, Please!

The flexibility in Sue's teaching position proved incredibly helpful, because she could be the conduit between what the child was learning in the classroom, in any special services received at school, and in the before- and after-school programs. Students who were dysregulated emotionally during the school day and had missed learning a skill or concept in class had a second chance after school. Students who shined and mastered a new concept in school could be bragged on and praised when Sue shared that news at the end of After School Club. Seeing children twice a day allowed for rebound and celebration.

We need to allow educators, teachers, paraprofessionals, families, and volunteers to collaborate with school and district leaders to think differently about the work that needs to occur on behalf of youth.

Tom Koch, the principal this book is dedicated to, recommended that we have more co-location. What did that mean to him? It meant being a living, breathing, caring adult and showing up everywhere to learn beside the families and the children: in the neighborhood, in the cafeteria, on the playground, at the ballpark, and in the classroom. Tom modeled this daily. As Don Carpenter of Trekkers preached, "It is a job, or it should be somebody's job, to sit beside youth wherever they are in the community or learning so we know how to intervene and help."

We need to allow educators, teachers, paraprofessionals, families, and volunteers to collaborate with school and district leaders to think differently about the work that needs to occur on behalf of youth. How might we reconsider roles and contracts to allow for summertime support for those students who are most at risk of the summer slide due to limited educational opportunities? How can we explore alternative teacher-contract structures during the school day and calendar year? Do all teachers need to work the same hours and follow the same yearly schedule? Could some teachers start and end their day an hour and a half later? Could some teachers work fewer days during the traditional school year to provide creative intervention programs in neighborhoods or at summer school?

> As educators and education constituents work to make education systems equitable and learner-centered, we must take a fresh look at what education systems are asking the people working in them to do. Without periodically revisiting the design of the education workforce, we risk continuing to do things as we have always done them, rather than how the people working and learning in these systems need things to be done. (Crabtree, Prince, and Righteous-Rogers 2024, 2)

We saw the greatest long-term success with Tier 2 learners, the youth who need extra support to catch up with grade-level peers. Academically, these are the students who benefit most from spending periods of time during the day in small-group settings with students who have similar academic needs. It's ideal when these small-group interventions take place in the classroom or with an intervention teacher during the regular school day. But that isn't always possible as often as needed. Also, there's a risk that when students are pulled out of Tier I classroom instruction, they miss exposure to grade-level vocabulary and subject matter, further hampering their ability to catch up. When we marry classroom instruction with high-quality, whole-child After School Clubs based on The Gear Model approach, learning outcomes are enhanced and youth are better prepared for future academic challenges.

Last Words as We Send You Off

The Gear Model was not designed to "save" youth and communities. Our work is designed to provide access to all so society benefits from the greatness of all its individual members. Every person has their own unique role to play. Only through collectively working together can we maximize the potential of this next generation and achieve our biggest goals.

Create Microcommunities: Schools cannot handle all the gears on their own. Schools are the centers of communities, and we need communities to rise up and surround schools with creative partnerships. We need to create microcommunities that surround learners with the conditions to envision and pursue the best versions of their future selves.

Start with Developmental Relationships: We cannot say this enough: Start with supportive and responsive relationships so all youth have a sense of connectedness and belonging. Go out, talk, and listen to youth and families. Focus on the whole child in the relationship. Without relationships in the center, all the work of all the people falls in a heap.

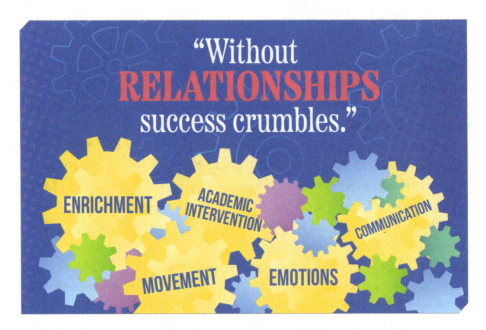

This Will Be Hard: Expect that making change on behalf of learners will not be easy. Aiming at the needs of the whole child and personalization is hard but rewarding.

Stay Future Focused: Be impatient enough to act, but patient enough to see the results. You are planting seeds that *might* not grow for a decade or more.

Long-Term Developmental Relationships = Success

The stories of struggle, success, and lessons learned that we shared in this book are just a few from our experiences. We have many more we could share. Reach out to us. We'd like to hear your stories and ideas for how to improve approaches to intervention.

We leave you with photos of a few of the now-grown students from the Neighborhood Homework Club that Sue and Martha refined and advanced from 2012 to 2020. One of the younger siblings benefited from the two-year implementation of the After School Club as well as from in-school intervention services. Almost all of the students pictured here benefited from in-school support in learning, and out-of-school enrichment too. The relationships took this group through elementary and middle school. Through community dinners, summer camp opportunities, and more, deep relationships developed between their families, teachers, and supporters that last to this day.

These photos show but a subset of the original group. The oldest are now in college, college graduates, and/or employed. The impact of strengths-based developmental relationships, both in school and out of school, delivered with a balanced blend of academic support and enrichment opportunities has indeed helped them become independent, contributing, and happy, healthy young adults.

Bonds remain so tight that a new tradition has emerged. Before someone in the group begins their college freshman year, they all visit Sue's house for ice cream sundaes and game night. Martha and the parents join when they can. The families have stayed in touch, and successes continue to be celebrated by their entire community. Tagging along for game night is the youngest sibling, who is watching, learning, and witnessing possible paths to the success they imagine for themselves.

Twister was always one of their favorite games—and ten years later, it still is!

"Together, all things are possible!"
—Cesar Chavez

Appendixes

A. Resources
    Asset-Based Framing
    Exemplary Programs
    Foundations: Learner-Focused and Personalized Learning
    Influences on Learning Beyond Academics
    Relationships
    School Models
    Systems Thinking
    Resources for the Gears

B. Sample Program Materials
    Invitation to Program
    Student Registration Form
    Questions for Prospective Partners
    Sample Partner Schedule
    Interview and Feedback Questions

C. Qualities of Effective Programs
    People
    Program Supports/Operational
    Focus on Learners and Families
    Program Design

Resources

Asset-Based Framing
360-Degree Assessment. Thrively. "Discover students' unique strengths, interests, and aspirations to build the skills they need for success in the K–12 classroom and beyond." thrively.com

Holistic Student Assessment (HSA). Partnerships in Education and Resilience (PEAR). "A data-driven tool to promote social-emotional development in young people in school and afterschool settings." pearinc.org/holistic-student-assessment

Exemplary Programs
Aspirations Incubator (Maine). aspirationsincubator.org

Banyan Community Family and Youth Development Center (Twin Cities, Minnesota). banyancommunity.org

Boys & Girls Clubs of Metropolitan Baltimore (Maryland). bgcmetrobaltimore.org

Casco Bay High School (Portland, Maine). cbhs.portlandschools.org

City Connects (Boston, Massachusetts). bc.edu/bc-web/schools/lynch-school/sites/city-connects.html

Harvard Medical School's MEDscienceLAB. hmsmedscience.org

Operation Breakthrough (Kansas City, Missouri). operationbreakthrough.org

ProvenTutoring Coalition, Johns Hopkins School of Education (Baltimore, Maryland). proventutoring.org

Trekkers (Rockland, Maine). trekkers.org

Yawkey Boys & Girls Club of Roxbury (Massachusetts). bgcb.org/findyourclub/yawkeyclubofroxbury

Foundations: Learner-Focused and Personalized Learning
"The ASCD Whole Child Approach to Education." ACSD. ascd.org/whole-child

"Improving the Equity in Personalized Learning Through a Multi-Tiered System of Support (MTSS) Approach." Aurora Institute. aurora-institute.org/event/improving-the-equity-in-personalized-learning-through-a-multi-tiered-system-of-support-mtss-approach

"Insights, Tools, Stories, and News on Learner-Centered Education." Education Reimagined. education-reimagined.org/news-resources/all

"Learn & Network." Aurora Institute. aurora-institute.org/learn-network

"Library of Resources." KnowledgeWorks. knowledgeworks.org/resources

"Whole Child Education." Learning Policy Institute. learningpolicyinstitute.org/topic/whole-child-education

Influences on Learning Beyond Academics
"Framework for 21st Century Learning Definitions." Batelle for Kids. static.battelleforkids.org/documents/p21/p21_framework_definitionsbfk.pdf

"What Are the Habits of Mind?" Institute for Habits of Mind. habitsofmindinstitute.org/what-are-habits-of-mind

Relationships
"Developmental Assets and Developmental Relationships." Peter C. Scales. 2018. In *SAGE Encyclopedia of Lifespan Human Development*, edited by Marc H. Bornstein, 564–566.

"Developmental Relationship as the Active Ingredient: A Unifying Working Hypothesis of 'What Works' Across Intervention Settings." Junlei Li and Megan Julian. 2012. *American Journal of Orthopsychiatry* 82 (2): 157–166.

"Developmental Relationships." Search Institute. searchinstitute.org/developmental-relationships

"Finding the Fluoride: Examining How and Why Developmental Relationships Are the Active Ingredient in Interventions That Work." Kent Pekel, Eugene C. Roehlkepartain, Amy K. Syvertsen, Peter C. Scales, Theresa K. Sullivan, and Jenna Sethi. 2018. *American Journal of Orthopsychiatry* 88 (5): 493–502.

"The Intersection of Developmental Relationships, Equitable Environments, and SEL." 2020. Insights & Evidence Series. Search Institute.

"Moving Beyond Relationships Matter: An Overview of One Organization's Work in Progress." Kent Pekel. 2019. *Journal of Youth Development* 14 (4).

School Models
"Canopy Project Data Portal." The Canopy Project. canopyschools.org/data-portal

"Exploring Innovative School Models in the Canopy Project's Interactive National Database." Aurora Institute. aurora-institute.org/event/exploring-innovative-school-models-in-the-canopy-projects-interactive-national-database

"Opportunities for Schools to Shape the Future Today." Katherine Prince. 2019. KnowledgeWorks. knowledgeworks.org/resources/opportunities-schools-shape-future-today

"The Value of Out-of-School Time Programs." Jennifer Sloan McCombs, Anamarie A. Whitaker, and Paul Youngmin Yoo. 2017. RAND Corporation. rand.org/pubs/perspectives/PE267.html

Systems Thinking
"Habits of a Systems Thinker." Waters Center. thinkingtoolsstudio.waterscenterst.org/cards

Resources for the Gears
Unless otherwise noted, the resources listed below are available at no charge.

Academic Intervention (Mathematics)
Funbrain. Math Zone. funbrain.com/math-zone

Fishtank Learning. Math and English Language Arts Units, Lesson Plans, and Assessments. "Helping teachers engage, challenge, and inspire students with quality curriculum materials." fishtanklearning.org

Tang Math. Math Games and Resources. "Interactive, visually appealing games that focus on building conceptual understanding through strategic practice." tangmath.com/games

Enrichment

Partners are not always easily found or available at the time of your work. If you are unable to secure a partner, consider an enrichment program run by the program leaders or others. Here are a few resources for creating your own Enrichment Gear.

Discovery Education. Watch virtual field trips on-demand. Field trip guides include standards-aligned, hands-on learning activities. Topics include SEL, science and STEM, literacy, and more. discoveryeducation.com/community/virtual-field-trips

Engineering Ambassadors Network. This network has programs at over 39 colleges and universities nationwide. engineeringambassadorsnetwork.org

National Geographic for Educators. Offers activities, lessons, units, games, reference materials, and interactive mapping tools, all based on the Explorer Mindset Learning Framework, which encourages curiosity, problem-solving, and critical thinking. nationalgeographic.org/education

National Oceanic and Atmospheric Administration (NOAA). Provides teaching and learning resources on our oceans and atmosphere. noaa.gov/education

National Park Service. Offers a wide range of educator resources, including lesson plans, materials for loan, primary sources, and more. nps.gov/teachers/index.htm

National Science Foundation Classroom Resources. Provides a rich collection of lessons and resources. The materials are arranged by research areas and include biology, chemistry, the environment, engineering, physics, and more. In a web browser, search "National Science Foundation Educational Resources."

Nature Lab. Find games, videos, teacher's guides, and more at nature.org/en-us/about-us/who-we-are/how-we-work/youth-engagement/nature-lab. Videos can be found at vimeo.com/tncnaturelab.

Science from Scientists. Real scientists deliver hands-on, inquiry-based STEM lessons in a collaborative, cost-effective program. sciencefromscientists.org

Stellarium. This online planetarium shows the stars and planets above your exact location. Details about specific stars can be found by clicking on them. stellarium-web.org

Communication

"250+ Best Would You Rather Questions for Kids." We Are Teachers. weareteachers.com/would-you-rather-scenarios-elementary

"Sentence Frames and Sentence Starters." Colorín Colorado. colorincolorado.org/teaching-ells/ell-classroom-strategy-library/sentence-frames

"Sentence Frames Based on Bloom's Taxonomy." Teaching Channel. teachingchannel.com/wp-content/uploads/2023/06/Downloadables-Sentence-Frames-Based-on-Bloom.pdf

Attending to Emotions

"Developmental Affirmations." Jean Illsley Clarke. extension.umn.edu/parenting-and-caregiving/developmental-affirmations

Mood Meter, Emotion Wheels, and so on. Search online for terms such as "emotional intelligence," "emotion plates," "emotion wheels," and "feelings/emotions posters."

Movement

"45 Best Cooperative Games to Promote Comradery and Healthy Competition." We Are Teachers. weareteachers.com/cooperative-games-for-kids

Action Based Learning. This company offers furniture and activity supplies (such as an obstacle course) that get children moving in the classroom. Requires funding. abllab.com

"Lead Outdoor Science Experiences." BEETLES (Better Environmental Education, Teaching, Learning and Expertise Sharing). Lawrence Hall of Science. Student-centered activities engage students directly with nature, encourage a scientific mindset, and ignite wonder and curiosity. beetlesproject.org/resources/for-field-instructors

Move This World. This is an evidence-based curriculum with interactive video lessons that encourage emotional exploration and engage students in real-world learning. Requires funding. movethisworld.com

Playworks. Game ideas available at no charge in addition to a fee-based program. playworks.org/resources

Invitation to Program

[Logo of hosting organization(s)]

Dear Family(s),

What: Your student is invited to **After School Club** where we will:

Celebrate individual strengths
Laugh and **play during team-building activities** in the gym
Challenge our MATH SKILLS
And, most importantly,
play with building materials to
take engineering to new heights

When: The program will run right after school until 5:00 p.m. on Tuesdays and Wednesdays.

Class Dates: February 22, 23
March 1, 2, 8, 9, 15, 16, 22, 23, 29, 30
April 12, 13, 19, 20, 26, 27
May 3, 4, 10, 11, 17, 18

Where: At [School name] media center and gymnasium

Why: The goal is to provide additional time, support, and opportunity for students to work toward progress in meeting their benchmark proficiencies.

How: Transportation home is available. A snack is provided.

Attendance: Children need to attend all sessions unless ill. We need the whole team there.

IMPORTANT NOTE: Please email your classroom teacher AND program leader the day of class if your child is sick or has a medical appointment: [email of program leader]

We look forward to working with your child. This will be a fun opportunity!

Questions?

[Contact name, phone, email]

Appendix B

Student Registration Form

Due to front office at [School Name on date]****

After School Club Registration

Child's name _____ Child's grade _____

Child's teacher _____

PERMISSION

My child has been invited to be part of the After School Club which will be held from 3:10 to 5:00 Tuesday and Wednesday.

_____I would like my child to participate in this program.

_____I am not interested in having my child participate in this program.

CONTACT INFORMATION

If your child is participating, please provide the following information:

Parent name _____

Email _____

Phone number _____

HOW WILL YOUR CHILD GO HOME?

Please choose one method that will be your consistent routine.

Examples: If you check the pickup option, that will be the plan every time. Your child will not take the bus. Only the children who check the bus option will be routed on the bus. If you check that option, we will count on your child taking the bus.

_____   **My child will be picked up and signed out at 5:00 in the main entry.**

Name of adult signing your child out: _____

_____ **My child should be signed in to school-based care at 5:00.**

_____ **Please send my child home on the bus**. (Note: *The bus route could take up to an hour.*)

Address for drop-off: _____

> **Photography Release:** Our After School Club might photograph and videotape activities for the purpose of showcasing the program in local media. Photos may be used by our partners, [name of partner], to report out to the donors.
>
> By initialing below, you are giving permission for the following:
>
> Use and reuse, in any manner, said photograph(s) and video, in whole or in part, modified or altered, in any medium or form of distribution, and for whatever purposes of showcasing the program for community members
>
> _____ (*please initial*) I represent that the subject of the photograph(s) is a minor and that I am the parent or duly authorized representative of the subject and have read the foregoing and fully and completely understand the contents.
>
> **Please Note:** If a student brings a cell phone, there will be texting/calling only to parents for purposes of pickup arrangements.

Questions for Prospective Partners

We recommend that you research your potential partners so you understand their intentions and past work. Consider any political or religious affiliations they have and the implications of that for your program.

Below are some questions and considerations to ask and think about when selecting partners:
- Are they part of your community? How does the community feel about them?
- What is their mission focus? Is there a conflict with your mission focus?
- What are your goals in offering an enrichment program (and do they align your program goals)?
- What are their goals or expected outcomes from the partnership?
- What do they believe about learners and growth?
- What background knowledge do they have about youth development? This will determine how much support you may need to give them.
- How will they engage students?
- How will you collaborate with them on behalf of youth? What is the cost to the partner? To you?
- Do they have results (data) from working with other groups of youth?
- What supports and supplies will they need from your program?

Below are some questions and considerations to ask and think about once you have partners selected:
- How will you make decisions together about the program?
- Will background checks be needed? Who will select the provider, timeline, etc.?
- Do you need a photo release or research approval for the work?
- How will you evaluate the success of your partnership?

Sample Partner Schedule

This schedule was for the University of Minnesota (UM) Mechanical Engineering Ambassadors.

Tuesday Schedule

2:15	Leave UM campus.
3:00	Sign in at school site. Get name badge. Find media center.
3:00–3:30	Sit beside individual students to assist in math/snack.
3:30–3:50	You set up while learners are in the gym. (Join us in the gym if you have time!)
3:50–4:10	Present your PowerPoint presentations to the whole group. (Sue displays the PPT using the Smartboard.)
4:10–4:20	Your Building Activity Time Large-group discussion: "What have you noticed?" "What are you wondering?"
4:20–4:30	Continue building/doing team challenge until ten-minute timer goes off.
4:35	Clean up.
4:40	Large-group quick written reflections chart. (Sue helps lead you and record learners' findings on chart paper to post again the next day.)
4:45	Sue gives reminders or we play a group game.
5:00	Learners head to bus or parent pickup while you clean up your supplies.
5:05–5:20	We "teachers" reflect on what went well and what could be better.

Wednesday Schedule

2:15	Leave UM campus.
3:00	Sign in at school site. Get name badge. Find media center.
3:00–3:30	Sit beside individual students to assist in math/snack.
3:30–3:50	You set up while learners are in the gym. (Join us in the gym if you have time!)
3:50–4:10	Your team leads a whole-group review of the reflections chart from the previous day. ▪ "What did we learn?" ▪ "What are we wondering now?" ▪ "What could we improve on today?" ▪ "How could we challenge ourselves and improve?"
4:10	Learners work at table teams on your activities. Large-group discussion: "What have you noticed?" "What are you wondering?"
4:20–4:30	Continue building/doing team challenge until ten-minute timer goes off.
4:30	Small group or individually written responses on activity sheet.
4:45	Sue gives reminders or we play a group game. Or, if you need more time, that is cool too!
5:00	Learners head to bus or parent pickup while you clean up your supplies.
5:05–5:20	We "teachers" reflect on what went well and what could be better.

Interview and Feedback Questions

Student Interview Questions

These three questions were almost always the same.

- How do you feel about reading and what could make it go even better?
- How do you feel about math and what could make it go even better?
- What else would you like us to know about your relationships with friends and adults here at school?

Volunteer Weekly Feedback Form

This feedback form was for the high school students. It was created in Google Forms, and we provided students with a QR code to access it.

- What is your name?
- What ideas for games that build teamwork do you have for our time in the gym?
- Would you be willing to be the designated person who gets the gym equipment out and puts it away perfectly?
- Did your group of learners all contribute to the STEM Challenge?

    ○ yes

    ○ no

    ○ everyone but…

- What ideas could help increase every voice being heard?
- Who did you meet that touched your heart?
- Who in the group do you want to spend time with next time?

Qualities of Effective Programs

The following list, highlighting the qualities of effective and sustainable tutoring, mentoring, and enrichment programs, was developed based on our research and site visits.

People
1. Programs had long-term leadership (1 to 2 decades).
2. Hands-on leaders worked with youth activities, families, and staff.
3. Paid volunteers or carefully selected unpaid mentors committed to 14 to 18 months (onboarding and continued training were provided).
4. Pride in their work; passionate staff were beyond surprised and delighted to have someone ask for their insights.
5. Programs grew their own staff over years from program participants.
6. Classroom teachers knew the site leaders to communicate with—and did so, often in person.

Program Supports/Operational
7. Funding started small. Funders came out of the woodwork when desired yearly gains were reported.
8. Transportation was available in one of these ways:
    - Program owned its own transportation (requires insurance and licensing)
    - Program was held in the students' geographic area so youth could walk
    - Program had dedicated space in public schools
9. Programs owned their own building or had permanent dedicated school building space.
10. Programs offered a flexible registration process, online and by paper, with staff to talk to at a central location.
11. Programs were open for operations and meeting in person during the COVID-19 pandemic.
12. Programs were beginning to measure long-term success based on how many alumni graduate from college or finish a trade school, not just high school.

Focus on Learners and Families
13. Staff meetings for reflection, planning, and data analysis happened bimonthly at a minimum, if not weekly.
14. Programs coordinated one-stop data collection with reports accessible and shared with all stakeholders.
15. People knew the strengths and needs of each *individual* child, no matter the program size.
16. Programs started with families when their children were young and maintained that community cohort. Or, they created cohorts of teens, meeting regularly for a minimum of 18 months, ideally keeping the cohort together 3–6 years.
17. Programs were outreach focused. They didn't wait for families to come to them.

Program Design

18. Programs were held immediately after school to maximize participation and avoid attendance issues.
19. All had experiential components to their programming. Students often helped plan the experiences. Experiences were not simply a carrot; they led to transformation.
20. Programs had a minimum of a dozen partnerships with easy access to reach out to them by text or phone for timely responses to minor issues.

Acknowledgements

This book wouldn't be possible without family, friends, and colleagues who have helped our thinking over many years. We would like to thank the team, especially Cathy Hernandez and Tom Rademacher, at Shell Education and Teacher Created Materials. They have helped us express our beliefs, work, and thinking so others could understand.

Our learning journey is with and due to the children and families who have influenced us and built relationships with us in and out of schools. We would like to express our deep gratitude to all the children and youth we have had the honor to work alongside in classrooms and in broader learning contexts. Watching you develop into the best version of your future dreams has been a pure delight. Our work is possible due to all that you have taught us.

Sue would like to thank the extraordinary teachers, youth workers, and child advocates she's found along her travels: Martha Grave, Beth VanOrsow, Principal Mary McKasy, Theresa Hunter, Joe Stevens, Don Carpenter, Adam Chaprnka, Andrea Swain, Jane Aibel, Jennifer Howe Heinemann, and Professor Al and Associate Professors Natasha and Nichole. Thanks to dedicated teaching partners like Dianne Gasch, Kari Wall, and all the other teachers who have always stepped up creatively for kids. To the tribe of volunteers who've joined in the out-of-school-time fun, thank you! You've all created conditions where relationships empower youth to become the best versions of themselves. I've been thankful to be a part of your joyful microcommunities bearing witness to the ways you celebrate and develop the whole child, never giving up hope.

Lucy would like to thank her husband, Lee, and close friends for their support of her many endeavors over the years. As collaborators and partners, you have pushed my thinking to always consider what is possible for young people and the adults supporting them. You have taught me to be bold and courageous in my work. You have helped me see the disconnects in educational systems that can be bridged through relationships and shared passion and purpose. You have been leaders and thought partners across different organizations, communities, and sectors of the education system. Thank you to the team at KnowledgeWorks, especially Anne Olson, for your thought partnership, advocacy, and collaboration over the past seven years. I look forward to what is possible when we all come together to personalize learning and center youth in our thinking and work.

A special thanks to Christine Parr at Pit Productions for professional visuals that are The Gear Model and to Linda Halverson for reading and providing feedback on early and final drafts.

References

Afterschool Alliance. 2022. "Access to Afterschool Programs Remains a Challenge for Many Families." August 2022. afterschoolalliance.org/documents/Afterschool-COVID-19-Parent-Survey-2022-Brief.pdf.

Allen, Kelly A., and Terence Bowles. 2012. "Belonging as a Guiding Principle in the Education of Adolescents." *Australian Journal of Educational and Developmental Psychology* 12 (December): 108–119.

Allen, Kelly-Ann, DeLeon L. Gray, Roy F. Baumeister, and Mark R. Leary. 2022. "The Need to Belong: A Deep Dive Into the Origins, Implications, and Future of a Foundational Construct." *Educational Psychology Review* 34 (2): 1133–1156.

ASCD. n.d. "The Whole Child Approach to Education." Accessed on March 12, 2025. ascd.org/whole-child.

ASCD. 2009. "The 21st Century Skills Movement." September 1, 2009. ascd.org/el/articles/the-21st-century-skills-movement.

Aurora Institute. 2020. "Improving the Equity in Personalized Learning Through a Multi-Tiered System of Support (MTSS) Approach." Webinar, recorded October 8, 2020. aurora-institute.org/event/improving-the-equity-in-personalized-learning-through-a-multi-tiered-system-of-support-mtss-approach.

Aurora Institute. 2021. "Exploring Innovative School Models in the Canopy Project's Interactive National Database." Webinar, recorded March 10, 2021. aurora-institute.org/event/exploring-innovative-school-models-in-the-canopy-projects-interactive-national-database.

Benson, Traci, and Sheri Marlin. 2021. *The Habit-Forming Guide to Becoming a Systems Thinker.* 2nd ed. Waters Center for Systems Thinking.

Bondy, Elizabeth, and Dorene D. Ross. 2008. "The Teacher as Warm Demander." *Educational Leadership* 66 (1): 54–58.

Boyes-Watson, Carolyn, and Kay Pranis. 2020. *Circle Forward: Building a Restorative School Community.* Living Justice Press.

Brackett, Marc. 2019. *Permission to Feel: Unlocking the Power of Emotions to Help Our Kids, Ourselves, and Our Society Thrive.* Celadon Books.

Cambridge Dictionary. n.d. "Enrichment." Accessed March 12, 2025. dictionary.cambridge.org/dictionary/english/enrichment.

The Canopy Project. n.d. "Canopy Project Data Portal." Accessed March 12, 2025. canopyschools.org/data-portal.

Clarke, Jean Illsley. 2021. *Words That Help: Affirmations for Any Age, Every Stage.* University of Minnesota Extension. pressbooks.umn.edu/affirmationsthathelp.

Costa, Arthur L. 2017. Foreword to *Students at the Center: Personalized Learning with Habits of Mind*, by Bena Kallick and Allison Zmuda. ASCD.

Crabtree, Maria, Katherine Prince and Jeremiah-Anthony Righteous-Rogers. 2024. *Envisioning Educator Roles for Transformation: Responsive Education Systems Need Responsive Educator Roles*. KnowledgeWorks. knowledgeworks.org/resources/envisioning-responsive-educator-roles-transformation.

Dweck, Carol. 2006. *Mindset: The New Psychology of Success*. Random House.

Farraj, Deena. 2018. "Movement Breaks: A Resource for Teachers to Promote Student Engagement." Master's thesis, California State University, Northridge. scholarworks.calstate.edu/concern/theses/0g354h92g.

Federal Reserve Bank of Minneapolis. 2019. "Executive Brief—Statewide Crisis: Minnesota's Education Achievement Gaps." October 2019. minneapolisfed.org/policy/education-achievement-gaps/executive-brief.

Fishtank Learning. n.d. "Fishtank Learning." Accessed March 12, 2025. fishtanklearning.org.

GoNoodle. n.d. "GoNoodle Movement and Mindfulness for Kids." gonoodle.com.

Gray, Peter, David F. Lancy, and David F. Bjorklund. 2023. "Decline in Independent Activity as a Cause of Decline in Children's Mental Well-Being: Summary of the Evidence." *The Journal of Pediatrics* 260: 113352. doi.org/10.1016/j.jpeds.2023.02.004.

Grissom, Jason A., Christopher Redding, and Joshua F. Bleiberg. 2019. "Money over Merit? Socioeconomic Gaps in Receipt of Gifted Services." *Harvard Educational Review* 89 (3): 337–369. doi.org/10.17763/1943-5045-89.3.337.

Hammond, Zaretta. 2014. *Culturally Responsive Teaching and the Brain: Promoting Authentic Engagement and Rigor Among Culturally and Linguistically Diverse Students*. Corwin.

Hammond, Zaretta. 2021. "Liberatory Education: Integrating the Science of Learning and Culturally Responsive Practice." American Federation of Teachers, June 3, 2021. aft.org/ae/summer2021/Hammond.

Hemingway, Ernest. 1998 [1967]. *By-Line: Ernest Hemingway: Selected Articles and Dispatches of Four Decades*. Scribner.

Institute for Habits of Mind. n.d.-a. "What Are the Habits of Mind?" Accessed March 12, 2025. habitsofmindinstitute.org/what-are-habits-of-mind.

Institute for Habits of Mind. n.d.-b. "Who We Are." Accessed March 12, 2025. habitsofmindinstitute.org/about-us.

Kallick, Bena, and Allison Zmuda. 2017. *Students at the Center: Personalized Learning with Habits of Mind*. ASCD.

Kohl III, Harold W., and Heather D. Cook, eds. 2013. *Educating the Student Body: Taking Physical Activity and Physical Education to School*. Committee on Physical Activity and Physical Education in the School Environment; Food and Nutrition Board. National Academies Press. doi.org/10.17226/18314.

Learning Policy Institute. n.d. "Whole Child Education." Accessed March 12, 2025. learningpolicyinstitute.org/topic/whole-child-education.

Learning Policy Institute and Turnaround for Children. 2021. "Design Principles for Schools: Putting the Science of Learning and Development into Action." Accessed March 12, 2025. k12.designprinciples.org.

Mahindru, Aditya, Pradeep Patil, and Varun Agrawal. 2023. "Role of Physical Activity on Mental Health and Well-Being: A Review." *Cureus* 15 (1): e33475. doi.org.10.7759/cureus.33475.

McCombs, Jennifer Sloan, Anamarie A. Whitaker, and Paul Youngmin Yoo. 2017. "The Value of Out-of-School Time Programs." RAND Corporation. rand.org/pubs/perspectives/PE267.html.

Minnesota Department of Education (MDE). 2022. "Minnesota Student Survey Statewide Tables." December 2022. health.state.mn.us/data/mchs/surveys/mss/docs/statewidetables/Heterosexual22.pdf.

Minnesota Department of Health (MDH). 2022. "2022 Minnesota Student Survey Results Released." December 23, 2022. health.state.mn.us/news/pressrel/2022/stsurvey122322.html.

National Center for Education Statistics. 2022. "Mental Health Services in Public Schools." National Center for Education Statistics Fast Facts, August 9, 2022. nces.ed.gov/fastfacts/display.asp?id=1130.

National Council of Teachers of Mathematics (NCTM). 1999. *Principles and Standards for School Mathematics*. National Council of Teachers of Mathematics.

National Council of Teachers of Mathematics (NCTM). 2014. *Principles to Actions: Ensuring Mathematical Success for All*. National Council of Teachers of Mathematics.

Operation Breakthrough. n.d. "Ignition Lab: Operation Breakthrough's NEW Ignition Lab powered by Eighty-Seven & Running." Accessed March 12, 2025. operationbreakthrough.org/ignition-lab.

Oxford English Dictionary. 2009. "Community." doi.org/10.1093/OED/1005093760.

Partnerships in Education and Resilience. n.d. "Holistic Student Assessment." PEAR. Accessed March 12, 2025. pearinc.org/holistic-student-assessment.

Prince, Katherine. 2019. "Opportunities for Schools to Shape the Future Today." KnowledgeWorks, March 29, 2019. knowledgeworks.org/resources/opportunities-schools-shape-future-today.

ProvenTutoring. n.d. "About Proven Tutoring." Johns Hopkins University Center for Research and Reform in Education. Accessed March 12, 2025. proventutoring.org/about.

Robinson, Carly D., Matthew A. Kraft, Susanna Loeb, and Beth E. Schueler. 2021. *"Design Principles for Accelerating Student Learning with High-Dosage Tutoring."* EdResearch for Recovery. February 2021. files.eric.ed.gov/fulltext/ED613847.pdf.

Safir, Shane, and Jamila Dugan. 2021. *Street Data: A Next-Generation Model for Equity, Pedagogy, and School Transformation*. Corwin.

Search Institute. n.d. "Developmental Relationships." Accessed March 12, 2025. searchinstitute.org/developmental-relationships.

Senge, Peter M. 2006. *The Fifth Discipline: The Art and Practice of the Learning Organization*. Revised and updated. Doubleday/Currency.

Slavin, Robert. 2018. "New Findings on Tutoring: Four Shockers." *Robert Slavin's Blog*, April 5, 2018. robertslavinsblog.wordpress.com/2018/04/05/new-findings-on-tutoring-four-shockers.

Taylor, Jill Bolte. 2008. *My Stroke of Insight: A Brain Scientist's Personal Journey*. Viking Penguin.

Taylor, Wendy. 2019. "Enrichment in the Classroom." *Learning Essentials*, January 10, 2019. learningessentialsedu.com/enrichment-in-the-classroom.

Teague, Jackie. 2000. "How California Ranks: Comparing States' Support for Schools." *EdSource*, March 2000. edsource.org/wp-content/publications/HowCARanks_3-00.pdf.

Tuchman, Sivan, and Travis Pillow. 2018. "The Enrichment Gap: The Educational Inequity That Nobody Talks About." Center on Reinventing Public Education. November 13, 2018. crpe.org/the-enrichment-gap-the-educational-inequity-that-nobody-talks-about.

Waters Center for Systems Thinking. n.d. "Habits of a Systems Thinker." Thinking Tools Studio. Accessed March 12, 2025. thinkingtoolsstudio.waterscenterst.org/cards.

Index

f denotes figure

A
Academic Intervention gear
  assessment of, 141–143, 141*f*
  described, 10, 73–86
  designing your own, 155–156
  getting youth feedback and evaluation on, 159
academic language, 108, 110–112, 145
academic support, in successful programs, 47–48
academics
  beyond academics as foundational concept, 13, 17–19
  focus on alone as not working, 169–170
access-to-enrichment gap, 89–90
achievement interventionists
  co-teaching by, 29
  creation of position of, 27–29
  as seeking input from families, 30–33
activities
  basic tips for running enrichment activities, 95
  collaborative movement activities, 133–135
  "45 Best Cooperative Games to Promote Comradery and Healthy Competition," 130
  Four Corners, 128
  Hidden Picture, 83
  math equation cards, 132–133, 133*f*
  Mix, Freeze, and Pair Up, 132
  opening circle activities, 114
  partner activities, getting started with, 132–133
  Partner Walk, Run, and Play (activity), 133–134, 133*f*
  research on physical activity, 126
  selecting movement activities, 130–131
  Ships Across the Ocean, 128
  A Skit Challenge (activity), 134–135, 134*f*
  small-group academic activities, 81, 82*f*–83*f*
  Spot the Difference, 83
  Team-Building Relay (activity), 134, 134*f*
affirmations, developmental, 119–123, 120*f*–121*f*, 132
After School Club
  building excitement for, 60
  evaluation of, 140, 140*f*–141*f*
  goals of, 55–56
  mathematics as initial academic intervention focus, 75
anchor charts, 94*f*
ASCD, 13
Aspirations Incubator (Maine), 42
assessments
  of Academic Intervention gear, 141–143, 141*f*
  of Attending to Emotions gear, 143–144
  of Communication gear, 143–144
  of Enrichment gear, 142–143
  Holistic Student Assessment (HSA) (PEAR). *See* Holistic Student Assessment (HSA) (PEAR)
  initial assessment, 14
  needs assessment as barrier to intervention success, 39, 39*f*
  of overall well-being, 144–145, 145*f*
  of resilience, 144–145, 145*f*
  Science Minnesota Comprehensive Assessment (MCA), 142–143
asset framing, as barrier to intervention success, 39, 39*f*
asset-based framing, as foundational concept, 13, 16–17
Attending to Emotions gear
  assessment of, 143–144
  described, 10, 12, 113–123
  designing your own, 156–157
  getting youth feedback and evaluation of social and emotional experience, 159–160

B
Banyan Community Youth Development Center (Minneapolis, Minnesota), 44
Beetles Science and Teaching for Field Instructors, 130
belonging, and emotional safety, 114–115
beyond academics, as foundational concept, 13, 17–19
Blanchard, Ken, 37
book club, formation of, 29–30
Boyes-Watson, Carolyn, 112
Boys & Girls Clubs of Metropolitan Baltimore (Maryland), 43, 46, 47–48, 49, 113–115
Brackett, Marc, 116
Britton, James, 103
building use, as barrier to intervention success, 39*f*, 40
Burch, Y'Landa, 49
Bussanmas, Corita (Sister), 44

C
calendar, limitations of, 169
Carpenter, Don, 41, 47, 170
Carpenter, Jack, 41
Casco Bay High School (Portland, Maine), 42
case studies
  Jesse, 21–23
  Kayla, 148–149
Challenging Growth, as element of Developmental Relationships Framework, 15, 127, 128
change fatigue, 168
Chaprnka, Adam, 42, 45, 46, 49
Chavez, Cesar, 173
Circle Forward (Boyes-Watson and Pranis), 112
circle practice, 111–112
City Connects (Boston, Massachusetts), 43
Clarke, Jean Illsley, 106, 119, 120, 120*f*–121*f*, 121
cloze procedures, 111, 111*f*
co-creation, as attribute of model of personalized learning, 14
collaboration, 26–27
collaborative movement
  activities for, 133–135
  benefits of, 135–136
  preparing for, 129–132
Collaborative Movement and Play gear
  described, 10, 12, 125–136
  designing your own, 157
co-location, 170
Communication gear
  academic language, 110–112
  assessment of, 143–144
  defined, 103–104
  described, 10, 12, 103–112
  designing your own, 156
  efficient, intentional strategies for, 104–109, 106*f*, 107*f*
  embedded communication opportunities, 108–109
  journals, 107, 108*f*
  nonverbal academic cues, 106–107
  rituals for greetings, gratitude, and goodbyes, 109
  sentence frames, 108
  verbal communication skills development, 104–106, 105*f*
communications
  importance of, 104

ongoing conversations everywhere, 147–148
with parents, 123
community. *See also* microcommunity
defined, 12, 33
growing students' community, 29–30
continuous improvement, key to, 157
Costa, Arthur L. (Art), 14, 18
co-teaching, by achievement interventionists, 29
curriculum, as barrier to intervention success, 39*f*, 40

D

data
as barrier to intervention success, 39, 39*f*
to inform improvements and demonstrate success, 157
need for to inform improvements and demonstrate success, 157
planning for tutoring based on, 79–81, 80*f*
review of in selection of participants, 58–59
use of student data for planning, 60–61
Design Principles for Accelerating Student Learning with High-Dosage Tutoring (EdResearch for Recovery), 74, 74*f*–75*f*
developmental affirmations, 119–123, 120*f*–121*f*
developmental relationships
as foundational concept, 15–16
long-term ones as equaling success, 172–173
starting with, 171
Developmental Relationships Framework (Search Institute), 15–16, 45, 105, 153, 170
Dudley Square Bike Club, 45, 67
Dugan, Jamila, 58
Dweck, Carol, 18

E

EdResearch for Recovery, 74, 74*f*–75*f*
effective programs, qualities of, 49, 185–186
Elementary and Secondary School Emergency Relief (ESSER), 154
emojis, emotions through, 117
emotional safety, belonging and, 114–115
emotions. *See also* Attending to Emotions gear
developmental affirmations, 119–120
identifying, 115–116
journaling about, 118–119
and learning, 116
through emojis, 117
tools for attending to, 116–123

endorphins, 126
Enrichment gear
access to, 89–90
anchor charts, 94*f*
assessment of, 142–143
basic tips for running enrichment activities, 95
building relationships and assessing prior knowledge, 96–98, 98*f*
celebration showcase highlighting success, 99
defined, 88–89
described, 10, 12, 62, 87–101
designing your own gear for, 156
getting youth feedback and evaluation on gear for, 159
lessons learned, 99, 100*f*
STEAM, 90–96, 91*f*–93*f*, 94*f*, 96*f*
why it is worth your time, 89
Erikson, Erik, 119
Essenburg, Joani, 44
Essenburg, Tim, 44
ESSER (Elementary and Secondary School Emergency Relief), 154
evaluation
of After School Club, 140, 140*f*–141*f*
as barrier to intervention success, 40
improvement of, 148
lack of good evaluation process as barrier to intervention success, 39*f*
of learners' increasing persistence in problem-solving, 142, 142*f*
of learners' meeting their academic goals, 141–142, 141*f*
of learners' possible improvement on standardized science tests, 143
need for data to inform improvements and demonstrate success, 157
from parents, 160–161
from partners, 146–147, 161–162
planning for, 157–158
of two-year program implementation, 139–150
from youth, 158–160
Expanding Possibilities, as element of Developmental Relationships Framework, 15–16, 100, 105, 128
Expressing Care, as element of Developmental Relationships Framework, 15, 105, 119, 127

F

families, seeking input from, 30–33. *See also* parents
Family Science Carnival, 146
feedback
improving collection of, 148
from parents, 146, 160–161

from partners, 146–147, 161–162
from volunteers, 146–147, 161–162, 184
from youth, 158–160, 184
Fishtank Learning, 78
Focused Math Intervention (TCM), 41, 78
Focused Reading Intervention (TCM), 41, 78
"45 Best Cooperative Games to Promote Comradery and Healthy Competition," 130
foundational concepts
asset-based framing, 13, 16–17
being learner focused, 13–14
building supportive relationships, 13, 15–16
influences to learning beyond the traditional three R's, 13, 17–19
systems orientation, 13, 19–20
Four Corners (game), 128
Framework for 21st Century Learning, 18
Fullan, Michael, 9
funding
as barrier to intervention success, 38, 39*f*
obtaining of, 154–155
in successful programs, 48
future focus, 172

G

Gear Model After School Club, 6, 17
The Gear Model
an afternoon/evening at program of, 53–55
benefits of, 6
components of (gears of), 10. *See also specific gears*
designing your own, 155–157
development of, 9–23
getting to know it, 53–71
graphic of, 11
importance of outreach and relationships in, 153
large gears as kept turning by small gears, 13
launch of, 59–61
logistics and calendar, 56–57
physical space for, 58
ratio of students to educators and volunteers, 59
selecting participants for, 58–59
starting with the end in mind, 152
structural considerations of, 57
time allocation for, 56–57
Gerrity, Anne, 113
goals
as barrier to intervention success, 39, 39*f*
collaboration on, 157–158
engaging partners with common goals, 67–68
evaluation of learners in meeting

their academic goals, 141–142, 141f
of The Gear Model After School Club, 55–56
GoNoodle (website), 128
Grave, Martha, 33
growth mindset, 18
Guiding Principles for Equitable Whole Child Design (Learning Policy Institute and Turnaround for Children), 13, 14f

H

Habits of a Systems Thinker (Waters Center for Systems Thinking), 20, 20f
Habits of Mind (Institute for Habits of Mind), 18, 30, 88, 104, 105f, 169, 170
Hale, Edward Everett, 125
Hammond, Zaretta, 1, 2, 89
Harvard Medical School's MEDscienceLAB (Massachusetts), 43
Hemingway, Ernest, 31
Hidden Picture (activity), 83
hierarchy of needs, 113, 114, 114f
Holistic Student Assessment (HSA) (PEAR), 39, 41, 42, 48, 55, 56, 61, 69, 143

I

Ignition Lab (Operation Breakthrough), 48–49
initiatives, handling of new ones, 168
Institute for Habits of Mind, 18. *See also* Habits of Mind (Institute for Habits of Mind)
Interfaith Outreach, 33
intervention
 academic intervention, 73–86
 identifying barriers to success in, 38–40, 39f, 41
 multi-age intervention strategies, benefits of, 30
intervention programs, primary goal of, 141
invitation to program, 179

J

Jesse (case study), 21–23
Johns Hopkins University, ProvenTutoring (Maryland), 28, 43, 47, 78
journals/journaling, 107, 108f, 118–119
Joyal, Julie, 43

K

Kallick, Bena, 14, 18
Kayla (case study), 148–149
Kelce, Travis, 48
Keller, Helen, 25
King, Martin Luther, Jr., 151
Koch, Tom, 4–5, 25–26, 27, 170

L

Langworthy, Maria, 9
leadership, in successful programs, 45–46
learner focused, as foundational concept, 13–14
learning
 emotions and, 116
 personalized learning, 14, 55, 169, 170
 play as supporting, 127
Learning Policy Institute, 13
"Liberatory Education" (Hammond), 89
location, finding one for your program, 164
logistical details, 56–57, 163–164

M

Maslow, Abraham, 113, 114
materials, for students, 85, 85f
materials, obtaining of for your program, 164–165
math equation cards (activity), 132–133, 133f
mathematics
 assessing disposition for rigor in, 83–84, 84f
 as initial academic intervention focus of The Gear Model, 75
MCA (Science Minnesota Comprehensive Assessment), 142–143
Mechanical Engineering Ambassadors (University of Minnesota), 55, 68–69, 76, 91, 95, 96, 97, 110, 111
microcommunity, 12, 13, 20, 22, 70, 128, 146, 151, 168, 169, 171
Mix, Freeze, and Pair Up (activity), 132
movement. *See also* Collaborative Movement and Play gear
 importance of, 126–127
 securing space for, 132
 selecting movement activities, 130–131
Muhammad, Gholdy, 73
multi-age intervention strategies, benefits of, 30
multi-tiered system of supports (MTSS), 169

N

National Blue Ribbon School (US Department of Education), 27
National Center for Education Statistics, on student mental health, 126
National Council of Teachers of Mathematics (NCTM), 76
needs, hierarchy of, 113, 114, 114f
needs assessment, as barrier to intervention success, 39, 39f
Neighborhood Homework Club, 5, 6, 30, 33

new initiatives, handling of, 168
Noam, Gil, 19

O

opening circle activities, 114
Operation Breakthrough (Kansas City, Missouri), 44, 46, 48–49
The Opportunity Myth, 89
Oriol, Nancy, 43
outreach, importance of, 153

P

parents. *See also* families
 communicating with, 123
 feedback and evaluation from, 146, 160
 tips for conversations with, 31–32
participants
 recruitment of, 163
 registration form, 180–181
 selection of, 58–59
partner activities, getting started with, 132–133
Partner Walk, Run, and Play (activity), 133–134, 133f
partners. *See also* partnerships
 as barrier to intervention success, 38, 39f
 engaging of with common goals, 67–68
 feedback and evaluation from, 146–147, 161–162
 questions for prospective ones, 182
 sample schedule for, 183
 using cohort reports for planning with, 69
Partnership for 21st Century Skills, 18
partnerships
 in broader ecosystem, 153–154
 building of, 62–70
 with multiple groups, 70
 school-university partnership, creation of, 25–27
 with university students, 68–69
Partnerships in Education and Resilience (PEAR), 39, 42, 61, 69, 144, 145
pay-to-play system, 40, 41
Permission to Feel (Brackett), 116
personalized learning, 14, 55, 169, 170
Person-in-Environment (PIE) theory, 49
physical activity, research on, 126
physical space, for The Gear Model, 58
Pillow, Travis, 90
planning
 based on needs of students, 130
 for evaluation, 157–158
 with partners, 69
 for small-group activities, 81, 82f–83f
 sticky note planning, 80–81, 80f
 for tutoring, 77–81, 80f

play
    importance of, 126–127
    kinds of, 127
    observations on state of, 127–128
    sounds of productive and collaborative play, 126
    structured play, 128–129
    as supporting learning, 127
    as supporting relationship building, 126–127
    unstructured play, 128
Playworks, 130
Plutarch, 87
Pranis, Kay, 112
Principles to Actions (NCTM), 76
problem-solving, evaluation of learners' increasing persistence in, 142, 142*f*
programs, successful ones. *See* successful programs
ProvenTutoring (Maryland), 28, 43, 47, 78
Providing Support, as element of Developmental Relationships Framework, 15, 105, 127

R

registration process
    as barrier to intervention success, 39*f*, 40
    for The Gear Model, 60, 180–181
relationships
    foundation of, 25–35
    importance of, 153
    play as supporting building of, 126–127
    through neighborhood program, 33–34
Relationships gear
    described, 10
    getting youth feedback and evaluation on, 159
resilience, assessment of, 144–145, 145*f*
resources, 175–178
Responsive Classroom, 114
restorative practices, 111–112
Rohn, Jim, 1
routines, development of for your program, 165
Rural Futures Fund, 42

S

Safir, Shane, 58
Sailer, Berta (Sister), 44
school structures, rethinking of, 169
school-university partnership, creation of, 25–27
Science Minnesota Comprehensive Assessment (MCA), 142–143
Search Institute, 15, 45, 153, 170
self-awareness, building, 113–123
self-discovery, as attribute of model of personalized learning, 14
sentence frames, 108

Sharing Power, as element of Developmental Relationships Framework, 15, 105, 127
Ships Across the Ocean (game), 128
Siegel, Dan, 116
site visits, key findings from, 168*f*
A Skit Challenge (activity), 134–135, 134*f*
Slavin, Robert, 28, 75
small-group academic activities, planning for, 81, 82*f*–83*f*
social and emotional experience, getting youth feedback and evaluation on, 159
social construction, as attribute of model of personalized learning, 14
The Special Ed Strategist (podcast), 88
Spot the Difference (activity), 83
staffing
    as barrier to intervention success, 38, 39*f*
    ratio of students to adults in The Gear Model, 59
    in successful programs, 46
standardized science tests, possible improvement on, 143
sticky note planning, 80–81, 80*f*
Street Data (Safir and Dugan), 58
structural considerations, of The Gear Model, 57
structure
    development of for your program, 165
    rethinking school structures, 169
structured play, 128–129
student buy-in, getting, 131
student materials, 85, 85*f*
student registration form, 180–181
students
    interview and feedback questions for, 184
    planning based on needs of, 130
    recruitment of, 163
    selection of, 58–59
    in successful programs, 46–47
successful programs
    identifying, 41
    visits to, 40–50
sustainability, 46, 48, 68, 147, 155, 157, 162–163
Swain, Andrea, 45–46
systems thinking, as foundational concept, 19–20

T

Targeted Services, 148, 154
tasks, five parts of, 106*f*
Taylor, Jill Bolte, 116
Taylor, Wendy, 88
Team-Building Relay (activity), 134, 134*f*
teamwork
    developing a team, 162–163
    emergence of, 135

Thrively, 61, 61*f*, 69
time, limitations of, 169
time allocation, for The Gear Model, 56–57
transportation, as barrier to intervention success, 38, 39*f*
Trekkers (Maine), 41–42, 47, 48, 170
Tuchman, Sivan, 90
Turnaround for Children, 13, 14*f*
tutoring
    curriculum for, 78
    defined, 74
    design principles of, 74*f*–75*f*
    homework support and, 78
    in math, 75–76
    planning for based on individual student data, 79–81, 80*f*
    program design considerations, 76–77
    what makes it effective, 74–75
    where to start planning for, 77–78
21st century skills, 18

U

University of Minnesota Mechanical Engineering Ambassadors, 55, 68–69, 76, 91, 95, 96, 97, 110, 111
unstructured play, 128
US Department of Education, 27

V

voice, as attribute of model of personalized learning, 14
volunteers
    as barrier to intervention success, 38, 39*f*
    feedback and evaluation from, 146–147, 161–162
    importance of, 62
    training of, 62–67, 64*f*–65*f*, 66*f*–67*f*
    weekly feedback form, 184

W

wall talkers, 129
warm demanders, 15
Waters Center for Systems Thinking, 19–20
well-being, assessment of overall well-being, 144–145, 145*f*
whole-child approach, 10, 13–14, 15, 16, 28, 44, 55, 56, 58, 60, 88, 132, 148, 151, 153, 154, 168*f*, 170, 172
Words That Help (Clarke), 120
work folders, 85, 85*f*

Y

Yawkey, Jean, 48
Yawkey, Tom A., 48
Yawkey Boys & Girls Clubs (Roxbury, Massachusetts), 42, 45, 46, 48, 49, 67

Z

Zmuda, Allison, 14

About the Authors

Sue Strom, M.A., is a veteran educator with 37 years of classroom experience, specializing in math and reading intervention. She holds a coaching certificate from the National Urban

PHOTO BY MARK BROWN

Alliance, is trained in the Orton-Gillingham approach, and has taught math and equity courses at the University of St. Thomas in St. Paul, Minnesota. Sue believes that the key to a child's success lies in strong relationships between schools, families, and community partners. Her commitment to these values led her to codevelop an innovative intervention model with Dr. Lucy Payne, combining in-school support with after-school tutoring and enrichment. Their model, informed by Sue's study of successful youth programs, aims to transform learning communities nationwide.

Lucy Payne, Ph.D., is a professional educator with over 35 years of experience. She holds a master's degree in reading education and a doctorate in early childhood and elementary

PHOTO BY SHANNON HUNTER

education with a focus on elementary math education and curriculum. Committed to improving reading education outcomes in Minnesota, she is a member of the Minnesota Path Forward Team. She has been appointed twice by the governor to serve on the teacher licensure and standards board. Additionally, Lucy has served over 10 years as an elected school board member, served on a cooperative school board, and served on various community arts boards. She is also a peer reviewer for the Council for the Accreditation of Educator Preparation (CAEP) and the Higher Learning Commission (HLC). In her role at the University of St. Thomas, Lucy teaches in the Teacher Education department, covering subjects such as elementary mathematics and science education, classroom environments, curriculum, technology integration, and assessment. She recently developed a new program focused on mental wellness for educators.